Imagining A Murder

Imagining A Murder

The Cartland case revisited

STOCKTON HEATH

Sandgrounder

First Printing, 2021
ISBN-978-1-9993591-9-5

Sandgrounder Publishing

Contents

Acknowledgements

I am indebted to numerous people without whose help the current project could never have come to fruition: Sue Reeve, Mike from the Late Niters and all the many people down in Pélissanne, Jouques, Saint Cannat, Aix and La Barben whose memories were jogged by the story: Jerome A Brgl, Gisele Turcan, Caroline Roger to name but a few. Special thanks to Pascal Lazarowicz for his invaluable help locating the site known as *Jas de Dane* and the electricity pylon no. 8 that still stands. Thanks also for their memories to Ann Smith, Patrick Benham, Fergal Roche, Peter Breakwell and Francis Lindsay-Hills. Archive material from a wide range of media sources was also invaluable especially from The *Daily Express*. Eastbourne Local Historian magazine (Issue 161 Autumn 2011) provided useful pointers too.

Map of wider Provence area (fig.1) and Pélissanne village (fig. 2) by Arlette Barletti. © OpenStreetMap contributors, Who's On First.

Front/back cover & *Jas de Dane* location sketch (fig. 3) by Sirajum Monira Nosaibha.

Preface

A question often asked of authors is how they came to write a particular book. Although I've tried to pin the moment down, I can't be sure when or how I first came across the Cartland murder. Whether via print, TV/radio or some other means, it must have been a passing reference because my knowledge of the case was never more than superficial. I knew somebody had once been murdered in France, but did not know the victim's identity nor any of the circumstances except that the crime had involved a caravan and arson. Possibly I watched the TV documentary that reconstructed the case. Not yet out of short pants, it's easy to imagine a young boy watching small screen images of a burning caravan, fully absorbed by the spectacle of it all.

Whatever its provenance, that image of a caravan burning in a faraway land, vague yet also distinct, haunted my adolescent mind for years to come. Somehow, it stuck in my subconscious and refused to leave. I suppose I must have assumed the victim had been murdered inside the caravan, which had then been set on fire to conceal the crime. It was an awful thought, more so than any horror film.

Certainly, the involvement of a caravan must have given the crime added salience. As a youngster I spent many summers on family camping holidays. The north Wales coast was a particularly favourite haunt. Camping I associated with care-free adventures, having fun. With this strange murder it had suddenly become less innocent, a pastime associated with shadows and as such an activity henceforth fraught with danger. That blazing caravan became to me totemic of something, of what I can't be certain - lost innocence perhaps, the encroachment into a child's world of darker realities.

Into adulthood my recollection of the crime, like my childhood years, must have melted away. At any rate I rarely, if ever, gave it a second thought. Decades later I was browsing through Roger Louis Bianchini's book about the Côte d'Azur. One of the chapters was devoted to what the author called the 'Oxford Murders' - all of which had occurred in the south of France and all of which had involved deaths of British subjects whom Bianchini linked together via their Oxford university backgrounds. But that wasn't the only link. According to the author, the victims had all worked for British intelligence services at some point in their careers.

One of the cases under review was that of a British professor who had been murdered in 1973. The victim's name was John Basil Cartland and he had been camping out in Provence in a caravan which his murderer(s) had set alight... In the pages of that book childhood phobias were once again resurrected. I was surprised how clearly it all came back, that image of an engulfed caravan, the incongruity of it all. I wanted to discover more about these cases. Above all else, I needed to discover exactly what had happened to Mr Cartland all those years ago.

Aye, but isn't it usually best to let sleeping dogs lie, to let bygones be bygones, go forwards not backwards? Not always. Something terrible happened on that moonlit Provence night, something unimaginable, incomprehensible. This is a story that needs to be told. And if not I, who else shall tell it?

Stockton Heath
June 2021

Truth will come to light;
murder cannot be hid long;
a man's son may,
but at the length truth will out.

The Merchant of Venice, Act 2 sc. II
William Shakespeare

1

In the forest of the night

Sunday March 18, 1973, a day like any other. A strong wind had been blowing all day, rattling the doors and windows of the Bouches-du-Rhône region of south-east France and now, as midnight approached, showed little sign of abating. The Mistral, so it is said, has driven people insane. Visitors beware for this unyielding force of nature will burrow inside the heads of the unwary, fray the nerves of the susceptible. Daylight vanished and with it the warm sun, the region's inhabitants knew to expect a chilly night.

It had indeed been a day like any other in La Barben, one of several communes that pepper the landscape between the Provences of Salon and Aix. Local farmer Francis Caire had spent the large part of this gusty day harvesting carrots for Monday's fruit and vegetable market in Châteaurenard, the largest of its kind in Europe. Tired from his exertions, he retired to bed around 10 o'clock. After she had finished watching television with the couple's daughter, Monsieur Caire's wife joined him.

'The dogs are barking,' she whispered slipping into bed.

'I know,' replied her husband. The farmer had initially ignored the barking and whining when it had started up. After all, the animals were only doing their job of protecting the Caire residency. However, tonight the dogs seemed more unsettled than usual; they had been barking for almost half an hour continuously.

'Shouldn't you at least check on them?'

'Yes, of course.'

Caire sighed. He wasn't exactly relishing the prospect of leaving the warmth of his bed to hunt around in the cold, night air. But the dogs *were* kicking up an unholy row. Something had clearly spooked them. Poachers perhaps? It couldn't be the wind. The Mistral is especially active throughout winter and spring, a fact of life. Both people and livestock have learned to live with it.

'I'll be back shortly,' said the farmer closing the bedroom door behind him.

Lying on the very edge of the La Barben commune, the Caire property occupied a spacious but secluded spot just off the Route Nationale 572 Pélissanne-Aix road. Opposite the farm lies a vast rocky plain, *Vallon de l'Apothicaire* - a rugged landscape of dirt tracks intersecting forests of pine beloved by hikers and off-road enthusiasts alike. Beyond the Caire farmstead the RN 572 continues east through open country. Tucked away behind oak and pine trees La Barben Zoo, the next sign of life, is a further two kilometres down the road.

Monsieur Caire stepped outside into the crisp, evening air. Such was the moon's luminosity it might have been the middle of the afternoon. Moonlight bathed the farmyard transforming it into a theatre stage: *la nuit de la pleine lune* - a full moon. Not a sound could be heard from the road beyond the farm. The silence was broken only by occasional gusts of wind rustling through oak and pine trees - that and barking. After settling his dogs down in their kennels, something caught the farmer's eye, 'a glow' of light. Shining from an easterly direction, Caire estimated the source of the light must have been about 400-500 metres away from where he stood as the crow flies.[1] The farmer assumed that the light belonged to a car, a side-light perhaps. Presumably a motorist had stopped for some reason. Dismissing the light from his thoughts and with the dogs now quiet, ten minutes after he had first breached the cold, Caire returned indoors.

Meanwhile, Frederic Delaude was driving home to Aix-en-Provence from Montpelier - a journey that had begun at 11pm. Approximately an hour and a half into this lonely two-hour drive, much of it skirting the vast regional parks of Camargue and Alpilles with their low-lying rocky mountain terrains, he had reached the environs of Pélissanne. Passing the pretty town of pastel pink and cream villas, the twenty-eight-year-old had entered the final leg of his homeward journey. With a clear road ahead the press officer could expect to be home in just over half an hour. The RN 572 was all but deserted.

Shortly after Monsieur Caire had returned to his bed, Delaude's Citroen 2 CV drove past the now silent farm. Ahead stretched miles of indistinct countryside what in Provencal dialect is known as *La Garrigue* - acres of woodland, scrub and forests infused with the essence of wild thyme, lavender and mimosa. He had not driven more than 200 yards past the farm when he spotted flecks of bright gold a little further on, a splash of unexpected colour in the darkness, alchemy in the night. Fire! A sense of foreboding gripped the young driver.

Forest fires had long since blighted this area of France. Once ignited, with the Mistral behind them, bush fires can spread quickly reaping disaster in their wake.

Approaching the bend in the road, Delaude's worst fears were confirmed: a substantial fire had indeed broken out in a clearing about twenty-five metres from the verge. He slowed the Citroen right down. Picked out by the car's headlights, arms waving, a dark silhouette had suddenly loomed out of the gloom. Delaude brought his car to a complete stop.

'What's wrong? Have you had an accident?' shouted the driver of the Citroen.

'I've been attacked,' called back a male voice.

The figure half walked, half staggered over to where the car had stopped. It was a cold Provencal night yet the man was wearing only a pyjama jacket and pair of blue slacks. Of athletic build and tall in stature, despite the signs of premature balding on the forehead Delaude guessed that the interloper to be a similar age to himself. Shocked as he was to find this apparition flagging him down in the middle of the night, the young Frenchman did not hesitate to offer what help he could. The press attaché immediately jumped out of the Citroen.

'I was knocked out. I've also been wounded,' gasped the stranger indicating his shoulder and stomach. The man spoke French with an English accent. He spoke calmly and did not appear overly agitated. When Delaude offered him a seat in the car, he almost collapsed into it.

'Are you alone?' asked the press officer noting with concern how the man clutched his abdomen.

'I don't know what has happened to my father.'

'Wait here,' instructed Delaude. And with that he scurried off leaving the groaning Englishman sat in the passenger seat of his car.

Such was the intensity of heat generated by the blaze, Delaude was obliged to shield his face as he approached. From what he could see it appeared that the Englishman must have been camping in the clearing and somehow his caravan had caught fire. Fanned by the wind and with flames curling all over its bodywork, the fire had already devoured much of the caravan; the top half had been completely destroyed. Delaude scanned the scene. Close by to this golden-orange inferno stood a white Hillman car. There was no trace of the stranger's father. Returning back to his own car, Delaude was relieved to see a Renault R6 arriving on the scene.

On their way back to Pélissanne, Madame Sobansky and her daughter Jeanine initially thought they had spotted a camp-fire. Upon noticing a couple of figures at the side of the road, the Sobanskys stopped their car. Could they be of assistance? While one of the men urgently explained what had happened through the car window, mother and daughter observed how his companion, a tall bearded blond with a distinct touch of the Viking about him, hung back. The poor fellow was clearly in some distress. 'Completely bewildered' is how Jeanine would later describe his countenance. Situation explained to them, the women readily agreed to inform the nearest gendarmerie. Not a moment to lose, the Renault sped away into the night. In an era before mobile phones the women needed to locate the nearest public telephone kiosk.

Delaude was once again alone with the wounded man who complained bitterly about the pain in his stomach. Apart from the burning caravan crackling and popping, it could have been a typically quiet Provencal night.

'It hurts. I need to get to a hospital,' pleaded the man.

With the fire threatening to engulf the car and perhaps the woodland too, the press officer needed to act smart. Moments later another Renault headed down the road, this time a white 4L model. Delaude stood in the middle of the road obliging it to stop.

'Hey! What do you think you're doing? Are you crazy?' The car's occupants were not best pleased.

'Can you help us please?' implored Delaude. The three passengers looked distinctly unimpressed. 'An English tourist has been attacked.'

Having spent the evening in Salon-de-Provence, friends Joseph Lorenzo (19), Michel Chambonnet (22) and Alain Weltman (21) had decided to search for some action in the larger conurbation of Aix-en-Provence. Beers drunk and in high spirits, the trio of Beaucaire natives had left 'The Splendid Bowling Bar' thirty or so minutes after midnight. Twenty minutes later they found themselves on the RN 572 at La Barben accosted by persons unknown.

'If the Mistral increases,' added Delaude desperately, 'there is no telling how far the fire will spread.'

True enough, all it would take is a blast in the wrong direction for the swirling wind to ignite the entire woods and more. A disaster of epic proportions could be a mere hair's breadth away. It was a powerful argument.

Persuaded by this message of impending doom, the young men agreed to help. Parking their car next to the Citroen, they came across the Englishman alluded to doubled-up in the driver's seat of that car, blood streaked across his dome-like forehead. He looked in a bad way. In between painful breaths, he was however able to confirm that he had been attacked while camping in the clearing.

Together with Delaude the trio of friends rushed over to the where the caravan burned. While Chambonnet and Lorenzo noticed a gas bottle still hooked up to the caravan, which they swiftly disconnected, Delaude spotted a plastic white container or jerrycan close by which he assumed might contain fuel and which he tossed into the thicket. Attention turned to the Hillman. The vehicle was in a perilous position - just a couple of metres or so from where the flames were shooting, though thankfully caravan and car were uncoupled. The right-side driver's door was closed but not locked, so the friends attempted to push the car to a safe place. However, the vehicle's steering lock system thwarted their efforts.

'Get the keys! Quick!'

Weltman ran back over to the Citroen where the injured man duly produced the ignition keys from his trouser pocket.

'Can you bring my jacket?' asked the man who, clad only in his pyjama top, was feeling the bite of the Provencal night. 'It's in the back of the car.'

The twenty-one-year-old dashed back, handing the keys to Lorenzo. As the interior of the car was dark and unfamiliar, he fumbled with various knobs and switches until succeeding in locating the ignition switch. An empty white plastic container inhibiting the use of the pedals, he moved over to the left-hand passenger side of the car. Thereafter, he drove the vehicle out of harm's way.

Destructive yet also magnificent, like a pack of lions that have overwhelmed a great beast the flames roared in triumph. Thinking on their feet, the four young men scoured the area for rocks and stones - anything which could be used to smother the blaze. Luckily, the caravan had stopped in a place used by locals as a kind of unofficial dump - *Jas de Dane*.[2] The clearing just so happened to be strewn with rubbish: cartons, bottles etc. Soon enough the young men began hurling an array of objects into the burning cauldron, collapsing what remained of the caravan's sides. Eventually, the fire came under a modicum of control. A job well done. However, Frederic Delaude's work was not quite over. The hero of the hour next hopped into the driver's seat of his Citroen, destination Salon-de-Provence. Provided nothing out of the ordinary were to occur, he could deliver the injured man to the town's hospital in a little over ten minutes. His English passenger could only groan. Delaude gritted his teeth

By now the Sobanskys had arrived in a deserted Pélissanne. Le Galion was just about to close its shutters for the evening when Jeanine Sobansky burst into the popular bistro.

'I need to call the police!' panted the student. 'There's been a caravan fire near La Barben!'

In a night of high drama where time had gone unnoticed, Salon police logged the call at 1.10 am. An unprovoked attack on English tourists - one of whom was reportedly missing - coupled with potential arson, the Sobanskys had just helped set off a chain reaction of late-night telephone calls amongst police and judicial top brass.

Back at La Barben the three Beaucaire friends watched the flames consume the lower half of a caravan that was clearly beyond salvation. A Peugeot 403 arrived at the scene. Guy Massieux had been just about to leave Le Galion when he had overheard the conversation to Salon police. He decided to head over to *Jas de Dane* to offer assistance. Some minutes before his arrival a Ford Cortina belonging to the Blasco family had been and gone. News of this curious occurrence was about to explode all over France and beyond.

Sirens wailing and blue lights flashing, having raced past Delaude's hospital-bound Renault, the Salon police and fire brigade arrived soon after. It was now 1.30 am. The fire service set to work subduing a fire which had almost burnt itself out. All that remained of the caravan and its contents was the burnt-out chassis, a charred outline of its final resting place on a bed of ashes.

However, the night was far from over. The Englishman had mentioned his father. What then had become of this second intrepid traveller who, for whatever reason, had chosen to camp out under the brilliant light of a Provencal moon? At this stage it seemed likely that upon being attacked, the terrified gentleman must have run off into the woodland of which there was an abundance. He could be anywhere out there, cold and alone, deep in shock no doubt. Flashlights at the ready, the police combed the area. By now fully immersed in the occasion, thoughts of Aix's all-night bars long since dismissed, Weltman, Chambonnet and Lorenzo hung back to lend their assistance.

'Over here! Quick!' The yells of one of the youths pierced the night. The errant father had been found, or so it appeared. The scream alerted the rest of the searchers who came rushing over.

Just a few metres from where the caravan had stood, thrived a thick clutch of bushes. In the midst of this thicket a lifeless body was lying face down the right arm tucked away under the torso. Torchlight revealed the body to be that of an older male. The deceased was wearing a thick blood-soaked mustard-coloured sweater. On the lower half of the body, he wore a pair of striped pyjama bottoms, which, it was noted, were rolled down around the ankles exposing the legs and buttocks. A pair of brown moccasin slippers completed the outfit.

When the flashlights settled on the head the true extent of the horror was revealed: a deep wound had split the base of the skull such as might be made in order to fell one of the mighty French oaks which stood nearby in shadowy silence.

The head and shoulders were caked in copious amounts of drying blood from what must have been a frenzied, angry attack. Although still warm, the unfortunate man was clearly dead, a formality confirmed at the scene by a local doctor. Further examination painted a truly grisly picture. Between clumps of matted hair, a large gaping wound emerged in the occipital region at the back of the skull. In what appeared to have been a series of attempts to cut the throat, the carotid artery had also been severed from which had sprung a pool of blood. The gruesome discovery was recorded as being made at 1.50 am.

Confronted by this macabre scene, some of the witnesses were aghast. What had started out as a roadside fire and search for a missing person had escalated into murder - cold-blooded murder.

Next the police searched the Hillman car. With the exception of the front right which was found to be unlocked, the other three doors were locked. Although nobody could have guessed it at the time, the question of locked or unlocked car doors would come to occupy an inordinate amount of time and space in the investigation to follow. Police also discovered all manner of items associated with travel: sunglasses, travel guides etc. Along with various items of clothing and food the Hillman's boot yielded a wallet containing various documents.

Warrant Officer Yves Salendre flicked through the passports his colleagues had retrieved. He'd briefly heard talk that the injured party currently en route to Salon hospital was English - a rumour that if true could only complicate matters further. Under torchlight he was at last able to establish the identity of the victim:

'John Basil Cartland. Born on the 19th of May, 1912 in London, England. Occupation: English teacher.'

The victim was indeed a British subject. Nor was he the first subject of Her Majesty the Queen to have been murdered this way on French soil. Twenty-one years might have passed since the murder of the Drummond family near the village of Lurs, fifty or so miles north of La Barben, but it was an episode forever fresh in the minds of French officialdom. Here then was a case bound to reverberate not only in La Republic but across the channel. Of more immediate concern to Salendre was organising a search of this inhospitable area. And so, with the time approaching two o'clock, aided by the floodlit moon and with the Mistral pausing for short breaths before gusting once again through this valley of pine and oak trees, the gendarmes began their search for clues.

So had begun one of France's most perplexing-ever murder cases. Over the coming months and years, the enigma of Pélissanne - as it would come to be known - would frustrate and elude all those attempting to grapple with it. There would be so many riddles to undo: how did this middle-aged subject of the British crown come to end up camping in such a remote spot of the Provencal wilderness? And the biggest puzzle of all: for what reasons and by whom had John Basil Cartland been so viciously butchered?

2

Daybreak

Aware of his passenger's discomfort, Frederic Delaude drove as quickly as his old Citroen would allow. The journey would retrace part of the route the unfortunate British tourists themselves had taken just a few hours ago.

'I heard a noise outside,' recalled the English passenger through deep intakes of breath. 'So, I left the caravan to investigate. That's when I was attacked.'

Upon arrival at the Salon hospital Delaude helped his stricken passenger out of the car. One hand pressed firmly into his abdomen, the athletic Englishman accepted the young Frenchman's arm and together they hobbled into the hospital's brightly lit reception area. Wounded he might have been, but the man's youth and vigour shone through. Of particular note was his auburn beard and balding pate the hair of which had all but receded despite its owner's relative youth. Paradoxically, the injured man exuded strength and vitality.

A decision was quickly made to send the patient to the hospital's emergency department. Jean Louvard, the doctor on duty, had already attended to one wounding on his shift so was not especially fazed when presented with another. While he made an initial assessment, the intern listened as the patient explained what happened; how he and his father had camped by the roadside and how he had heard a noise and had stepped outside the caravan to investigate.

'Then somebody hit me on the head from behind knocking me unconscious,' continued the young man. 'After some time – I don't know how long - I woke to find the caravan on fire and my father missing.'

Louvard observed the man with a medic's eye. The patient did not appear to be exhibiting the clinical signs usually observed in a person who has come round from coma following a blunt force trauma injury. He also complained of a painful shoulder. Be that as it may, Louvard was unable to identify any physical signs of injury to this area.

The doctor next checked the patient's skull. A crack on the head delivered with force would likely result in hematoma - the body's natural response to trauma whereby blood vessels break allowing blood to collect in surrounding tissue. Scalp hematoma usually manifests as swelling in the shape of a bump or lump. However, upon examination the emergency doctor was unable once again to find evidence of hematoma although Louvard did note the presence of several superficial scratches on the right side of the patient's forehead. Of more concern were two wounds to the torso. Just above the right nipple was a 2 cm deep, 1.5 cm wide cut into the pectoralis muscle. The other wound presented in the left hypochondrium, the area around the lower part of the ribcage and which, at a depth of 5 cm and width of 4 cm, had penetrated the abdominal wall. From the angle of insertion, the doctor concluded that both wounds had been caused by a sharp object thrust from a downwards trajectory.

The intern did not though consider the injuries serious enough to seek the advice of his head of department. Instead, Dr Louvard sutured both wounds with two stitches apiece. As with all such cases, after the procedure the patient was admitted to hospital as a precautionary measure and would thus spend the night in the hospital's General Ward.

'Where is my father?' anxiously asked the patient as he was transferred by stretcher to the ward. He repeated the question several times, but the medics either failed to hear or did not know the answer.

All was quiet in the hospital's General Ward. Neither the clatter of the trolley nor the whispered voices of nurses unduly disturbed the residents and the wounded man was soon comfortably installed in bed. With the exception of a few coughs and wheezes, peace once again descended. The bearded Englishman began to doze. On the stroke of 3am he stirred. Officer Christian Gandon of the Judicial police stood at his bedside. Despite the late hour, the officer had come to take a statement.

'My name is Jeremy Bryan Cartland,' replied the patient when asked by the officer to identify himself. 'I was born on February 4, 1944, in Brighton.[1] I am a British subject.'

Over the course of the next two hours the young Brit would relate an extraordinary tale which had begun with a father and son setting off together on a peripatetic adventure from the south coast of England, a journey which had, one week later, come to an abrupt and gruesome end in the south of France. By the time the interview had finished dawn was breaking. Exhausted, the patient tried to rest. But sleep when it did come was fretful. On top of the pain from his wounds, the young Brit's shoulder ached.

A few hours later the sound of the hospital breakfast trolley doing its rounds roused the young man from his fitful slumber.

'Where is my father?' he asked.

The nurses shrugged. Nobody seemed to know what had happened to John Cartland. Later, the young Englishman was taken by wheelchair to an x-ray suite on the hospital's first floor where several plates were taken of his upper body: head, shoulder, chest, stomach etc. For a man who had been badly assaulted just hours previously it was an uncomfortable affair and Jeremy was relieved when it was finally over. Returned to the ward, he tried to sleep - without much success.

Meanwhile, news of the attack had rapidly spread. Locals from the communes of La Barben, Pélissanne and beyond had been stopping by the site as per human nature upon such occasions. Like moths attracted to light, all morning vehicles had been pulling up at this lonely stretch of the RN 572, sight-seers eager to confirm the rumours that a couple of British tourists had been slain. Although the corpse of John Cartland had by now been removed, evidence of the attack was stark and plentiful: the caravan's burnt embers suggestive of a funeral pyre while the victim's blood had stained the earth a dark, scarlet-brown colour.

Daylight having broken some hours ago, the murder location began to slowly reveal itself: a patch of waste ground strewn with rocks and rubbish slightly elevated in comparison to the road beside which it ran. Typical of the area, olive groves and pine trees abounded. Behind where the caravan had been pitched rose a mountain surrounded by wild, untrodden hills. Further east, jewel in the Bouches-du-Rhône crown and dating back to the 11th century, the magnificent turrets of La Barben chateau peeped out of the forest.

Warrant Officer Salendre's eyes took in the debris which littered the site: broken bottles, cartons, newspapers and even parts of household appliances. Salendre and his officers, it must be said, faced a tricky task. The hunt for evidence could hardly be helped by so much debris lying around.

'A strange choice of campsite,' remarked the Warrant Officer to a colleague who shrugged.

Indeed, the bumpy nature of this terrain on the very edge of the Provencal wilderness was hardly the most suitable location in which to temporarily site a caravan and the clearing's rather isolated position might have deterred many casual campers. As a place to camp out the general consensus was that there were many better places in the vicinity. Maybe, but how could a pair of British tourists have known?

The police search resumed at 9am. It didn't take long to recover several bloodstained items scattered around the immediate area: a handkerchief, an axe, a kitchen knife with a 15" blade and a large piece of concrete covered by a bloodied pillow case. The knife was found in a bush fifty metres south of the caravan. Manufactured by W Marple and Sons in Sheffield, England, the axe meanwhile was discovered seventy metres in the opposite direction underneath a concrete slab in what appeared to have been a crude effort to conceal its whereabouts. A lucky break, detectives were both delighted and surprised to find key pieces of evidence in such close proximity to the crime scene. Experience taught that murder weapons are all too often never discovered.

By the time the fire service had arrived the fire had almost burned itself out. Thus most, if not all of the victims' personal effects had perished. As for the caravan's contents, virtually nothing survived the blaze. A suit, a camera, tins of food, a porcelain teapot... a few items were just about recognisable - crisp, blackened remnants, the morning after the night before of an especially fierce barbecue. The Hillman Avenger yielded a little more fruit. Amongst the items removed from the vehicle was a white plastic container/jerrycan which, judging by the smell, had been used to store paraffin and still contained vestigial remains of that fluid. Also discovered was a blue gas bottle, umbrella, walking cane and Dee Brown's book chronicling the Indian history of the American West from 1970, *Bury My Heart at Wounded Knee.*

At 11.30 am Judge André Delmas arrived at the scene. As the examining magistrate serving the Aix-en-Provence district, procedure dictated that Delmas would assume overall command of the investigation relieving Warrant Office Salendre of his duties: a changing of the guard. Close to retirement, the judge had chanced upon an especially delicate affair with which to close a hitherto unremarkable career. It would be the first case of its kind Delmas had presided over. Indeed, this somewhat diffident scooter-riding magistrate, not to be confused with Monsieur Hulot - creation of French comic actor Jacques Tati - would be thrust into the kind of limelight he had always actively avoided.

Delmas arrived in time to witness the police sniffer dog Wolf at work. Starting from the locations where the axe, knife and concrete had been discovered dog and handler attempted to pick up the assailant's trail. Alas, each sortie ended with Wolf returning back to the caravan.

Meanwhile, news of the attack had naturally come to the attention of the press. Already there was much interest in this brutal attack on a pair of British holidaymakers, an English professor and his son camping out in the French countryside. Diabolical and bloody, it was a story that instantly captured the media's imagination. The first despatch from *Agence France Presse* had been in circulation since early morning:

> A father and son were brutally attacked last night around 1am, when they had just stopped their caravan in a pine forest, at the exit of Pélissanne along the national road 572. The father is dead, the son seriously injured.

Having been tipped-off by police contacts, a couple of journalists from local newspaper *Le Provencal* were conducting enquires of their own. That morning Paul-Claude Innocenzi and Francois Luizet had originally been intending to join colleagues at a cinema just off Marseille's famous La Canebière thoroughfare for the premier of *The Dominci Affair*. It would have to wait. Stocky and owl-like thanks to his large black-rimmed glasses, Innocenzi was one journalist who knew a trick or two about getting that story. He and Luizet had certainly had a hectic Monday morning. The duo had already spoken with both farmer Caire and a petrol pump attendant named Augusta Chauvet, and were now, as lunch beckoned, driving like the wind to Salon hospital where they hoped to find the victim's son.

Shortly after midday the *Provencal* colleagues slipped past hospital reception. It was like a prison break, but in reverse. Scenting they were on the cusp of securing an exclusive, the hacks held their breaths. A pretty nurse had just seen them. She flashed the pair a quizzical look.

'Is the injured Englishman here do you know?'

Expecting to be shown the door, Innocenzi and Luizet were delighted instead to be directed to a room on the ground floor. Hardly daring to believe their good fortune, they entered the General Ward.

With the sharpness of the journalist's eye the interlopers quietly appraised the patient. After his exertions in the x-ray theatre the Englishman was back in bed, lying on his side, dozing peacefully. His Shakespearean forehead framed by ash-blond locks and a well-kept beard, there was a definite air of regality about this young man. King Alfred sprung immediately to mind. For its part, the French media would develop the habit of comparing him to a Viking.

Jeremy greeted the strangers with a little smile. Their presence at his bedside did not appear to disturb him and he answered their questions with equanimity. In the few minutes they managed to snatch, the journalists were able to obtain several facts: that the victims were attacked while camping overnight in a caravan and that they were both teachers based in Brighton. This rather charming young man answered questions freely and in proficient French. The partners were not only impressed by his mastery of their native language, but declared themselves 'amazed' at the young teacher's composure. Coolness personified, Jeremy did not break down or become emotional at any time during the interview.

'Do you know what has become of your father?' Innocenzi put the question as delicately as he could.

'No, not at all,' replied the wounded man, 'have you heard anything?'

The fate of John Cartland remained a mystery, at least to the unfortunate man's son. In fact, the murdered man's corpse had been taken by the fire service to Rue Fontainebleau where the mortuary of Pélissanne cemetery was located and where the earthly remains of this English gentleman now reposed on a cold, stainless steel slab. An autopsy had been scheduled for later that day. Naturally, the *Provencal* comrades said nothing.

'We have just spoken to a witness in Pélissanne,' said

Luizet, 'who says she served you 15 francs worth of petrol yesterday afternoon.'

'What else did she say?' asked Jeremy.

'That a pink and yellow caravan arrived at her garage at about 5pm on the afternoon of the murder and that she spoke to a man who matches the description of the victim.' Although they could not have known it at the time, the journalists might just have imparted a vital piece of information to the stricken man. The questions continued: *why had the Cartlands come to France? How long were they planning to stay*? etc.

By now the *Provencal* duo had been joined by a freelance English journalist based in France. Word of the murder was spreading quickly. Over the next 48 hours Salon-de-Provence hospital would find itself under siege by local, national and even international media.

Later, when the journalists had been shooed away by a less accommodating nurse, Jeremy was transferred to a private room on the hospital's first floor. It was to these much quieter surroundings that the British Vice Consuls, Frank Benham and John Edmonds were ushered.

'Do you know where my father is?' asked Jeremy before the diplomats had even had chance to seat themselves.

'He's been very badly beaten around the head,' replied Edmonds gravely. 'He's still unconscious.' It seemed the British diplomats were under orders to disclose only that which was necessary.

The diplomats began by providing some practical advice, not least regarding what to expect in terms of the police investigation. They pointed out that the French judicial system operated in a wholly different fashion to that of its Anglo neighbour and Jeremy was reassured to discover that one or both of these two imperturbable gentlemen intended to be present tomorrow when the police were scheduled to visit. Jeremy was also heartened to hear that his sister Liz would probably be flying out on the morrow. Upon hearing the news, the young man's mood immediately improved.

A day which had begun with what the young Brit had described as an unprovoked, violent attack on himself and his father was coming to a close. It had been an exhausting as well as bewildering twenty-four hours. There was much to ponder. No doubt the police would have plenty of questions to ask. Jeremy tried to sleep but was interrupted by nurses going about their duties.

Just seven days earlier the Cartlands had left England for the continent on a trip which would take them to Cartland senior's beloved Provence among other places. Business and pleasure combined, they would travel at their leisure, dropping in on associates while taking the opportunity to visit sites of interest, whatever took their fancy. It should never have ended this way.

3

Jeremy's tale

Every summer the south coast of Sussex transforms into a hub of activity as thousands of foreign students arrive to undertake vacation courses in English language. Demand for EFL (English as a Foreign Language) summer schools reaches a peak in July. Thanks to their fine pebbly beaches, turquoise waters and elegant Georgian architecture, the towns of Eastbourne and Brighton have been attracting students eager to improve their English language skills for decades.

John Cartland opened Careers Tuition Centre in 1972. Located on Dyke Road in the heart of an area of Brighton known as Preston, like many similar operations in the area the school provided English language courses to students from all over the world, especially from the southern Mediterranean region. The summer EFL market has always been a lucrative one but also highly competitive. It pays to cultivate good relations with partners. And so, as part of a recruitment drive for the school's 1973 summer programme, the Cartlands intended to market their courses to their overseas' contacts.

Marketing then was one reason why father and son had embarked on their trip that spring. There were others: as Mr Cartland wished to turn the running of the school over to Jeremy, he wanted his son to meet his various business partners – language travel agents as they are known in the business. Given that hardly any appointments had been made in advance of the trip, father and son it seems intended to drop in on their contacts unannounced.

Business aside, there was yet another reason for the trip. Two years previously Cartland senior had purchased a caravan from a couple he had met while holidaying in Ibiza for the sum of £300.[1] He had bought the caravan unseen, on a whim. The time had now come to pick it up. Once collected from its owners who lived in Denia on Spain's Costa Blanca, Mr Cartland intended pitching the caravan somewhere in France – likely Marseille. Collection of caravan, recruitment of students and introduction of Jeremy to partners as his father's successor, the trip would thus kill several birds with one stone.

On the evening of Monday, 12th March, John Cartland set out from his home at 11 Powis Square on what would prove to be a fateful journey, the bloody culmination of which he could never have guessed - even in his wildest dreams. It took but a few minutes to drive to his son's flat at Highcroft Villas.

And so begins a version of events, Jeremy's tale.[2]

After arriving outside his son's house, Mr Cartland opened the boot of his car for Jeremy to place his luggage. What, with all the accoutrements required for a European road trip – maps, torches, hurricane lamp, candles etc. the Hillman Avenger was packed to bursting point. Cartland knew just how cold a spring night could be when spent in a caravan – even along the Med, so had packed plenty of warm clothing too – wool pullovers etc. A seasoned traveller, Mr Cartland was all set for the expedition. Jeremy meanwhile brought his own luggage out and placed it into the boot of the car. While doing so he noticed a large felling axe. It was one used by the Cartlands to chop down trees at various properties they owned around Brighton and Eastbourne.

'What's with the axe?' asked a bemused Jeremy.

'Oh, you never know when it might be needed,' replied his father airily.

'Don't be silly,' laughed the younger Cartland taking the instrument out of the boot and back into the kitchen of his flat.

Later, Jeremy pretended not to notice his father smuggle another smaller axe out from the house and place it into the boot of the car. Cartland senior was, in his son's words, going through his 'current mania for protection.' It seems the older man may have had concerns over his safety, believing himself to be a target of nebulous actors. His son smiled to himself. If it made his father happy, he could take the axe.

After Jeremy had loaded up his travel things, the pair drove back to Mr Cartland's home for a bite to eat and to drop off Jeremy's pet dog, Lara with Mr Cartland's housekeeper, Janet Gibson. Of Scottish antecedents, Ms. Gibson performed a range of duties for Cartland senior, both domestic and secretarial and which now included dog-sitting. Eventually, the fifty-seven-year-old waved her employer off. It was a dark, chilly evening on England's south coast.

'I wish I wasn't going,' said an apparently rueful Cartland senior as the car pulled out of Powis Square, the well-to-do area of Brighton where he owned an elegant, three-storey Regency house. 'I'd rather be at home with Janet's cooking and the television.'

Heading first for Denia and thereafter France, Italy and Switzerland, father and son expected to be gone for anything up to three, maybe four weeks. Apart from appointments in Denia and Marseille their plans were rather vague. Just how vague is apparent in a letter Mr Cartland wrote in early March to his business partner, Jacques-L. Mont-Reynaud, director of The International Centre for Educational Tourism in Marseille. 'Dear Jacques,' it begins:

> This year my son will be taking over the summer school as Director of Studies, and with this in view we are going to do a tour of Europe this March, together in our caravan. We hope to be in Marseille about 18/19th March. We would be grateful if you would do some small service for us. We want to leave our caravan somewhere preferably "permanently". Do you know anyone who will give it a home? We look forward to seeing you later in the month.

Cartland senior had also written to Nicholas 'Nikko' Lyon, the owner of the caravan, confirming that he and his son would be arriving in Denia on the 15th March.

Leaving Sussex behind, the Cartlands drove along the coast to Southampton where they were booked on the overnight ferry to Le Havre due to leave at 2300. On board they bought some bottles of Glenfiddich whiskey. Before arriving at 7am at the French port, they snatched a few hours' sleep.

Once on French soil a southwards journey of some 1500 km lay before them. After leaving Le Havre, they crossed the River Seine via the Pont de Tancarville suspension bridge. Thereafter, the journey south took them virtually the entire length of France, a gruelling eight-hour drive. Stopping overnight at hotels in Toulouse and then Tarragona in north-east Spain, true to his word, late in the afternoon of the Thursday 15th, the Cartlands rolled up in Javea where Lyon had a yacht moored in the town's pretty harbour. The three men spent a pleasant couple of hours on board *The Tabriz* chatting and drinking tea.

Later, they drove the short distance back to Denia. Lyon had kept the caravan on the front drive of his home, part of a small development called *Los Cortijos* situated just off Cami Pou de la Muntanya. For the elder Cartland this was in fact his second visit to the Lyons. In December 1971 he had arrived in Spain intending to take delivery of his purchase, but had fallen ill with bronchitis. The mission had been aborted. Mr Cartland returned home to Sussex empty-handed.

During the twenty-four hours the visitors would spend in his company, Lyon noticed some changes in John Cartland since that last meeting. The sixty-year-old had become frailer and somewhat forgetful. 'He seemed to me,' remarked the ex-pat in a statement 'to have become irresponsible.'

While his father retired to bed early, Jeremy visited a cinema in Denia in company with Nikko. That night the Cartlands slept in the caravan on the Lyons' forecourt. Caravans can be chilly places at night, even on Spain's Costa Blanca. Anticipating as much the Cartlands had brought a paraffin heater along. And so, the next day, the host accompanied Jeremy into town to buy a gas bottle and where the young Brit had a white plastic jerrycan filled with paraffin. After carrying out some repairs, later that afternoon the decision was taken to relocate the caravan to the nearby Camping Las Rotas on the beachfront of the same name.[3] Lyon hade his guests farewell on what was turning into a stormy afternoon.

Now towing a 1965 Sprite Musketeer 4-berth caravan in

their wake, father and son set out early the next morning from the campsite, Jeremy at the wheel. Like their contact in Denia it seems the young teacher, who had dreams of becoming a famous poet or writer, did not entirely trust his father - not enough to drive on the continent at any rate. Launched in 1970, The Hillman Avenger was catalogued as 'a small family car.' Progress thus must have been leisurely. The vehicle had not exactly been designed to tow 800 kg of caravan.

Valencia, Tarragona, Barcelona, mindful no doubt of the caravan they towed, father and son skirted round these busy urban areas as they progressed northwards along Spain's east coast. Glimpsed to the right, the brilliant blue expanse of the Balearic Sea was never far away. On the night of Saturday, 17th March, the Cartlands settled down for an icy night in a car park near the town of Girona. That paraffin heater brought all the way from the UK must have come in handy.

The next morning the convoy of Hillman Avenger and Sprite caravan crossed the border into France at Col de Perthus, a steep mountain pass sometimes used in the Tour de France cycle race. it was hot and sticky inside the little car, hot enough for Mr Cartland to take off his shirt at one point. By 4 o'clock that afternoon the Cartlands had arrived in Arles. Father and son visited the town's famous Roman landmarks. According to Jeremy, just before closing time they manged to dip into the town's splendid amphitheatre, which in its heyday could seat up to 20,000 spectators.

On a windy but warm Sunday afternoon, rather than heading south towards the city of Marseille to keep their appointment with Mont-Reynaud, the Cartlands headed east towards Salon-de-Provence and the village of Pélissanne. Father and son were now en route for the pretty village of Jouques where Cartland senior had owned a plot of land since

1963 and where the academic was a well-known if transient figure. For whatever reason the schedule had changed. Thus, the Brits did not visit Mont-Reynaud that Sunday as arranged.

Next, the Cartlands stopped to refuel at a garage where they purchased petrol before continuing their journey. The significance of where and when this transaction occurred will be appreciated later.

It had been a long day and now, as daylight began to fade, sixty-year-old John Cartland started to feel tired. A creature of habit, the businessman-cum-teacher rose early and went to bed even earlier. As the Cartlands threaded car and caravan through the narrow streets of a seemingly unknown place, they had begun to think about pitching up somewhere for the night.

Two kilometres after the village of Pélissanne, the Brits spotted a clearing on the right-hand side of the road. It seemed like a suitable place for an overnight stay. Turning off the road, the Hillman followed a stony pathway with the caravan bumping along behind. Once they had uncoupled car and caravan, positioning both vehicles in the direction they had just come in readiness for their departure in the morning, father and son began preparations for their stay: stabilising the caravan, hooking up the gas bottle, laying out the beds etc. While his son prepared supper, John Cartland stretched his legs.

Meanwhile, Jeremy poured himself a glass of whiskey, one eye cocked on the pans bubbling away on the little stove.

'That smells good,' said Cartland senior upon his return to the caravan.'

'Just tinned meat and veg,' laughed Jeremy. 'Hardly Cordon Bleu.'

Accompanied by a glass of red wine, the two men ate their modest dinner. Mr Cartland finished off with a tin of rice pudding and jam - 'an execrable concoction' in the words of a disapproving son. In the meantime, the Provencal landscape had imperceptibly transformed itself from benign haven to a silvery, crepuscular landscape of moonlight and shadows. Darkness had fallen.

Having read a little, Mr Cartland was asleep by nine o'clock. Jeremy did some accounts and made some notes for a novel before falling asleep a short time after his father.

And then it happened. A disturbance.

Woken by what seemed to be voices outside the caravan, Jeremy hurriedly dressed. For all their experience of France, its people and customs, the British tourists were clearly in a potentially vulnerable position. It was dark. The caravan was parked in a fairly remote spot on the edge of a small commune.

'I can hear voices,' whispered Jeremy as he shook his father. 'I'm going to check outside.'

Slipping on a pair of trousers over his pyjama bottoms and then his desert boots, Jeremy stepped out of the caravan into the cold, night air. He was met by a disturbing sight: one foot resting on the ground, a figure leaned inside the Hillman's passenger seat. Thieves!

'Que faites-vous?' Young Cartland stood by the boot of the car from where he demanded to know what was going on. It appeared from his vantage point that somebody was trying to hot-wire the Hillman in order to steal it. Jeremy could make out the back of somebody's head and shoulders, a dark and sinister silhouette but nothing else.

Before he knew what was happening, multitudes of tiny stars were dancing before his eyes. Everything went fuzzy. His ears buzzed. The young teacher had been hit on the back of the head so severely he had, as the French say, 'seen thirty-six candles.'

Fade to black.

Sometime later the young man came round, groggy and in pain. He immediately felt the searing heat from a fire. His attackers had fled the scene, setting the caravan alight before departing or so it appeared. Jeremy had one thought: where was his father? Despite the immense heat being generated by the flames, he rushed over to the burning caravan. There was no sign of Mr Cartland. In fear for his life the older man must have escaped. Was he hiding somewhere in the bushes, cold and terrified, having just witnessed the attempted murder of his only son?

It was at this moment Jeremy noticed that he was bleeding profusely. He had been stabbed in the stomach and chest. Disorientated and in agony he knew he had to get help fast. Pressing a handkerchief tightly over the wound in his abdomen, he staggered over to the road hoping to flag down a passing motorist.

A short time later a Citroen 2CV driven by Frederic Delaude approached. Jeremy waved it down.

4

Manic Monday

News travels fast, never more so when the topic is murder. By daybreak on Monday there was hardly a soul left in the Bouches-du-Rhône region of France unaware about what had occurred overnight at La Barben. Correspondents of all major news outlets in France and the UK were already heading down to Provence or making plans to do so.

Just hours into the investigation, the *Jas de Dane* murder location was indeed awash with people. Salon police force had its hands full. As well as being engaged in tasks such as cataloguing the contents of the Hillman Avenger motor car and analysing the smouldering remains of the caravan, the police were busily occupied preventing a curious public from collecting souvenirs – although criticism would later be levelled that this is precisely what they failed to do: preserve the integrity of the site. In addition, in their hunt for clues officers were also searching the site to a radius extending 300 metres into the surrounding scrubland and forests. Come daylight the murder site had been crawling with officers.

Police had also started to collate their impressions into a scene of crime report which would subsequently come under heavy fire from all directions. Some of the report's initial comments were undeniably imprudent. Most noticeably, it seemed to reject the possibility the crime could have been committed by a local person because people of the region had what it described as 'unblemished reputations' and possessed 'good character.' When it came to murder, the report observed, machine guns were apparently the choice of weapon among the local criminal fraternity, not axes. It also intimated that given unprovoked attacks of this nature were uncommon in the area, prowler theories could also therefore be precluded. With its various hypotheses and a tone teetering on the edge of certainty, it would be all too easy to conclude that here was a case over before it had begun.

Compiled by the type of local constabulary with only limited experience of such matters prior to the arrival of the specialists from the criminal divisions of Aix and Marseille, this hastily compiled document would prove to be somewhat of an albatross round police necks. Hasty as well as presumptuous, it was there to be shot at.[1]

Initially, officers had searched the scrubland in darkness, guided by torches and moonlight. It was only upon their return the following morning that they had been able to make a full assessment of the site, draw conclusions. As they had walked around, dewy sunshine on their backs and birdsong in their ears, it must have been hard to reconcile the carnage before them with an otherwise serene landscape. They would not have expected to stumble across the blood-encrusted weapons presumed to have been used in the attack; but there they were, axe, knife and concrete slab, strewn carelessly around the site. And then there was the caravan, melted into the earth, parts of which even now still smouldered. Officers of the Salon brigade had never seen anything like it. Perhaps it was the sheer unusualness of this crime that prompted the report with all its hypotheses and conjecture.

While their colleagues puzzled over the scene of crime, officers of the brigade had started to interview potential witnesses. Door to door enquiries were conducted in La Barben and the surrounding area. Local farms and building sites known to employ migrant workers – largely of north African descent – received visits. Enquiries were made near the coast where a new highway was under construction. Flights out of Marseille's airport at Marignane were also checked for last minute departures which might raise suspicion. At this stage of the enquiry, it appears that investigators were working on the tentative assumption the murder had occurred as a consequence of a robbery gone wrong even if they might have started to believe otherwise.

'I remember that day very well,' recalls a lady still resident in Pélissanne. 'My future husband and I had been to the cinema on that Sunday evening. The following day he was interrogated by the police. They wanted to know all about his movements of the previous night.'

One witness in particular attracted the attention of both press and police. As soon as she heard what had happened, Augusta Chauvet had made herself available. The 66-year-old vividly recalled an encounter with a couple of caravaners which had taken place late on Sunday afternoon and she wondered if this information might be relevant to the police investigation. Her instincts turned out to be correct. Officers listened closely as this neat, grey-haired lady related all that she had witnessed on that fateful day.[2]

As the proprietors had been away on Sunday, 18th March, the pensioner had been minding the pumps of the Total garage situated on Allée de Craponne, a boulevard lined with platanus trees and elegant thoroughfare which leads to Pélissanne's medieval village centre. Between 5.00 and 5.15pm a caravan had arrived on the garage forecourt. Its colour she recalled was pink and straw yellow. Inside the (white) car which towed the caravan she noticed two men, the older of whom got out of the passenger door and whose age she estimated as 60. The younger man remained in the car, reluctant, or so it seemed to leave the wheel. Madame Chauvet did however manage to catch a glimpse of the vehicle's somewhat reticent driver. His hair had been long 'like young people have it now.' This young man, she also recalled, had looked 'sullen.'[3]

Speaking excellent French though with a foreign accent, the older man requested 15 francs of super grade petrol. It was a request which surprised Madame Chauvet who had been expecting to supply rather more fuel than this trivial amount. While stood at the pump, attendant and customer chatted about the Mistral, which was currently blowing at a blustery 35 mph. When it came to payment, the younger man passed the money to the older gentleman in what the witness described as an 'off hand manner.' She also added that during the transaction the driver's attitude towards his companion had 'shocked' her and that he had not spoken a word during the stop either to herself or to the older passenger.

From her position inside the station, Chauvet watched the men. Rather than leaving the forecourt immediately, they waited several minutes. When they did eventually re-join the road, they did so abruptly, obliging a passing motorist to swerve in order to avoid an accident.

When *Le Provencal* duo Innocenzi and Luizet had spoken to this same witness, they had pressed the old lady for more details. What had she and her English customer spoken about at the pumps? The weather replied Chauvet. What about it? 'This Mistral bothers us a lot,' so had apparently said John Cartland in his perfect French. 'We will not be going far.'[4]

A potentially vital witness had come forward. So, would she now be able to identify the British traveller to whom she had served petrol?

'That's him,' she said when police showed her the deceased man's passport photo. 'That's the man I served yesterday.'

'Are you certain?'

'Absolutely.' Madame Chauvet had no doubt whatsoever.

Currently recovering in his hospital bed, as far as Jeremy Cartland was concerned the lady's (police) testimony might prove to be inconvenient for two reasons: firstly, it placed the British visitors in the vicinity of Pélissanne much earlier than the young teacher had intimated; secondly, it suggested there had been a certain amount of tension between the vehicle's two occupants that bright and blustery afternoon. Further, her recollection of a scowling, uncommunicative driver disdainful of his older companion hinted that all had indeed not been well between the travellers that afternoon.

With this testimony investigators could now begin to piece together the Cartlands' movements that Sunday, 18th March. The Brighton teachers must have certainly driven through the centre of Pélissanne. According to how Jeremy would recall events the elder Cartland had been required to check their bearings on a road map as they traversed the village.[5] Like the seasoned travellers they were, John and Jerry had packed plenty of maps and travel guides prior to setting off from the UK. Indeed, police recovered no fewer than three maps from the Hillman. They also found a couple of manuals specifically aimed at the international camper and published by the AA - *Continental Handbook* and *Camping & Caravanning Overseas*.

Armed with information a-plenty, minutes after leaving the forecourt of the Total garage, the caravanners arrived at *Jas de Dane* on the RN 572. How? And more to the point, why? What exactly were the Cartland's intentions that afternoon?

At this juncture the issue of time becomes crucial. If Mme Chauvet's recollections could be trusted - and coming less than twenty-four hours after the event, why wouldn't they be? – the tourists should have had ample time to reach their avowed destination of Jouques before nightfall. Barring accidents, the Cartlands could expect to complete the 45-kilometre (28 mile) journey directly eastwards in about an hour or thereabouts.

The journey across to Jouques might have been relatively short yet the travellers never made it. Clearly, police would need to work out why; in order to do so they would need to check the Cartland's movements even more carefully. It might have been a gut instinct, but detectives felt the route the visitors had chosen to take might be significant - even if they couldn't yet determine why. Maps and routes were consulted. Soon, police had a fair idea of the route they believed the tourists had taken that March afternoon.

After departing from Arles sometime on Sunday afternoon, forty minutes later the Cartlands would have skirted the peripheries of Salon-de-Provence before arriving at the start of the RN 572. Almost immediately after joining this national road the travellers must have branched off to enter Pélissanne via Allée de Craponne which conveyed them to their meeting with Mme Chauvet and the petrol pumps at the Total garage.[6]

Fuel purchased, the Cartlands had two options, both of which would deliver them to their overnight destination at

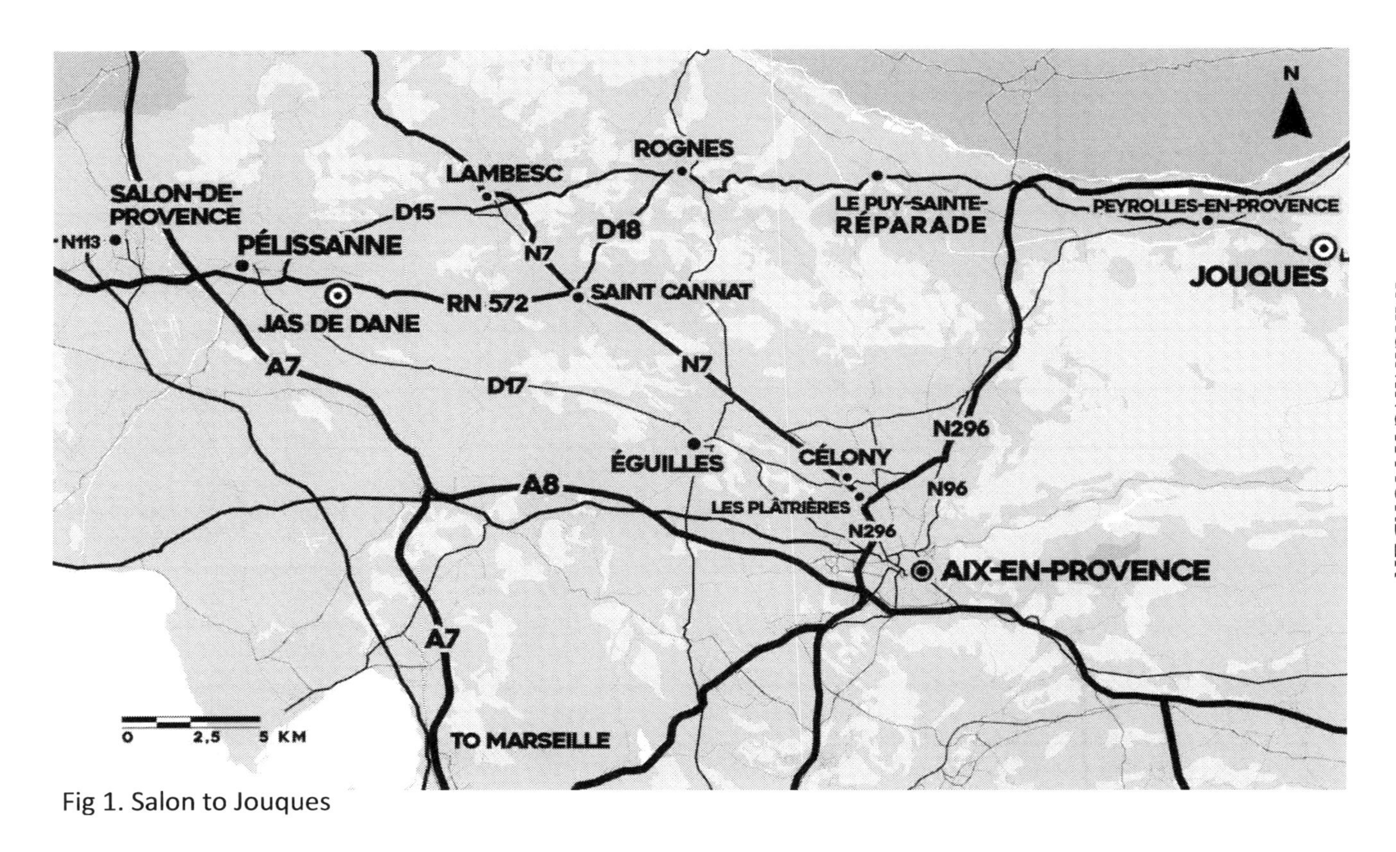

Fig 1. Salon to Jouques

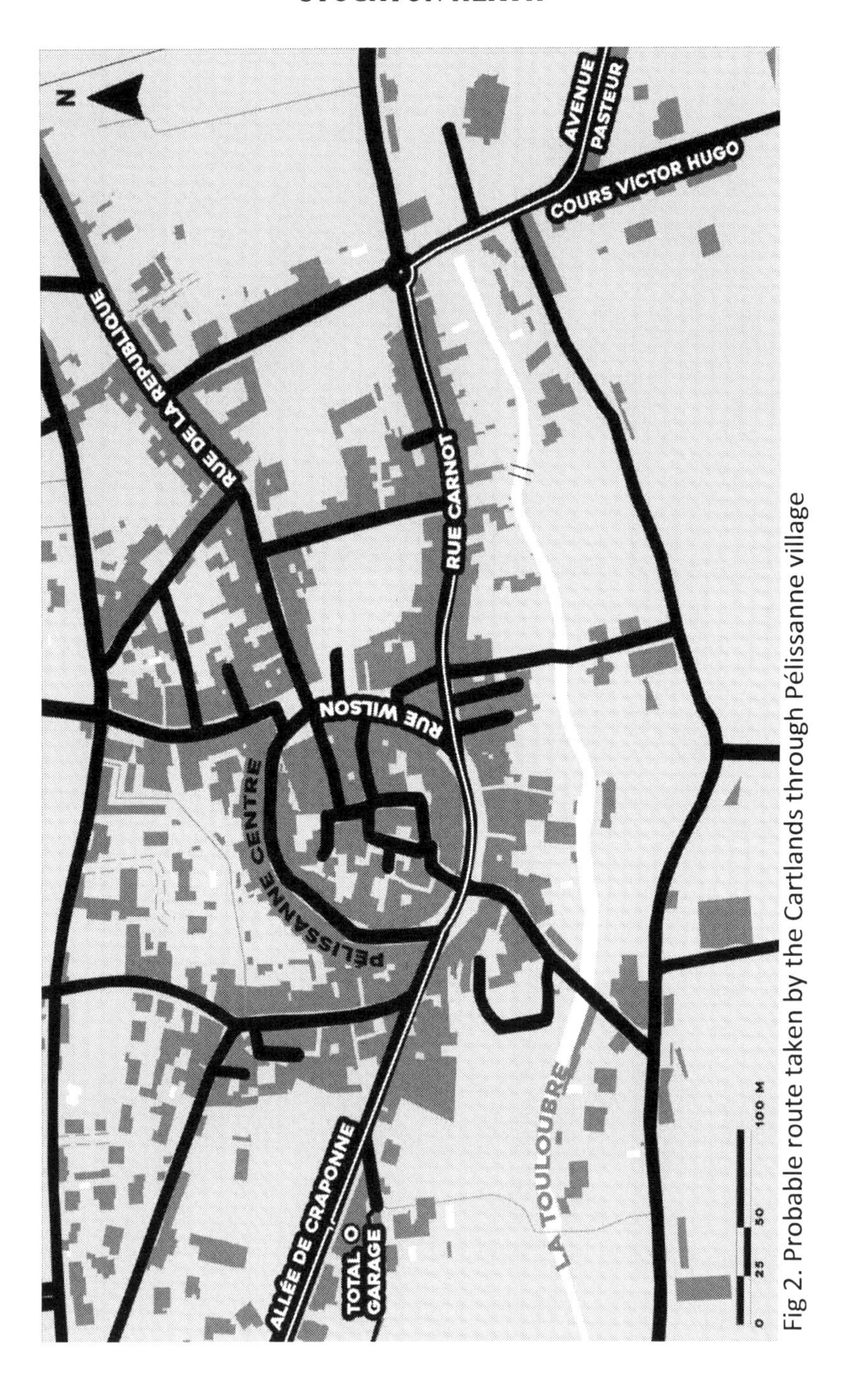

Fig 2. Probable route taken by the Cartlands through Pélissanne village

Jouques. Option 1 would have seen them take the D15 road. Taking the motorist through the attractive towns of Lambesc, Rognes, Le Puy-Sainte-Réparade and Peyrolles-en-Provence, the D15 would have been the most direct route and therefore one upon which the chances of getting lost would have been minimised (see fig. 1.). As it happened, when they left the Total forecourt, the Cartlands had in fact been just around the corner from the Rue de la Republique, the road leading out of Pélissanne and which subsequently merges into the D15 Route de Lambesc.

The second option was the one the caravanners actually took. After leaving the garage, the Cartlands would have continued past Pélissanne's ancient village centre along Rue Carnot 250 metres onwards to the crossroads at Cours Victor Hugo. (See fig. 2) Rather than continuing straight over, they must have turned right and then left onto Avenue Pasteur, a manoeuvre that ensured they remained on the RN 572A. Were they then following a specific route? It looked that way.

The British visitors, so it appeared, had decided to take what locals call the 'scenic route.' For soon enough the A road becomes the National 572 road taking the visitor to the commune of La Barben with its zoo and spectacular chateau. From here it would have been a short drive to the town of Saint Cannat. Although it would have been possible to head north-east to Rognes and join up with the D15 at this point, rather than taking this minor link road the more logical course of action would be to take the National N7 road south-east in the direction of Aix-en-Provence. According to Jeremy however the Cartlands had wanted to avoid this city of fountains sometimes dubbed France's most beautiful town.[7] This they could have achieved by branching off prior to hitting the city's environs.[8]

Having opted for the RN 572, a couple of kilometres after leaving the Total garage for some unknown reason the Cartlands pulled off the road at the clearing known as *Jas de Dane*. As a course of action, it puzzled detectives. Had not the father and son stopped for petrol in the late afternoon? Sunday had been a warm, sunny day. It would have been a pleasant enough drive over to their land, mistral notwithstanding. And yet rather than heading directly for Jouques where Cartland senior not only owned land but also had acquaintances and colleagues, the Cartlands had chosen instead to camp out by the side of the road in an unfamiliar place.

Why stop so short of their destination? As a decision it just seemed illogical. Early theories suggested Cartland senior and junior might have had a disagreement and had pulled off the road in order to cool down or avoid an accident. Whatever the reason, one thing seemed clear enough: *something* had prevented them from completing the journey and police wanted to discover what.

5

'With savage fury'

Early on Monday evening Commissioner Gregoire Krikorian arrived at the mortuary of the Pélissanne Cemetery where colleague's Dr Jacqueline Jouglard and Dr Jean-Marc David were preparing to conduct an autopsy on the corpse of John Cartland. Nicknamed 'Boumédiène' due to a supposed resemblance to Algeria's President of the same name, as evidenced by the seniority of his rank Krikorian was regarded as somewhat of a high-flyer within the Aix police department. The detective had been appointed by Judge Delmas to take over the case from the Salon brigade. Recently, he had helped crack a huge real estate scandal wherein investors had been swindled out of millions of francs.[1] Reputation preceding him, it was hoped and assumed the Aix officer would wrap the case up with minimum fuss.

After spending much of the day at the *Jas de Dane* murder location, Krikorian had hurried straight over to the mortuary.

The detective was eager to observe proceedings first hand. Tomorrow, Tuesday, he planned to interview the injured son at Salon hospital. He wanted to be prepared.

On the face of it the case seemed clear enough: persons unknown had targeted the British registered Hillman motor car together with the caravan pitched alongside it at what was an admittedly isolated spot at the side of the RN 572. Presumably, the motive had been theft. However, for reasons yet to be established, robbery had escalated into murder. It was just a case of tracking down the individuals responsible. Krikorian though had other ideas. Something was not sitting right with this thoughtful, analytical man of Armenian extraction - a hunch, a gut instinct, the kind of intuitive feeling no instruction manual can ever teach. For now, he put his instincts to one side. He wanted to concentrate on the post mortem.

At 6pm Dr David and Dr Jouglard began their grisly task. The cadaver before them, the doctors remarked, was that of a 'robust' man 1.75 metres tall, 43 cm broad. First, they washed all traces of congealed blood from the body, the majority of which centred around the head, neck and shoulder areas.

On the exterior of the body, they observed several lesions as well as bleeds (hematoma) mainly to the right forearm, knee and hip. In particularly, the forehead displayed numerous small lesions. Hematoma was also observed on the left side of the face. Some time prior to his death it thus appeared the victim may have been involved in some sort of fracas which had resulted in this series of largely superficial abrasions. By contrast, the hands and nails remained intact, free of lesions.

Next the doctors examined the scalp area noting immediately two significant wounds to the left side of the skull. One of these wounds presented just behind and above the ear. Described as 'star-shaped' it was accompanied by a large underlying hematoma. The other wound presented closer to the top of the skull. It measured six centimetres in diameter and had caused the bone to fracture into small pieces.

External examination over, attention turned to the interior of the skull where the doctors fully expected to find serious damage. Opening the cranium with an electric saw duly revealed copious quantities of blood. Mr Cartland had suffered massive internal haemorrhaging. David and Jouglard now observed yet more wounds. Of an especially serious nature was a large occipital fracture, the bone which sits at the base of the skull cupping the lower part of the brain whence it protects the delicate tissue contained within. Overall, the left-side of the skull had suffered serious trauma. Fractures to this side of the cranium doctors described as 'particularly serious' adding that they had been made with 'considerable violence.'

In the neck area, David and Jouglard observed a series of ten lesions, the longest of which measured some 15 centimetres in length. The doctors concluded that these wounds – some reaching a depth of 5-6 centimetres - had been inflicted by a blunt cutting tool such as an axe. One blow had been delivered with such ferocity it had detached a piece of the lower jawbone. A clean cut to the carotid artery was also observed. According to the report, this series of sustained blows had been 'carried out with precision' and had been 'particularly mutilating and mortal.' Mr Cartland's attacker had been determined, so it seemed, to cut the unfortunate man's throat.

As the doctors went about their work, a pensive Krikorian stood close by. Though he seemed calm enough, inwardly he was wrestling with an acute anomaly: Mr Cartland's wounds bore no resemblance to those of his son. The older man had been hacked to death; in sharp contrast his son had suffered superficial cuts. How to account for such a grave disparity?

The autopsy continued. Examination of the internal organs revealed the presence of a 'creamy white pulp' in the stomach. Following microscopic analysis of proteins and lipids, the doctors concluded that this mulch was the remains of a meal consumed 4-8 hours prior to death. Large hematomas also were noted in the trachea and oesophagus. Analysis of the bladder revealed some potentially interesting information; it contained 350 ml of urine. The bladder capacity of an average adult before urination becomes necessary is somewhere in the range of 300 and 500 ml, though the aging process decreases the organ's elasticity and explains why the doctors classed the deceased's bladder in this instance as being 'full.' Meanwhile, in the rectum faeces were observed having formed though 'not necessarily implying a need to defecate.'

Krikorian's ears pricked up. Hadn't the victim been found in a recess within the thicket, pyjama bottoms down around the ankles? Police initially suspected that Mr Cartland had been murdered while in the process of *faire ses boissons* i.e. going to the toilet. Thus far it was a hypothesis the autopsy appeared to support.

In general, the post mortem showed that at the time of his death John Basil Cartland had been in a fairly good state of health for a man of his years.

Having performed their various test and analyses, including alcohol (negative) and blood group (A) David and Jouglard addressed the circumstances of death. What did the evidence reveal about how the victim had died? More specifically, could the doctors shed light on the likely sequence of events? Based on their analysis they were able to describe a likely scenario: Mr Cartland was first violently struck in the back of the head by a blunt object causing him to fall to the ground. Then, the attacker delivered several more blows to the stricken man's skull. Of the wounds observed, the fracture of the occipital bone at the nape of the neck would certainly have resulted in unconsciousness, and in contrast to the other wounds had probably been delivered by an axe or such like instrument. In all likelihood, when knocked to the ground, the victim had not been dead.

While lying motionless, next his throat had then been slashed multiple times using a blunt cutting tool. The doctors described this phase of the attack as being carried out 'with savage fury.' Severing of the carotid artery had not however produced jets as might be expected from this type of injury; rather blood had largely flowed into the victim's pullover and directly into the ground where it formed a large pool. In other words, blood had not been spraying all over the location. There had been no scarlet fountain. It was a hypothesis already confirmed by forensics at the murder scene.

The doctors further deduced that when he or she had been hacking at the throat, the attacker had been standing level with the victim, at his side, one or both feet planted close to his throat. And then came a crucial observation: no signs of a struggle were detected. Mr Cartland had apparently not fought for his life. The abrasions already observed to face and body were of a minor nature, hardly commensurate with a life-or-death struggle. Nor were there any signs of the body having been dragged. On the contrary, the evidence indicated he had fallen at the spot where he had first been struck. Thereafter, he had lain motionless, semi or more likely fully unconscious.

Finally, Drs David and Jouglard tested the blood-stained handkerchief which had been found close to Mr Cartland's body. Whose blood was it, that of father, son or a third party? Testing established the blood belonged to group A. Thus, it could have been stained with the victim's blood or that of another person with blood group A. What, if any, significance this suggested was not entirely clear. The autopsy was over. It was getting late. But a much clearer picture of what might have occurred on the night of Sunday 18-19th March had started to emerge.

Krikorian considered what he had seen and heard. All the evidence seemed to indicate that the deceased had indeed been taken by surprise. On this point the policeman found himself in agreement with the doctors' hypothesis. Moreover, when attacked, it seemed likely the 60-year-old may have been making a final visit to the toilet before settling down for the night. Hadn't the bladder been almost full? Further, the body had been found just six metres from the caravan door in a clump of bushes, pyjamas rolled down. Maybe the victim had also been intending to defecate. If so, then the poor gentleman must have thus been a sitting – standing – duck.

According to the doctors, a 'blunt object' had been used to inflict the horrific injuries to the skull just witnessed on the mortuary slab. As to the weapon, Krikorian had a more than likely candidate: the blood-stained pillow case retrieved from the scene of the crime. By placing a heavy concrete slab inside it, whoever killed John Cartland had assembled a potentially lethal weapon which could be slung at some velocity. It was an effective as well as macabre creation. Regarding the concrete itself, it seemed probable that it had been sourced from amongst the rubble which abounded at the murder location.

In the middle of his/her frenzy, the killer had apparently swapped concrete sling for an axe in order to hack at Mr Cartland's neck. Two murder weapons, three if including the knife. A cool customer indeed, determined, or so it seemed, to finish the job. Hence, there was absolutely no doubt in the policeman's mind nor those of the doctors: the perpetrator(s) had definitely meant to kill the teacher-cum-businessman. The sheer ferocity and prolonged nature of the assault proved as much. Would opportunistic prowlers, wondered Krikorian, commit such a violent crime - even if they had been disturbed? After all, the difference between petty theft and murder is vast. The one could result in a fine or short jail term; the other could lead all the way to the guillotine.

Rather than a random attack on a couple of vulnerable tourists, the commissioner was starting to develop other lines of thought. Theft might not necessarily have been the motive. If not theft, then what?

Of course it might have been the Cartlands misfortune to have met a psychopathic killer on that night of the full moon. Such an explanation might help explain the level of violence meted out on the dead man. This hypothesis, handy as it was, begged another question however: why had the killers gone to such lengths to ensure the death of Cartland senior, but spared his son? As Krikorian had vividly come to realise, the older man's wounds, multiple and mortal, bore no resemblance at all to those of his son, described by one Salon nurse as 'mere scratches.'

'We know that frenzied attacks of this kind are more often than not the result of the offender acting on the basis of cumulative wrongs – real or imagined,' notes Professor David Wilson when discussing murders which exhibit a high degree of overkill. 'He is retaliating against the victim for perceived insults or injustices . . . he is therefore acting in a rage; he is hyper emotional and out of control.'[2] Had the killer of John Cartland been acting out of anger, slashing the victim's throat multiple times in an act of retribution?

Krikorian thanked David and Jouglard before walking out

into the cool, night air thankful it was all over. Although the post mortem had provided answers to several questions, it had raised several others: why had the prowlers been so intent to murder just one of the campers? How had they managed to obtain the axe belonging to the Cartlands? Where had the pillow case come from housing the concrete block used to fell Mr Cartland?

Indeed, there were all sorts of anomalies to consider. One of the most insoluble concerned logistics. If Mr Cartland had been in the process of *faire ses boissons* when the killers had struck as seemed likely, it implied that he had failed to notice their presence when leaving the caravan. It seemed odd, for had not Jeremy already been attacked? Surely, Mr Cartland must have heard the attack. Had not Jeremy woken the older man to inform him that prowlers were outside the caravan? Despite this warning and the fact his son had disappeared outside to confront these unwelcome midnight callers, Cartland had wandered over to the thicket. However strange it sounded, this was the only explanation that could reconcile Jeremy's version to the facts suggested by the forensic evidence.

Far from confirming the account of the night's events given to police by the victim's son, the autopsy seemed to point in another direction. There was much for Krikorian to ponder over. The thirty-five-year-old detective had no illusions; he and his officers would need to prove any theories with the type of evidence that would stack up in a court of law.

'I knew that Krikorian would have to produce evidence,' reflected Jeremy a few years later, 'to back his theories . . . I also knew that there could not possibly be any evidence to support these accusations.'[3] Jeremy had called it correctly: some if not all of it having been destroyed in the burning caravan, evidence of the type required by law would surely be difficult if not impossible to obtain.

The commissioner got into his blue, Simca 1100. Despite his misgivings, he felt satisfied the case would soon reach a satisfactory conclusion. On the forty-minute drive home to the quiet suburb of Marseille where he lived with his wife and two children, the detective had plenty of time for reflection. If nothing else he had achieved what he had set out to do that evening - to confirm the many misgivings which had struck him earlier that day while surveying the murder scene.

Tomorrow he would meet the surviving Cartland. Questions racing through his mind and with them a theory evolving which the autopsy appeared to have confirmed, the detective felt sure a breakthrough was within his grasp.

6

Witness no. 1

Having come under siege by journalists hungry for a scoop, during a hectic Monday, the decision had been taken by Salon-de-Provence hospital to transfer the British patient to a private room. Not surprisingly, the hospital had been quite unprepared for the media interest generated by this vicious, seemingly unprovoked attack on a couple of British tourists. And so, later that day, Jeremy had been duly transferred to a room on the first floor of the hospital.

The young Briton thus awoke on Tuesday morning in a quieter, more serene environment than he had encountered in the General Ward. No sooner had breakfast ended, than the first of what would be many visitors that day arrived at his bedside. Much to the patient's dismay, a mobile X-ray unit was wheeled into the room. Not again! The technician took yet more exposures: head, shoulder, abdomen, with Jeremy just wishing it could be over.

Fresh from the post mortem of the previous night, it was Dr Jouglard who arrived next in order to conduct a physical examination of the British patient. Jeremy was apparently unaware that Mr Cartland was dead. 'Where is my father?' It was a question he would persistently ask medical staff, but nobody seemed to know. The police were biding their time. Under strict instruction not to divulge any information, Jouglard performed her task with diligence and compassion.

Immediately after lunch an operator wheeled an electro-encephalograph (EEG) into the room. EEG records brain activity and can therefore be used following trauma to the head to assess the extent of any damage. Jeremy was far from happy.

'What are you doing this for?' he asked a technician busily attaching sensors to a scalp still sore.

'Checking for brain damage.'

'But there's nothing wrong with my brain,' he objected.

Nonetheless, the test went ahead. According to his own testimony, Jeremy had been coshed hard enough on the back of his head to lose consciousness. EEG testing was a precautionary measure therefore. After a painful procedure in which virtually all the patient's reflexes and responses were checked, the tests finally came to an end.

'Don't worry,' said the technician undoing the multitude of wires, 'everything's fine.'

Awake since dawn, the young British teacher by now was exhausted. Alas, his exertions had only just begun. Police had just arrived and were waiting in the corridor to commence interviewing. From the commotion outside it seemed half the population of Salon was waiting to pay homage to the English patient whose name was now making headlines around the world.

Some of the nurses brought extra chairs into the room and began arranging them. A typewriter was set up on a table. Propped up in bed, a bemused Jeremy watched as a coterie of officials crammed into the small room. Detectives were joined by a police interpreter as well as by a couple of British consular officials, Frank Benham and John Edmonds, who had arrived from Marseille to represent as best they could the young man's interests. No requirement under French law for third parties to be present at preliminary police interviews – not even lawyers – the officials' attendance was a courtesy of the presiding judge, M. André Delmas.

Krikorian made his entrance with his usual nonchalance, a trait which had wrong-footed many a criminal. For underneath the casual exterior lurked a razor-sharp mind. On this, their first meeting, Jeremy would later describe the commissioner's distinctive black moustache as the type, 'favoured by lounge lizards in pre-war films.' No love lost there then.

Once the introductions had been made, Inspector Jean Ettori took up a place at the typewriter, fingers poised over the keys. Jeremy was about to be questioned as a witness. It was almost half past three on a warm, sunny Provencal afternoon.

To begin with, the young teacher recounted his story. It was essentially the same one he had told police in the early hours of Monday: exhausted after a long day travelling from Spain, he and his father had decided to pitch up by the side of the RN 572 where later that same evening they had been attacked by prowlers. Knocked unconscious, Jeremy had not seen his attackers. He had come round to discover his father gone and the caravan on fire. But there were some additional details:

1. Around 7pm that Sunday evening, the Cartlands purchased 21 francs of petrol 'a little after Salon.' Jeremy

could not however recall the location of the garage itself.

2. Jeremy had been knocked unconscious following a blow to the jaw.

3. Shortly after pitching the caravan at *Jas de Dane*, Mr Cartland had spoken to persons unknown parked in a vehicle close to the clearing.

However, the more he expounded the more issues arose with the teacher's story. Upon admission to Salon hospital, Jeremy had not mentioned any blow to the jaw. The details of the petrol stop, vague and yet precise at the same time, were contradicted by the testimony of Madame Chauvet. And who were the mysterious occupants of the car with whom Cartland senior had conversed, but whom his son claimed not to have seen or even heard?

As Jeremy spoke, Krikorian made a mental note of these and other anomalies, occasionally exchanging a look with Ettori. It was a tedious process. Tedious because police questions as well as Jeremy's answers required translating from English into French and vice versa.

'Can you describe either of your attackers?' asked Krikorian quelling the exasperation he felt.

'No. I only saw the silhouette of the one sitting in the car,' replied Jeremy. 'I saw nothing of the one who struck me from behind.'

It transpired that the police's main and only witness had been unconscious virtually the entire duration of the incident. Jeremy had seen nothing but shadows and was thus unable to provide any kind of description of his attackers. Thus, many of the questions which followed led to dead end after dead end yet had to be asked.

'What did your attacker use to hit you?'

'How could I possibly know that?' replied Jeremy with a sigh. Questions were now being fired from all angles. When Krikorian paused, Ettori or another colleague would step in.

Of particular interest to police was the condition in which the Hillman had been found. According to Jeremy, he had seen someone leaning into the vehicle via the left-hand front passenger door, presumably in an attempt to steal it - though why thieves would wish to steal a rather ordinary family saloon car readily identifiable by its English registration plate YYU 999H was never adequately explained. Delaude and the three Beaucaire pals had testified that although the Hillman's doors had been closed, its right-front door had been unlocked and thus they had been able to gain access to the vehicle via this, the driver's door. Jeremy maintained that both vehicle's front doors had in fact been unlocked, right and left. However, when checking the Hillman upon their arrival at the murder scene, police had found the left-front locked.

'How do you explain this discrepancy?' asked Krikorian.

The English patient was not warming to this detective with the hunched shoulders whose prowess had earned him the honour of being called 'the Maigret of the south.'

'Somebody must have locked it,' replied Jeremy coolly, 'while moving it away from the caravan.'

'The witnesses disagree.'

'Then I can only assume they may have forgotten. The door was certainly unlocked when we left Arles.'

Much to the Englishman's irritation, Krikorian continued to press the point home. Upon investigation police had found several items of value and/or importance in the Hillman such as traveller's cheques, passports and other documents and the detective wanted to know why the tourists had not taken even more care to ensure the security of the vehicle overnight. The commissioner viewed the issue as incontrovertible proof that his interviewee had been lying all the time about the nocturnal disturbance. It was a detail he would return to again and again.

'Fact: the door was most certainly locked when we found it,' barked Krikorian. 'Nor was there any sign of breaking in. Admit it Mr Cartland – the door was never unlocked. You are not telling us the truth!'

Jeremy appealed to the tall, sun-tanned figure of Frank Benham sitting in the corner of the cramped room. The Vice Consul's look said it all. His presence in the hospital room had been granted on the proviso that he would not, at any time, intervene in proceedings and Benham was sticking to his word.

This particular line of enquiry leading to stalemate, next Krikorian unrolled the items discovered at the scene of the crime: kitchen knife, concrete slab and axe - all of which bore the scarlet stains of extreme violence. Jeremy recognised only the last of these artefacts. It was the same axe, he confirmed, that he had seen his father smuggle into the Hillman's boot at the start of their voyage. As for the knife, he had never set eyes on it. The same for the pillow case housing the concrete block: it was the first time he had seen this gruesome combination.

'Is this the same knife which you used to kill your father?' demanded Krikorian unimpressed by the patient's denials.

'I told you, I've never seen it before.'

Inspector Ettori snorted. The veteran detective had a reputation for cutting to the chase. Thus, it was the man sitting at the typewriter who finally put the police theory, and bluntly so, to the bed-ridden Brit:

'Isn't it true that you and your father had drunk too much that evening and that you quarrelled? And isn't it also true that later, when your father went to relieve himself in the bushes by the caravan, you followed him out and killed him with the axe you had brought with you for that very purpose?'

'No, that's not true!' protested Jeremy.

'Then how did the murderers come to be in possession of the axe – *your axe*?' snapped Krikorian now pacing up and down the small room. 'You yourself said it was stored in the caravan, in a drawer by your father's bed!'

'Father must have taken it outside with him when he heard me being attacked. The attackers must have disarmed him.'

Whenever he spoke, the young man did so without any sign of apparent agitation. Moreover, during the interview this softly-spoken, imperturbable English patient tended to look detectives straight in the eye; not once did he raise his voice or shout. A cool customer indeed thought Krikorian. Despite his attitude often verging on arrogance, the commissioner almost admired the Viking his boldness.

'Perhaps you could explain why your father felt it necessary to bring an axe to France in the first place? It seems a rather strange item to pack for a holiday!'

'I've already explained that father wanted it for protection. He has been worried lately about his safety and so he decided to bring it as a precaution. I tried to stop him but he insisted.'

Krikorian cast a doubtful eye on the young man now lying serenely in his hospital bed. What was it about him that disturbed the detective so? His apparent nonchalance? His unflappable manner or the rather cool indifference he seemed to display towards the whole saga? The Commissioner and his colleagues had already established certain facts regarding the victim's background, enough for the son's various explanations to seem contradictory. Police knew for example that Mr Cartland owned land in the region; they also knew he had business contacts in Marseille, Aix and Jouques and that he spoke fluent French. In fact, Cartland appeared to have many connections with France and yet this same country had suddenly and inexplicably become dangerous enough for him to need protection. If, as the son claimed, his father had been so concerned about his personal safety he had felt it necessary to bring along an axe, why had the Cartlands decided to go to France in the first place? Moreover, why set up camp at an isolated spot such as *Jas de Dane*? These did not seem to be the actions of a man worried about his safety.

At 6 o'clock questioning stopped for refreshments. Hostilities at last suspended, Krikorian, Ettori and co. became almost friendly towards their English adversary, chatting casually about this and that in a manner that suggested there was nothing personal about the sometimes-gruff exchanges of the previous two and a half hours. The cops had just been doing their jobs. It was a welcome break from the tension. Aware that the truce would soon end, a thoughtful Jeremy sipped orange juice. Krikorian and Ettori might be chatting and smiling now, but the Brit sensed this pair of sleuths represented a very real threat to his liberty and would soon enough reassume the cynical demeanour of the past few hours.

In the meantime, Jeremy's sister had arrived at Salon hospital after being met and escorted from the airport by John Edmonds.

Elizabeth 'Liz' Cartland had been informed of her father's murder while on duty at the Hertfordshire secondary school where she worked as Head of English. She had caught the first available flight to Marseille from Heathrow the following day. Her arrival at the hospital recalled the type of scenes usually witnessed down the coast at the annual Cannes festival. Even before she had stepped out of Edmond's car the flashbulbs had started. Journalists scrambled and jostled with one another. In the short glimpse they had of her skipping out of Edmond's car straight into block 5 of the hospital, the hacks knew that the addition to the story of a glamorous sister could only help sell more newspapers. And Miss Cartland *did* turn heads. From the start, the French press simply adored this most English of roses. Love at first sight. Or, as the French say, *le coup de foudre* ('a shot of lightning.')

While Edmonds negotiated with officials to enable Miss Cartland to gain access to her brother, the lady herself waited in the hospital corridor with a journalist friend who had flown out with her. The sheer number of people outside shocked her. It dawned upon her that the Cartlands were in the middle of a very big story. All she wanted for now though was to see her brother. But it wasn't quite that simple. Naturally, the police were rather anxious to take a statement from this key witness. The young teacher agreed to speak - anything that would allow her to gain access to Jerry.

'My father and my brother were on very good terms,' she told police. 'My father lived for his children. Jeremy loved him.' The slim, undeniably attractive 26-year-old added that her brother was a 'fundamentally non-violent person.'

The investigation was moving into tricky waters - family relations. If Jeremy had, as investigators increasingly suspected, murdered his own father, then what had been the motive? Had it indeed been a quarrel gone badly wrong or had there been deeper, underlying reasons? Was the relationship between father and son quite as simple and straightforward as portrayed by Miss Cartland? Delicate questions such as these would clearly need to be addressed.

Statement completed, Miss Cartland was granted permission to see her brother. It was an emotional reunion. Upon seeing his sister enter the sickroom Jeremy finally betrayed some emotion. The Cartlands comforted one another before being gently reminded that the police interview was not quite over. Liz left the room promising to take her brother home as soon as she could.

The interview resumed. Scrunching their coffee cups up and stubbing out cigarettes, detectives prepared for what they knew would be a long night. They were not wrong about that. As the hospital's night lights came on still the interview went on, Krikorian seemingly indefatigable.

Not long after the resumption, Frank Benham found an opportunity to have a quiet aside with his compatriot. 'I'm afraid I have some bad news. Your father is dead.'

At nine-thirty, and with little sign of the end in sight, Benham stood quietly up and left the room. Krikorian and Ettori stopped in their tracks. The Vice Consul had made a typically discreet gesture, but one that could not be ignored. It was time to call it a night. Jeremy was exhausted, so too was police interpreter Madame Diamantidis. Defeated, Krikorian snapped his briefcase shut. Bidding good-night to Jeremy, the detective took his leave. A long and draining day had finally come to an end.

Huddled together in small groups or dozing in their cars, the sight of the slim figure of Krikorian emerging from the hospital instantly energised journalists some of whom had been waiting since lunchtime. Correspondents from the UK (BBC, *Daily Express, The Times* etc.) had been chatting and comparing notes most of the day while their counterparts from *Le Monde, Le Provencal* and the French broadcast media had been doing likewise.

'Mr Jeremy Cartland replied to all my questions freely,' said the detective while the gentleman of the press thrust their microphones under his nose. 'He is absolutely free to leave. He is simply a witness, most certainly an essential one to whom I may listen to again if necessary.'

'Commissioner, is the Englishman a suspect?'

'Do you think he killed his father?'

Head down, the Commissioner pushed and squeezed his way through the crowd of journalists. Firing questions with the rapidity of a machine gun, the gaggle jockeyed for position while pursuing the phlegmatic detective over to his car. Something was not quite right and the hacks knew it; witness interviews don't last for over six hours.

Krikorian drove away tired but hopeful. Despite what Jeremy Cartland might believe, the interview was not over by any stretch of the imagination. In fact, it had only just begun. Tomorrow the commissioner intended to confront this somewhat imperious English teacher with more inconsistencies and yet more contradictions until the young man realised the futility of his position. While the media spoke of prowlers and robberies gone awry, Krikorian felt certain the key to the mystery lay not within the gypsy camps of Provence nor the area's farms and the army of itinerant workers who worked them, but rather it lay much closer to home: within the Cartland family circle.

7

Worshipper of the Provence sun

Almost from its inception the gory 'French murder' captured the imagination of both press and public. Its Mediterranean climate and idyllic lifestyle long since drawing British travellers to Provence and with lurid reports of one such tourist's 'decapitation' filling newspaper front pages, interest in the crime intensified. For once tabloid reports were not that far from the truth. The unfortunate Mr Cartland had been the victim of a frenzied attack, butchered in his pyjamas while holidaying in a country he adored.

Early in the investigation there was thus just one question on everybody's lips: who could have done such a thing and why? In its sheer brutality the crime hinted at motivation beyond just a robbery gone wrong. Petty criminals rarely kill – not with such apparent fury. Had the victim been killed because of a grudge or in an act of retaliation then? 'John Cartland' was a name on many lips. Finding out about the victim, the life he had led and the type of man he had been, became a priority.

At the time of his death the media invariably described Mr Cartland as a 'Brighton headmaster' who ran a private language school. That much was true, but as a description it did justice to neither the man's intrinsic complexity or his colourful background. The picture which accompanied the majority of press reports shed little more light, depicting as it did a still ruggedly handsome man in late middle life. Anthony Quayle with a dash of Errol Flynn, a touch of the archetypal matinee idol lingered on in Cartland's face. Closer inspection revealed a glint in the eyes. Though undoubtedly well-thumbed, the book of John Cartland might still have had a few chapters waiting to be writ.

Over the coming days and weeks a much more detailed picture of this remarkable man would emerge. Thrice married and divorced, the deceased had lived and worked all over the world and spoke several languages fluently including French, Italian, Arabic, Urdu and Pashto. Whilst studying at Worcester College he had won a coveted Gibbs' bursary for outstanding scholarship. He had left Oxford with a First in Modern History. During the war, it was whispered, he had worked with Free France, the resistance unit which had been active in southern parts of the country, Provence included. Amongst his acquaintances it was said he counted British prime minster Ted Heath and former French president Charles de Gaulle - a signed portrait of whom took pride of place in the dead man's office.

Persistent rumours of a background in British wartime intelligence circulating, journalists sensed there might be hidden depths to this story. Perhaps there was more to this respectable Sussex headmaster than met the eye. The media began to search for clues.

The ever-resourceful Paul-Claude Innocenzi scooted up to Jouques. This charming village of stone houses was apparently where the Cartlands and their caravan had been headed until fate decided otherwise. Here the journalist heard plenty of stories about the ex-pat: of easy-going temperament, sociable, a true English gentleman, he was apparently also well known for his thrift – tight-fisted as some might say. 'He always managed to casually avoid paying for drinks,' recalled a local associate with a chuckle, 'but believe me he wasn't averse to raising his elbow!' While rarely seen with his family in and around Jouques, the deceased man would sometimes be glimpsed in the company of 'young people' of all creeds and colours whom he would, until its sale in 1969, entertain at his villa of red shutters and whitewashed walls. Much of this village gossip Innocenzi would present in his book about the case, *The Enigma of Pélissanne* in a chapter devoted to Mr Cartland entitled, 'A gentleman, bizarre and stingy.'

'He was an extremely brilliant man, a great humanist,' Jacques Mont-Reynaud told *Le Monde*. 'He loved Provence and the sun.' Mr Cartland's fellow headmaster went on to reveal that his British business partner had been a keen naturist preferring to sleep nude and who would, upon arriving at his counterpart's Marseille home, invariably strip off his clothes and thereafter walk around naked.

In an obituary written in The *Times*, former ambassador to Tehran, Sir Denis Wright, recalled that his old university friend – whom he still referred to as Basil Cartland - had been, 'brilliant and unconventional to the point of eccentricity.' He also observed that Cartland had been, 'a warm-hearted character with a great sense of fun who never quite fulfilled his early promise.' All those who had known the dead man spoke of a warm, friendly if unusual character.[1]

John Basil Cartland and his older brother had been brought up on the Sussex coast after moving from London in the 1920s. Educated in the independent sector he gained a scholarship to Oxford in 1932 where he made the acquaintance of a pre-ennobled Denis Wright in the Officer Training Corps (OTC). Thereafter he secured a teaching job. It was a respectable position no doubt and one young Cartland was eminently well suited for, but above all else he yearned for adventure. The youthful teacher had an undeniably romantic, whimsical side to his nature – impractical some might call it. And so, when the opportunity arose, he gladly exchanged the humdrum life of a school master at an English boarding school for an infinitely more exotic role at the recently founded Peshawar University. Cartland had landed close to the North-west frontier, the Khyber Pass within range.

A man apart, like Orwell's anti-hero John Flory in *Burmese Days,* Cartland happily threw himself into local culture oblivious seemingly to any disapproval his behaviour might incur. Photographs would come to light of him participating in tiger hunts and hiking in the Himalayas. According to Sir Denis Wright, his friend had been 'totally lacking in colour or class prejudice.' Colonial sahib he most definitely was not.

At the outbreak of war, ever the nomad, Cartland transferred to North Africa where he saw action with the British-led Sudan Defence Force in its engagements with the Italian Royal Army on the Abyssinian border. He also served under General Wavell in Cairo. Here Cartland would have been part of a small force defending Egypt from attack by Italian held Libya. Early in the war this restless spirit joined the Intelligence Corps where he attained the modest rank of Second Lieutenant. The unit specialised in the collection of intelligence and the production of counter intelligence. Amongst other activities, operatives would be parachuted into occupied France. With his flair for languages Cartland may not only have worked behind enemy lines in France, but may also have been involved with the unit's work in East Africa, specifically in the de-briefing and interrogation of Italian POWs captured in Abyssinia.

War over and back on civvy street, his attentions turned to politics. Now rakishly styling himself as 'Major J B Cartland'[2] he unsuccessfully contested the Willesden West seat for the Conservative Party in the 1945 General Election. At other times he would be 'Captain Cartland.' Post-war roles also included a stint in Geneva working for the UN and Kuwait in the petrochemical industry.

Wanderlust finally satisfied, the rover returned to Sussex armed with a store of anecdotes that would delight friends and family, related with humour and punctuated as always by a loud, hearty laugh. From the Normandy landings in which a unit under his leadership captured the port of Cherbourg, to battling Mussolini in the deserts of Libya, the dashing young man had an endless store of exciting Boys' Own stories to tell.

By the 1950's Cartland was looking for a new direction. Newly affluent he bought several properties in Eastbourne and Brighton. He also became a partner in a boys' prep school at Staveley Court, a fine building with a commanding view of the Eastbourne seafront, which still stands and where young Jeremy once attended. The story of how he acquired this wealth was vintage Cartland. During the war, so the story went, the gallant young officer had found himself fighting alongside Mohammad Al-Sanousi, future king Idris I of Libya. A few years later, homeward bound from East Africa, Cartland dropped in on his old friend. Upon parting, 'Snusi' presented his trusted English comrade with a gift in the shape of a suitcase, telling him not to open it until he reached home. Curiosity getting the better of him, Cartland opened the case while sitting on a bus to Tunis. It was stuffed full of US dollars! Whichever way he acquired his wealth, a new chapter had begun as a landlord, school principal and not to mention raconteur.

In terms of his personal life Cartland had his ups and downs, but who doesn't? Whether due to immaturity or some other character flaw, it appears that domesticity never truly suited this somewhat eclectic at times awkward character. His first wife cited violence in her divorce petition. In typical Cartland style he had proposed marriage just two weeks after meeting Joan Wheeler at the hospital where she worked and where he was being treated for a minor ailment. Apparently, he had decided to marry her at that first meeting. The couple had two children: Jeremy (b.1944) and Elizabeth (b. 1946).

His next wife Kathleen he met while she was headmistress of Fairlie Place in Brighton, a finishing school that attracted wealthy girls from all over the world. Headmaster and headmistress married in 1955.

'He would turn up at our college and lunch with us girls,' remembers a former pupil. 'Once he sat opposite me and we had great fun with him guessing where I was from. Belgium! You're Belgian, he said in triumph. We all laughed. Actually, I was one of the few English girls at the college!' Was the headmistress' husband flirting with his wife's students? Perhaps. Traditional lady-killer he might not have been, but Cartland had a way about him, a boyish unkempt quality that might have attracted women who wished to mother him. The formerly beautiful and vivacious Kathleen Cartland would end her days in a spiral of depression and alcoholism.

Cartland met his third wife in France, marrying in 1965.

Like her predecessor, children's illustrator Leila Hirschfield had been quite the beauty in a youth spent in her native New Jersey.[3] She could still turn heads, even at forty-nine years of age. However, life in an English seaside town did not quite captivate the new Mrs Cartland. The marriage did not last long. Cartland's third wife had a taste for the high life while her husband preferred TV, plain food and an early night. Certainly, he was much more at home in a pair of old shorts and boots than a tuxedo.

By 1973 John Cartland was living a bachelor life of a genteel retirement on the Sussex coast. As well as ownership of his summer language school situated on Dyke Road, Brighton, his business interests included a share in a nursing home and rental income from his property portfolio. Financially he was more than comfortable. The 'Major' was thus able to indulge his passion for foreign travel on a whim, and he did just that. It was on a package tour to Ibiza that he had first made the acquaintance of Nikko Lyon and brokered the deal to buy his caravan unseen, a characteristically impetuous decision. Lyon relates how, upon returning home to Denia, he was shocked to find a £300 bank transfer already deposited in his account in lieu of the purchase! His own home at Powis Square, the ever-canny Cartland had sub-divided into bedsits of which the 60-year-old occupied the ground floor unit. The remaining units were often let to Sussex University students.

Powis Square was and remains a jewel in the Brighton crown. A timeless oasis, its tastefully appointed villas huddle round a shaded garden providing residents lucky enough to live there with serenity by the spadeful. The town centre is a short walk away. Brighton's famous pebbly beach, promenade and pier lie just beyond.

Overall, Cartland was a well-known, popular figure in and

around the south coast environs where he lived and worked. Possessing the vigour of a much younger man, as he approached his sixth decade he still retained an air of the absent-minded professor either not caring about or blissfully unaware of what his neighbours and peers might think. Charming, civilised and interesting, he was the type to liven up any occasion. If he tended to embellish the odd anecdote here or there, no harm was intended.

'I remember a tall stooping man who owned a caravan in France,' recalls a lady still resident in the same Brighton street where she first met the English professor[4] in the early 1970s. 'My mother invited him to a dinner party one evening and was horrified when he turned up wearing a pair of slippers!'

In some ways this well-spoken gentleman with his stories of tigers, emirs and wartime espionage taking place to a backdrop of snake charmers in the bazaars of Tripoli, Cairo and beyond must have seemed like the archetypal ex-colonial, a relic from a bygone age. Cartland though had always been somewhat of a paradox. On the one hand, he enjoyed the company of younger people, was receptive to their ideas, and therefore would have seemed 'with it' to use the lingo of the times. On the other hand, he could come across as obdurate, a man set in his ways. Indeed, there had always been an irascible side to his character. He could and did easily fall out with people. Back in 1952 a teacher at his Staveley Court school had taken him to court alleging wrongful dismissal. The judge agreed with the plaintiff. Cartland and his business partner were ordered to pay £150 in compensation.[5] Not long after he sold his share of the school after falling out with his partner too.[6]

All told, John Cartland ought to have been satisfied with his lot in life. His marriages might all have ended in failure, but it's probably true that temperamentally some men are just not cut out for married life. Besides, in Janet Gibson the businessman had found what must have seemed the perfect solution: a woman who performed a number of wifely (and secretarial) duties asking for nothing in return except of course her salary. If there was a darker, less convivial side to his nature then he wouldn't have been unique: who amongst us does not have positive and negative attributes? Ok, so in Cartland's case not one but *three* wives had divorced him suggesting that life with the school principal might have come with irreconcilable drawbacks. And there are certainly more than enough clues indicative of a character who could sometimes be impetuous, over-bearing and argumentative to the point of dogmatic.

John Cartland may have come across as convivial, but underneath the jovial exterior lurked an altogether more sombre, introspective character. When he surmised that his old friend had not fulfilled his potential, Sir Denis Wright had been correct. Political ambitions thwarted long ago, Cartland now watched from the side-lines the rise of his protégé Ted Heath, a vicarious pleasure at best. Overall though it appears life had disappointed this ambitious, eclectic and always unconventional man.

Intellectual, raconteur, adventurer, romantic and entrepreneur, John Basil Cartland was a paradox, a man of many parts, some of which he had taken extra special care to hide well away from prying eyes.

8

The gangbuster

Wednesday broke bright and warm over the valleys and meadows of Bouches-du-Rhône. That same benign Provencal sun so beloved of John Cartland greeted the region's residents as they flicked through the pages of *Le Provencal* or *Nice-Matin*, the working day about to begin. In the cafes and bistros speculation was rife: who killed the English professor?

In some places there was talk of vengeance, of old scores being settled – possibly by the Maquis, the French resistance fighters who had been based in just this part of France in the second world war, networks of whom were still rumoured to be active. In other quarters the word 'parricide' was being whispered. However, by far the most popular theory centred on prowlers, specifically gypsies. In August of the previous year an engaged British couple from Croydon, Robert Latter 23, and Joyce Jaffe 21, had been brutally murdered by gypsies near the village of Ondes while also returning from Spain. Mr

Latter had been stabbed 18 times and Ms Jaffe had been raped.[1] The couple's throats had been cut. Was the Cartland murder another case of tourists being targeted?

Within the cool interior of the Marseille gendarmerie HQ located opposite the city's La Major cathedral, detectives huddled together deep in discussion, jackets cast aside, sleeves rolled up. Six foot two tall and built like a rugby union prop forward, Chief Commissioner of the Criminal Division, Emile Gonzalves cut a reassuring figure in their midst, calmness always his watchword. His appearance this fine morning had only helped fortify the investigative team. But what was the famous sleuth even doing here?

Forty-eight hours after the murder of the English tourist pressure for a breakthrough had been mounting. With the press resurrecting the Drummond case at every turn and a nervous public haunted by the spectre of an 'axe murderer' on the loose, police badly needed a result. And fast. Enter the talismanic 'gangbuster,' Emile Gonzalves.

Gonzalves' reputation certainly preceded him. Earlier in his career a Parisian industrialist, Roland Lecomte had been shot dead during a pheasant shoot at an estate in the countryside north west of the French capital. With thirty-nine suspects all armed it had been pure Poirot. Everybody had been shooting, but which guest had fired the fatal shot? To much acclaim the dogged young Commissioner had eventually got his man. A decade later his exploits would once again hit the headlines. Following his role ending a tense prison siege with typical gung-ho bravura, the 10th February 1971 front page of *Le Parisien* had hailed him a hero for preventing a potential massacre. In between times he had taken on Marseille's heroin gangs, and won. A leader of men this swarthy, unconventional policeman not only inspired the respect of his colleagues, but

Marseille's criminal fraternity - no mean feat.

Together with Krikorian, the gangbuster reviewed the case. Much of what Jeremy Cartland had said so far seemed frustratingly vague. And when the young teacher did say something more concrete his replies appeared to contradict the known facts. Often his explanations confounded expectations. For example, upon being disturbed that night by noises outside the caravan, in the detectives' opinion Jeremy had not acted in the way most people might in similar circumstances: he had not looked out of the window in order to assess the situation; he had in fact walked straight out into the night unarmed.

'It appears he did not once check his wristwatch the entire day,' remarked Krikorian bringing his colleague up to date. 'He doesn't know the time he left Arles, the time he arrived in Pélissanne or the time he heard the prowlers outside the caravan. Nor can he remember at which petrol station he and his father stopped to refuel, nor the woman who served them, nor the two figures he claims attacked him. Oh, and he didn't see the car or its occupants with whom his father chatted on Sunday evening at Jas de Dane.'

By way of response the gangbuster smiled: 'Not the most observant fellow in the world young Mr Cartland, is he?'

Maybe so, but this pair of seasoned detectives knew hunches would only carry them so far. Awaiting the results of forensic analysis of the Cartland's clothes, all they had in the absence of scientific proof were just doubts and suspicions, a shared conviction that somehow things didn't ring true. It wasn't enough.

Nonetheless, by the end of the morning the detectives had drawn up a list of anomalies which they intended to use in their next interview with Jeremy scheduled for later that day. In effect, the list brought together all those aspects of the young teacher's testimony police found less than convincing.

One of the first anomalies to present itself concerned the choice of location. What Gonzalves and Krikorian had learnt about the travellers so far made them question why the Cartlands had chosen such an isolated place in which to camp out. While it was conceivable that casual tourists might have chosen such a desolate spot, when it came to travelling in France the Cartlands weren't exactly novices. They had in fact been roaming back and forth to the region for a decade and longer. It would be no exaggeration to suggest that Provence was practically a second home.

Moreover, having spent some time at the murder location himself the previous day, Krikorian understood its geography better. Something in Jeremy's account of how the Cartlands ended up camped out that night troubled him. The Commissioner had stood on the main RN 572 road, seen for himself what the tourists would have seen as they trundled along, looking for a place to park up for the night. A couple of kilometres out of Pélissanne approaching the area known as *Jas de Dane* woodland becomes denser, thicker. A few hundred metres after passing the Caire family farmstead, to their right would have been a dirt road which ascended further up into the wilderness – not the type of route to take on an evening wherein, according to Jeremy, dusk was rapidly falling. Just past this turn off was a narrower rocky pathway running more or less parallel with the main road. Clearly, this path led deeper into the woodland. The Cartlands had branched off and followed it.

'Why did they decide to drive down this pathway?' asked Krikorian rhetorically. 'From the turn off it looks just like – well, a stony pathway. The clearing is much further along, some eighty to ninety metres. Why would they take this path not knowing to where it led? How could they possibly know that it would lead to a suitable place to camp overnight for a car and caravan? They were taking a chance. Unless . . .'

'Unless they had been to the clearing before,' continued Gonzalves finishing his colleague's train of thought. 'Or at least knew of its existence.'

'Besides, it's little more than a dump in the middle of nowhere. A little further on they would have come to a campsite, several in fact.'

'Perhaps they wanted to camp out somewhere private,' replied Gonzalves evenly. 'So, they wouldn't be disturbed.'

Krikorian nodded. 'Quite.'

Next, the colleagues discussed what police felt was yet another anomaly: the positioning of car and caravan at the site. Once they had arrived at *Jas de Dane* the Cartlands unhooked the caravan and turned it through 180°. They performed the same manoeuvre with the Hillman, turning it round on itself. Thus, both car and caravan eventually faced Pélissanne, the direction from where the Cartlands had just arrived. At that time the rocky path which the tourists took to leave the RN 572 re-joined the road again some ninety metres beyond where they had chosen to camp.[2] It was a piece of information that would have taken almost no time to establish, a matter of taking a few paces further along the clearing to enable a view of the land beyond. Police concluded the volte face operation, reversing and turning both car and caravan back and forth, as well as being an elaborate escapade had been completely unnecessary.

Gonzalves frowned. 'It's odd. Why not remain facing the direction they wished to take in the morning? It was just a temporary stopover, a place to sleep. So why go to all that trouble?'

'That's what I'd like to know,' said Krikorian.[3] 'You know how narrow that stretch of road is. A very sharp turn – several in fact would have been required to re-join it the next morning.'

It had already been noted that while the majority of Mr Cartland's personal effects had perished in the fire, most of Jeremy's items had been preserved in the Hillman where they had been left overnight. When the tourists had collected the caravan in Denia, Mr Cartland had transferred most of his personal effects to the caravan. Jeremy, however, had left his inside the car.

'Perhaps Master Cartland wanted to ensure the car would be safe in the event of something untoward occurring to the caravan that night,' offered Gonzalves. 'A fire maybe.'

'Thereby preserving his own papers and valuables,' said Krikorian returning the compliment.

'Indeed. What else have we got?'

Among the list of eleven anomalies the way in which the suspected murder weapons had been discarded especially puzzled the sleuths. Police discovered the axe lying seventy metres to the north of the crime scene; the knife they found fifty metres to the south west while the concrete block lay twenty-five metres to the south east. It seemed a strange way for fleeing murderers to behave, shedding the tools of their bloody trade at disparate points around the crime scene. Would they have had either time or inclination? Police sensed intent in this apparent random dissemination.

Nor did the anomalies end there, especially with regards to the axe. The bloodied weapon had eventually been found under a block of chipboard in what appeared to have been a clumsy attempt to conceal its whereabouts. The detectives were puzzled. Rather than taking it with them to discard of in say, a river or some other place where police would almost certainly never find it, Krikorian and Gonzalves wondered why the murderers had left it behind at the crime scene. Could the reason be that nobody had actually fled the murder scene and therefore the opportunity to dispose of the weapons as far away from *Jas de Dane* as possible had not been an option for the perpetrator(s)?

Nor was this the only anomaly to surface with regards to the axe. The policemen reminded themselves that, according to the dead man's son, the axe had been kept in a cupboard inside the caravan next to John Cartland's bed. How then had the attackers got their hands on it? Had they discovered it while ransacking the caravan? If so, by this time Mr Cartland must have been lying in the thicket, unconscious. It seemed odd: after all, the old man no longer represented a threat to the prowlers. Yet for some reason they decided to take the axe back over to the thicket and launch a frenzied attack on a man they must have assumed was as good as dead. Why the overkill? The detectives were stumped. Instead of checking for valuables, it appeared the prowlers had opted instead to engage in an orgy of violence.

Indeed, nothing about these prowlers rang true. From the somewhat eclectic arsenal of weapons brought along – club, knife and concrete slab concealed in a pillow case – to their behaviour during and after the robbery, their actions seemed illogical. Rather than pillage these thieves had seemed more intent on committing acts of wanton violence – murder and arson. Krikorian and Gonzalves knew enough about opportunist thieves for their suspicions to be instantly aroused. What kind of prowlers operated in this bizarre way?

'What do you think?' asked Krikorian. There had been a lot of information for the Chief Commissioner to digest.

With his stocky build and imposing bearing, he might have resembled some people's opinion of a street brawler, but Gonzalves was just as cerebral as the next detective. From what he could make out certain parts of the young Englishman's testimony were not consistent with the known facts. That much was clear. 'Let us assume for the moment that the son's recollections are correct,' he said after a while. 'If so, then something like the following sequence of events must have occurred from the point where the son was knocked unconscious.'

'I'm listening,' said Krikorian appreciating the input from Marseille's legendary buster of crooks and villains.

'Mr Cartland hears the confrontation between his son and persons unknown and instinctively reaches for the axe he has luckily brought along for protection. Upon exiting the caravan, he spies a prowler. Worryingly, there is no sign of his son. Now, according to the autopsy the victim was attacked from behind, is that right?'

'Correct,' said Krikorian. 'So, it is safe to assume the second prowler must have crept up behind the father as he had done with the son.'

'A logical deduction commissioner,' returned Gonzalves. 'So, the professor confronts this prowler holding the axe in one hand and a handkerchief in the other – a pretty picture I think we can agree. The victim's handkerchief was found next to the corpse I believe? Anyway, while Cartland is distracted by the first prowler, his accomplice approaches from behind. It must be the case, as you say, that Cartland was taken by surprise in a similar manner to his son.'

'But the body is not discovered in the vicinity of the caravan as might be expected,' interjected Krikorian. 'It is found inside a cramped clump of bushes.'

'Which means, if we follow the logic of Jeremy's story, that, after striking Mr Cartland from behind, for some reason the prowlers must have moved the body over to the thicket - all the time ignoring the younger man who lays some distance away. So, both Cartlands are 'out cold.' It is the perfect opportunity to commit theft. But no! Instead, they collect the axe as well as the handkerchief and return back to the thicket. Even though he no longer represents a threat to them, they have decided to murder John Cartland.'

'Which in itself makes little sense,' said Krikorian. 'The older man was going nowhere – not with that hole in his skull. But the younger man could have woken any moment. He'd only been punched.'

Gonzalves and Krikorian exchanged glances. The more they tried to apply logic to the witness' story, the less sense it made. The Chief Commissioner continued.

'And then what happens? After butchering the older man, they find the son still unconscious and inflict two superficial wounds upon him with a hitherto unused kitchen knife. And then, they scratch his face! Preposterous! And rather than stealing whatever they can from the caravan and car, they leave clues at various points around the clearing – the axe, concrete slab and knife.'

'And yet they kept hold of the cosh,' observed Krikorian.

Gonzalves flashed his colleague a quizzical look.

'We still haven't found the weapon – we think it was a club or a stick – used to knock the son unconscious.'

The conversation moved onto the topic of fire. Ascribing a motive why the would-be thieves had decided to torch the Sprite proved a difficult task. It might simply have been a random act of vandalism. If so, the policemen needed to know by what means the fire had been started. In all likelihood the jerrycan would provide the answer, but until the analysis came back from the lab the detectives could only speculate.

Marseille's famous gangbuster reflected on what he had learnt so far. The team of detectives had produced a list of improbabilities, but to what end? There were suppositions a-plenty but not much in the way of actual evidence. In themselves each of the anomalies amounted to little more than a list of doubts, some more glaring than others. However, when taken together the inconsistencies became much greater than the sum of their individual parts.

The detectives had done all they could. It was time to head over to Salon police station.

'One aspect of this crime cannot be disputed,' said Gonzalves as the detectives drove through Marseille's busy lunchtime streets. 'And that is this: whoever killed this man hated him, *really* hated him.'

9

Under pressure

Meanwhile, back in Salon-en-Provence, Jeremy Cartland was preparing to leave hospital. Having dressed himself in spare clothes and wearing his dead father's ill-fitting boots for lack of any others, a couple of police officers now escorted Jeremy from his sickroom, the tap-tap of their footsteps echoing through the hospital's empty corridors.

'Don't say a word to anyone,' the officers warned. 'Not a word!'

Their escortee shrugged. He just wanted to see his sister and get away as far as possible from Salon, Provence and from France itself.

Blinking in the warm sunshine, Jeremy's appearance at the hospital door had journalists scrambling. Many of them had been camped in the car park since Monday morning. The Cartland murder was still making headlines and would continue to do so through spring and summer.

Two dozen photographers reached for their cameras. Startled by this reception, Jeremy allowed himself to be shepherded through the press pack to where a vehicle awaited. He carried with him an overnight bag and couple of paperback books. Though a little hesitant the young man certainly looked in rude health. He walked freely, without support. Cut and grazed around the forehead he could have been a boxer emerging into the light the morning after a slug-out for the light heavyweight championship of the world, a warrior of Anglo-Saxon legend.

For their part, the journalists seemed somewhat nonplussed. Young Cartland had made a speedy recovery. What, not even a wheelchair? Camera shutters clicking behind him, Jeremy dove into the back seat of the waiting Fiat Simca. The English passenger was driven away shielding his face, absorbed in thought.

A few minutes later the pale green vehicle arrived at Salon police station. 'Out jumped Jeremy,' observed one newspaper report further emphasising his health and vigour in its next sentence: 'He bounded up the five stone steps.' Much to his chagrin, Jeremy soon found himself waiting in an anonymous room somewhere deep inside the building. His main worry now was the whereabouts of his sister. What was Liz doing?

Half an hour later, at 3pm, the arrival of a second car sent a frisson of excitement through the courtyard.

'Look! It's Gonzalves!'

'What's he doing here?'

Obliging the assembled journalists to scatter like skittles, Emile Gonzalves made a customary low-key entrance into the courtyard at the wheel of his Citroen GS. The gentlemen of the press nudged one another. They understood all too well what his appearance here signified; for the Chief Commissioner himself to attend today's interview Jeremy Cartland must surely be more than a mere witness to his father's murder.

No sooner had Gonzalves entered the building than another vehicle roared into the courtyard. It was hard for the press to keep up.

Much to the appreciation of the assembled hacks, out stepped the slim, shapely figure of Liz Cartland along with the gentleman rumoured to be her fiancé. Vice Consul Frank Benham followed. The trio hurried into the station. Members of the press pack could not help but be impressed with Jeremy's younger sister. 'Blonde, feminine and quite beautiful,' was how Innocenzi would describe her.

One or two of Innocenzi's media brethren seemed a little envious that one so beautiful could care so much for a mere brother.[1] They had a point; at times her devotion to Jerry would border on the Shakespearean. It was a familial bond the strength of which would not go unnoticed. While certain factions of the French media expressed puzzlement at the Cartland's reaction to their father's demise, noting the obvious delight brother and sister took in one another's company, the fact is that people do react to major life traumas in different ways, some of which may appear baffling to outsiders.

'I never experienced the full emotional impact of it,' Jeremy later remarked when reflecting on his lack of emotion in the immediate aftermath of his father's death. What the French media assumed to be British frigidity or even callous indifference could thus have been something much more complex - delayed shock, internalised grieving etc.

The Cartland's father might have indeed been brutally murdered, but this was no time for grieving. There was work to be done. Sometime over the next 24 hours the police would likely charge Jeremy with his father's murder. Thereafter, he could spend anything up to 18 months in prison awaiting trial. As tenacious as she was alluring, Ms Cartland had thus spent Wednesday morning arranging legal representation. Her task had led thus far to Christopher Mitchell-Heggs, a Paris lawyer who would in turn direct her to Maitre Paul Lombard the flamboyant Marseille-based celebrity lawyer. For the moment all she wanted though was to see her brother.

The three Brits were ushered up to the first floor of the station to a corridor where a group of officials chatted in hushed tones. Benham approached the group. He already knew police had petitioned Judge Delmas to withdraw the privilege which had allowed him to sit in on the previous days' interview. Irritated by this move but professional down to his fingertips, the consular official conducted himself with his usual aplomb. After a short conversation he turned back to his companion.

'Where's Jeremy?' asked an anxious Liz Cartland. 'Can I see him?'

'Only for a moment,' replied Benham. 'The police will be interviewing him shortly.'

After she had briefly spoken to her brother, Benham led the fraught young woman into a quiet room where they were joined by Gonzalves and other officials. There was much to discuss. Uppermost in the minds of Benham and Miss Cartland was the tricky question of where Jeremy would be spending the night - in a prison cell or as a 'free' man? Much would hinge on the next few hours.

Meanwhile, in a room close by Jeremy waited, wondering, or so he would later claim, why he had been escorted to Salon police station. After all, had he not co-operated fully with investigators? Following his discharge from hospital the young teacher had therefore been expecting to fly home – a surely unrealistic hope that was fading fast. Jeremy sat stiffly in his chair, 'bewildered' by the whole affair. Until this point his demeanour had always been that of supreme indignation, as if the very suggestion of any involvement in the crime was simply unthinkable. Investigators would surely realise the absurdity of their position soon enough.

'I was sure that he had realised his mistake and that I would hear no more of it.' Jeremy wrote these words when reflecting on his interaction with Krikorian of the previous day. However, it looked as if his confidence had been misplaced. If he now seemed a little sullen, it was perhaps only to be expected. Rather than further cross examination Jeremy seemed to believe he should have been flying back to the UK.

Eventually, a procession of officials entered the stark interview room for what would be Jeremy's third confrontation with police in as many days. Along with several other high-ranking officials, Commissioner Krikorian, Inspector Ettori, Warrant Officer Salendre and interpreter Madame Diamantidis seated themselves around the table from where a somewhat edgy English teacher appraised them. Jeremy's apprehension increased even more when Gonzalves, hitherto unknown to him, sidled up and looked him directly in the eye. Jeremy took an instant dislike to the Chief Commissioner. He instinctively sensed that this hulking detective from Marseille - rugged yet undeniably intelligent - and who appeared to have taken over running the investigation, represented a serious threat to his freedom. The Cartland circle would come to refer to Gonzalves as 'freak features.' According to Jeremy, the gangbuster bore a striking resemblance to Jack Palance, the American actor renowned for his portrayal of pathological characters.

Over a dozen officials now sat round the table either side of the British teacher. 'Despite the presence of all these officers,' Jeremy would later write, 'I in my naivety, still did not expect to be treated like a suspect.'

The interview began with some general questions about the trip, but soon moved onto the night of the attack. Questions came from all quarters - what the ever-indignant Brit would refer to as 'absurd suppositions.' One such absurdity emanated from the Chief Commissioner:

'Why did you not arm yourself,' asked Gonzalves voicing the thoughts of many of those present, 'when you heard what you say were strange voices outside the caravan? Surely it was the prudent thing to have done in the circumstances?' For reasons the detectives could not fathom, upon hearing what he suspected were prowlers outside the caravan, the Brit had walked straight out into potential danger. He hadn't even glanced through the curtains in order to assess the risk.

'In England it is quite normal behaviour,' returned Jeremy coolly. 'I didn't expect to be attacked.'

'Very few people do - expect to be attacked.'

The detectives seemed unconvinced. Had not the elder Cartland supposedly insisted on taking an axe along on the trip specifically for the purpose of protection? Yet Jeremy was asking them to believe that he had blithely walked out into darkness unarmed, not knowing what danger he might face. Logically, it was a course of action that made little sense. It made even less sense when the isolated nature of *Jas de Dane* was taken into consideration.

During the interrogation, Jeremy glanced over at Krikorian. He was much less prominent than he had been the previous afternoon, further proof he thought that the commissioner knew a dreadful mistake had been made in accusing him of parricide.

'Why did you choose to camp out in that place?' If Krikorian was feeling remorseful, his colleagues weren't. Questions were being fired from all directions.

'Because father was tired.'

'But it was you who was driving.'

'Maybe so,' shrugged Jeremy, 'but that's how it is.'

And so the die was cast; when it came to anomalies Jeremy would typically do one of two things: either provide what his interrogators considered were highly implausible answers or respond with a phrase in the way of 'I don't know how', 'I can't explain why' or 'That's the way it is.'

'Tell me Jeremy,' invited Gonzalves fixing a steady eye on the man sitting next to him, 'those stab wounds of yours, you say you were knocked out by a blow to the head - or was it the jaw I forget which?'

'I can't remember precisely. Both.'

'Indeed. So how do you explain these wounds? They must have been made when you were unconscious . . . '

'Yes, I suppose so.'

'And yet according to the hospital they were little more than superficial cuts. But your father's wounds were fatal and multiple – more than a dozen. How do you explain that?'

'I can't explain it.'

'Neither can we Jeremy,' smiled Gonzalves. 'Neither can we.'

'Unless they were self-inflicted,' chimed in a detective called Georges Roustan. In common with virtually all the police he interacted with Jeremy had taken a dislike to a man who according to the young teacher 'clearly fancied himself.'

'Ridiculous!' Jeremy glared at the man he called 'leather jacket' due to his habitual style of dress. 'I did nothing of the sort.'

Questions relating to the young Brit's injuries were one of

the most puzzling anomalies on the detectives' list. According to Jeremy, upon stepping out of the caravan he had received a very severe blow to the back of the head. Subsequently, he incorporated an equally vicious blow to the jaw in his version of events, which had been delivered with enough venom to knock him clean out. Examination at Salon hospital failed however to locate any swelling or bruising to the back of the head (Jeremy did not mention a blow to his jaw, so it was not assessed.[2]) Nor did medical staff observe the classic symptoms associated with concussion. Concussed individuals typically exhibit a range of both physical and psychological symptoms e.g. dizziness, amnesia, nausea, confusion, double vision, slurred speech etc. On the contrary, upon admission to hospital Jeremy had appeared lucid. 'Speaking calmly' and 'not in a panic' is how Monsieur Delaude had described his passenger's comportment on the journey to hospital.

What the victim had presented with were a couple of flesh wounds to the stomach and upper right pectoralis, which had required just two stitches apiece. Inspector Roustan was not the only one sat around the table who thought such wounds bore the hallmarks of self-infliction.

As he sat before them, calmness personified, answering their questions in the manner of one going about a chore which he found rather boring, it was difficult if not impossible for detectives to square the mutilated corpse of John Cartland with the ruddy exterior that was the dead man's son with whom they now conversed. The disparity in their respective fates had indeed been stark. Mr Cartland had been subjected to a series of mortal blows, one after another, while his son had suffered nothing more serious than a couple of inconsequential flesh wounds. Why not kill both witnesses? Here was an anomaly that stubbornly resisted explication.

'Take a look at this! What do you think?'

Without warning leather jacket thrust a graphic image of John Cartland's mangled head in the line of Jeremy's vision. Police photographers had captured the aftermath of the attack in all its grisly detail. Unable to look at an image that seemed as if it originated from hell, Jeremy turned his head away.

Next, the blood-stained axe was thrust towards the young man once more. He looked appalled.

'Is this the axe with which you killed your father?'

'I did not kill my father!' protested Jeremy.

As to what happened next, it all depends on sources and which to trust. No doubt originating from his contacts within the Aix and Marseille police departments, Paul-Claude Innocenzi reported that Jeremy was unable to look upon the axe encrusted with his father's life-blood and that he turned away horrified. To those assembled it seemed the mere sight of the murder weapon had had a profound effect. Jeremy appeared to tremble. Gonzalves placed a reassuring hand on the young Brit's own hand. In the meantime, Jeremy composed himself. Some moments passed in silence.

'One hundred and twenty,' calmly announced the gangbuster withdrawing his hand. Gonzalves had only gone and taken the unwitting Brit's pulse! At rest, the human heart rate is between 60 and 100 beats per minute.

'Come Jeremy,' said the Chief Commissioner solemnly, 'it is better to tell the truth.'

All eyes looked towards the young English man. Until this moment he had seemed imperturbable, bullet-proof - at times contemptuous. All that bravura had suddenly evaporated. Had the psychological game of chess played out between these two intelligent men reached the point of check-mate?

'I don't know anymore,' mumbled Jeremy, head bowed, eyes

fixed on the floor. 'I'm tired . . .'

A hush descended. The room crackled with anticipation. Was the teacher-poet about to make a confession?

A beat.

'Coming back, if I may, to the precise meaning of a word that was just said . . .'

In her attempt to clarify a point of translation and inexperienced in the wiles of the police, Mme Diamantidis had inadvertently broken the spell. Jeremy swallowed hard. After taking a slow drink of water the young Englishman seemed to regain his old composure. The moment had gone.

Although this is the way Innocenzi tells it, for his part Jeremy would later state categorically that he could not recollect any of this high drama as chronicled by the *Le Provencal* journalist.

The interview turned to focus on the marks still visible on the teacher's handsome face. By his own admission Jeremy had not struggled with his attackers on the night of the murder; he had been knocked clean out. However, to have acquired the type of minor injuries manifest on that impressive forehead (i.e. scratches and bruises) logic dictated that he must have been involved in some kind of altercation or brawl. Scratches like that don't just appear of their own accord. How then had he acquired these battle scars? Police thought they knew the answer – it involved alcohol and a family quarrel - but wanted to hear Jeremy's explanation.

'Since I was knocked unconscious from the outset, I can't remember how I got them,' replied the young Brit sounding a little ruffled. The implication seemed clear enough: Jeremy's scratches, bruises as well as his wounds must have indeed been administered while he had been out cold. But why attack an unconscious man?

It was yet another less than satisfactory reply to one of the police's list of anomalies. And the more Gonzalves probed, the less assured the young man sounded. The Marseille gang-buster was getting under Jeremy's skin. Even so, without an actual confession his British adversary rightly calculated that only stalemate could ensue – from his point of view a more than satisfactory outcome. All Jeremy had to do was stick to his guns, maintain his discipline, keep his cool. Thus far the Brit had fended off wave after wave of attacks.

'Coming back to the murder weapons.' Gonzalves indicated the axe, knife and concrete cosh all of which still lay on the table. 'The attackers left these items strewn all over the site. Why do you think they did this?'

'You'd have to ask them that question.'

'Why not dispose of these vital clues as far away from the scene of the murder as possible?'

''Perhaps they were in a hurry to get away.'

'The prowlers stole nothing of value. How is that possible?

'Maybe they couldn't find anything.'

'Not especially skilled prowlers, more like amateurs.'

'It seems that way.'

There was a palpable sigh of relief when it was decided to break for refreshments. Jeremy sipped orange juice and took a drag on a cigarette, a habit he had resumed after a long period of abstinence. The air in the interview room was thick with the stench of stale Gauloise smoke. What, with the humidity of the night and the intensity engendered within it, the atmosphere inside the room was stifling. For how much longer would the interrogation continue?

Coffee over, battle was re-joined. The police intended to go through their entire list of anomalies. Jeremy prepared himself for what promised to be another late night.

10

Rendezvous a Marseille

Outside darkness had fallen on Salon. Clocks having struck half past eleven, the town's bistros were bidding adieu to their final customers prior to rolling down their shutters. The streets were all but silent. Salon might have been winding down, but its police station was a hive of midweek activity, a merry-go-round of comings and goings. This provincial outpost of law and order had never been so busy.

Together with Frank Benham, Liz Cartland had already left the building. While her departure had not gone unnoticed, for the moment the media had bigger fish to fry: Jeremy Cartland, rumour had it, would soon be transferred elsewhere - to Marseille perhaps. What did this mean? Were police going to charge their prime witness with murder? If so, why not detain him overnight in Salon? In situ since 5pm sustained by sandwiches and flasks of coffee, the gentlemen of the press could only speculate. Had Gonzalves cracked the case? Had the famous gangbuster managed to extract a confession? The balmy night air was charged with anticipation.

One of the Cartlands was certainly headed to Marseille that night. Liz Cartland had a date with possibly one of only a handful of men in La Republic who could come to her brother's aid: Maitre Paul Lombard. Forty-five minutes after departing Salon, Frank Benham's car arrived at Rue Neuve-Sainte-Catherine in the Mediterranean city's old port area where Lombard's junior clerk greeted them at the door of an elegant building. The visitors found themselves in a luxurious duplex apartment where the mistress of the house awaited. Mme Lombard explained that her husband had himself only just arrived home from Monaco where he had been dining with clients at the Hôtel de Paris and from where he had taken the call asking him to represent the English tourist earlier that afternoon. He would be with them shortly. In the meantime, there was time for the guests to appreciate the apartment's stylish décor. The Lombard's taste in art was as impeccable as their taste in home furnishings. Success permeated the air.

Philosopher, writer and humanist, Maitre Paul Lombard was indeed a lawyer of some renown; clients included superstar actor Alain Delon, the artist Pablo Picasso, Greek shipping tycoon Aristotle Onassis and Olympique Marseille Football Club. The rich and famous apart, a lifelong penchant for the underdog meant Lombard invariably found himself defending not only some of France's most high-profile cases but on occasions some of its most notorious ones too. The Cartland case thus had more than enough to recommend it. Along with the whole of France, Lombard had heard all about the horrific 'Pélissanne murder' and had not hesitated to accept the brief. The case intrigued him. Lombard level of expertise however did not come cheap. Nonetheless, determined that her brother should obtain the very best legal advice money could buy, the indefatigable Liz Cartland had been busily arranging loans with various banks. By the end of Wednesday, she had raised the first instalment of £1500.[1] Jeremy Cartland's supporters had done him proud; they had secured for him the services of arguably France's most astute legal mind. It was quite a coup.

Refreshed from his journey, Lombard breezed into the parlour with typical dynamism. Every inch the sophisticate, he glided over to a distraught Liz Cartland.

'Oh please sir, will you help us?'

The lawyer seemed impressed. 'Be assured my child,' he said giving her hand a gentlemanly kiss, 'I will do all that I can. Come into my office, please.'

With the assistance of Benham's concurrent translation, Liz petitioned the bemused lawyer, throwing herself upon his mercy. 'You have to defend my brother. He's an intellectual, a poet - incapable of violence. Please Master do something for him, I beseech you.'

Like all men she encountered, young Miss Cartland had seemingly cast her spell on this man of culture. Lombard said all he could to reassure her. He then called his associate Jean Chiappe, President of the Marseille Bar, who within minutes of taking the call had arrived at the apartment. As good as his word Lombard also called a colleague in Salon for an update. The contact informed him that Cartland had just left the town's gendarmerie but the interrogation would continue on Thursday. Police were convinced of Jeremy's guilt, so said the contact, and felt certain a confession was close at hand. Lombard and Chiappe conferred. The lawyers started to speak rapidly and with growing excitement. Benham gave Liz a reassuring smile. Unlike his companion whose French was basic, having been based in Marseille since 1964 the Vice Consul spoke the language like a native. After a lengthy discussion, heralded by a typically dramatic flourish, Lombard addressed his guests:

'Do not worry Miss Cartland. I assure you we will do all that we can for your brother.'

'Oh, thank-you so much,' said Liz, relief etched into her pretty face.

'She was becoming of serious beauty - pathetic almost,' Lombard would later write in one of his memoirs in which he recalled the Cartland case and the evening he first made the acquaintance of this most devoted of sisters. 'I'm no advocate for sentiment, but I found this woman sincere, beautiful. I was deeply touched.'[2]

While his sister was beguiling France's most eminent legal eagle, Jeremy Cartland was being bundled into yet another unmarked police car, a Renault 16 – this time in the compound of Salon police station. Exhausted after his sparring session with Gonzalves, he too was about to depart for Marseille. In keeping with the Consul's policy in relation to DBS (Distressed British Subjects) wherein the British Consul assume duty of care for British citizens on foreign soil, police had, after much debate, agreed that Jeremy should spend the night in the care of John Edmonds at his Marseille home.

It was only when the gates to the compound suddenly swung open the press boys realised what was happening: as predicted the English witness was being transferred. Before anyone knew what was happening the car conveying Jeremy Cartland streaked past a somnolent pack of journalists. *Allons! Allons!* A dozen cars and several motorbikes scrambled into action, screeching onto the main road. Innocenzi jumped into his colleague's Triumph and joined the convoy.

Midnight and save for this impromptu car chase tearing up its streets, the environs of Salon were silent. Pedal-to-the-metal in an effort to drop the pursuing pack, the R16 crossed the RN 572 emerging on the southwards autoroute to Marseille - the direction John Cartland had no doubt been expecting to take just a few days earlier in order to keep his appointment with his business partner, Monsieur Mont-Reynaud.

Hitting 125 mph, the Renault attempted without success to shake off its pursuers. The chasing pack slipstreamed one another, drawing level with and occasionally nudging ahead of the police vehicle. Each time a car pulled level, camera lens pointing his way, Jeremy would duck down into his seat. But the hacks were nothing if not persistent; a frontpage picture in tomorrow's papers might keep the lucky photographer in Pernod for months if not years. At the A7 motorway toll dozens of cars flew past startled officials. In the back seat of the Renault Jeremy and Edmonds clutched onto whatever they could. Fair to say the Brits were not exactly enjoying their white-knuckle ride.

Eventually the Renault arrived at Marseille's old port. At the city's police station Jeremy was transferred into another vehicle. With the case delicately poised, the authorities were naturally keen to keep him away from the media. While journalists caught their breath and wondered what might happen next, the British teacher was whipped through the deserted streets of Marseille along the Quai du Port, haven to a fleet of yachts bobbing gently in the dark, midnight waters of the city's marina. From here, the car flew past the eerily quiet shops on the fashionable Rue St. Ferreol. Pursuers finally dropped, the Renault eventually rolled up outside a grand building at a development known as La Cadanelle, official residence of the British Consulate. Here Jeremy was greatly relieved to be met by Liz and Frank Benham who had not long since left the home of Paul Lombard.

Defeated, journalists gave up the chase and returned home. Some like Innocenzi already were home. Others headed back to Salon, Aix and even further afield. Despite its silent air and darkened windows, one or two lingered outside the British Consulate building on Avenue du Prado.

Brother and sister embraced. A lot had happened in the past few days. Jeremy heard the welcome news that there was a good deal of sympathy for his plight among both the ex-pat community in France and back in the UK. He was even more buoyed to learn that Maitres Lombard and Chiappe had agreed to represent him. The Brit's legal team had thus expanded to four: the Marseille lawyers would team up with Christopher Mitchell-Heggs and his Parisian colleague Jacques Sagot. It was a formidable quartet. And with the ever-dependable Benham and Edmonds providing back-up, the young man's position suddenly looked much stronger than at any time over the past three days. Liz Cartland had done her brother proud.

Yet Jeremy's status was far from assured as he tucked into his first proper meal in days - a late, late supper prepared by Mrs Edmonds. For now, he savoured the meal and the company of friendlier British faces. Even if for a brief moment, he could forget his predicament. Conversation revolved around any number of mundane topics, welcome respite after the marathon at times bad-tempered interviews with Krikorian and Gonzalves of recent days.

Somewhere short of freedom and uncomfortably close to detention, Jeremy Cartland was indeed in a sort of limbo on this sultry March evening. Under French law a suspect could be interviewed for a maximum of 48 hours. Thus far Jeremy had wisely co-operated with police. Wise, because it was within their power for police to hold a suspect in custody for the 48-hour duration if deemed necessary. In fact, the teacher had undergone 14 hours of interrogation over the preceding two days. From a purely technical point of view this preliminary stage of the enquiry had therefore not expired; thirty-four hours remained on the clock. Ostensibly then Jeremy was still a witness. He was 'assisting' police with their enquiries. As such he was free to come and go as he chose and so could, at least theoretically, return home to the UK. Had not Krikorian intimated as much the previous day? Ok, so the Brit would almost certainly not wish to leave France under such a cloud - not without first clearing his name - but as Lombard appreciated, sooner rather than later his client would be charged. The fallout from the Drummond case never far away, it appeared that French authorities ideally wanted to obtain a confession prior to charging their British suspect. It was just a matter of time. Under ever more pressure the Brit would eventually crack and Marseille's gangbuster would duly charge him with murder.

Unlike his new client, who revelled in the hospitality laid on by Her Majesty's Consulate, Maitre Lombard did not sleep too well that night. His mind was racing. Despite accepting the brief to defend Jeremy, there was nothing he could actually do until the enquiry progressed to the next stage wherein the *juge d'instruction* André Delmas would direct proceedings, by which time it might be too late to save the young teacher from an appointment with Madame Guillotine.[3] Not until 1981 would capital punishment be abolished in France.

Lombard urgently needed a way to check the police's next move before they made it. Time was of the essence. A stroke of genius, when he awoke on Thursday morning the lawyer knew just how the initiative could be seized.

Once an investigation is under way in France the family of a victim of murder can constitute themselves as civil parties (*partie civile.*) Taking out such an action confers upon the bereaved family certain benefits e.g. they are allowed access to the police dossier; in order to keep track of developments they can also arrange interviews with the *juge d'instruction*; they can also petition the judge to order ancillary investigations. It is also an essential pre-requisite towards securing financial reparation by way of damages. Under French law it ought to be borne in mind that the *partie civile* is the person who considers themselves a *victim* of an offense. Given the presumption of guilt hanging over the Brighton teacher, Lombard's plan to make him a civil party to his father's murder enquiry was an audacious as it was ingenious plan, unprecedented in French law. Customarily those suspected of murder do not assume the role of victim. It simply isn't done.

The next morning Lombard drove the short distance to the British Consulate residence at La Cadanelle where he and his new client met at 10 o'clock. Jeremy, Liz and a BBC reporter Ian Smith, the man described as her fiancé, had just finished breakfast when Lombard arrived at the spacious apartment usually reserved for official consulate engagements. Like his sister, Jeremy made a favourable impression on the lawman. Lombard was struck by his client's 'Viking face' and what he detected to be his 'will of steel.' The lawyer outlined his proposal: Jeremy (and family) should become *partie civiles* in the murder enquiry of John Cartland.

A potential game changer, becoming a civil party achieved several things at once explained the lawyer. On a practical level, Jeremy could only be interviewed henceforth by the presiding judge and only in the presence of his lawyers in the highly formal and ritualised setting of the Aix-en-Provence Palais de Justice. Gonzalves and Krikorian would thus be effectively side-lined. Any hopes they might have harboured of pressuring Jeremy to confess would now be dashed. Via the judge, police would now need to submit their questions to the defence 24 hours in advance of interview thereby removing the element of surprise. And it just got better. Rather than the intense and sometimes explosive duo of police Commissioners he would now face the far less pugnacious *juge d'instruction*, André Delmas. Moreover, he would face this mild-mannered magistrate in company with his legal quartet of Lombard, Chiappe, Mitchell-Heggs and Sagot. Delmas would be supported by his clerk. Numerically the tables would turn: five against two. At Salon police station recall Jeremy had been one man pitched against more than a dozen officials – intimidating by any standards.

From Jeremy's perspective the many practical advantages of instigating a civil suit were apparent enough. But the benefits did not end there; there was also a symbolic value. In the eyes of the law becoming a civil party would instantly transform him from the status of accused into *accuser*; it would signal very clearly that he, his family and his legal team rejected any accusation of guilt. In effect by becoming a *partie civile* Jeremy was declaring that he would do all he could to assist the authorities in their quest to bring the real culprits to justice.

'In summary, for the reasons just stated, as your lawyer I strongly recommend that you become a *civil partie,*' said Lombard radiating as always, an inner confidence that reassured politicians and nobility alike.

The thought of crossing swords again with either Gonzalves or Krikorian filled Jeremy with dread. Shrewd, perceptive and highly diligent, in this duo of highflying French detectives Jeremy sensed he had met his match even if he did habitually portray the police in a less than a complimentary light. He could see it in their eyes, scepticism and just the occasional flash of disdain. These two police commissioners unnerved him. And now the immaculately dressed lawyer sat beside him was promising to neutralise this threat.

'What do you think Mr Cartland, shall I proceed?'

'Yes, by all means,' replied Jeremy who had all but resigned himself to yet more interminable interviews with the 'Maigret of the South' and 'Jack Palance.' 'But can it be done? Is it possible?'

'Be assured Mr Cartland, it is more than possible. It is in fact the law!'

Lombard now needed to inform the appropriate authorities. Without further ado he called *juge d'instruction*, André Delmas at his Aix-en-Provence base. After an exchange of pleasantries, Lombard came to the point.

'I make it my duty judge to inform you that I am engaged to act on behalf of Jeremy Cartland.'

'Dear Master I thank you for this courtesy,' said Delmas affably, 'but your client has not been charged at this time and therefore your call is a little premature.'

'You misunderstand me your honour,' replied Lombard suavely. 'I know Cartland has not been charged, nor will he ever. I merely inform you that I wish to bring a civil action on behalf of the same young man.'

Silence.

'Judge? Are you there?'

'I'm here,' said the good judge eventually. 'Could you repeat that Master? Perhaps I misheard.'

'Certainly. I wish to notify you of my intention to make Mr

Jeremy Cartland a civil party to the enquiry into the murder of his father.'

'I see. It is your prerogative, master.'

'Indeed.' Ordinarily a lawyer might be obliged to wait several days if not longer to lodge a suit – a stipulation of no use whatsoever for a defence team needing to act swiftly. But this was not just any old lawyer, it was Paul Lombard. 'Shall we meet later today your honour, say 3pm?'

In the subtle game being played out between police and their prime suspect, the defence had just played an ace nobody – not even Krikorian or Gonzalves - could have seen coming and one which in the coming days and weeks would have a profound impact on the direction the case would take. If he were never to set eyes on Jeremy Cartland's Viking features again or the pretty face of his sister, if he were to make no further contribution to the case from hereafter, Maitre Paul Lombard had already done more than enough to justify his substantial fee and much, much more besides.

11

When the inspectors called

Intent on locating the man of the moment, French and English media descended on Marseille en masse. By now certain Jeremy was not being held in custody, they had one aim: an exclusive interview with one of France's most talked about personalities. No such luck at the British consulate, these determined souls began checking the city's hotels. The teacher had vanished, but to where?

Once Lombard and the legal team had set off for Aix and the Edmonds had left the apartment, along with Liz Cartland and her 'fiancé,' Jeremy had wisely remained cocooned within the protective realms of La Cadanelle whose elevated position offered expansive views of Marseille's long, sandy Prado beach and beyond that the azure waters of the Mediterranean. Like it or not the Brit's face was, at that particular moment in time, one of the most recognisable in France and beyond. Together the Brits glanced at the lurid headlines in newspapers. Much to his horror, Jeremy realised that some factions of the French media had all but convicted him of murder.

Meanwhile, Judge Delmas had informed the Marseille police of the startling development that Jeremy Cartland had become a *partie civile* in his father's murder enquiry. The implication was not lost on the investigating officers:

'*Sacre bleu*! Cartland has bewitched us!'

Emile Gonzalves frowned. Between the thumb and fingers on his right hand it was the detective's habit around this time to rotate a little sponge ball – therapy for a hand injured in one of his heroic acts in the line of duty. He squeezed the ball harder. The news that Jeremy had managed to wriggle out of further interrogations was a major blow. From this point forwards the detective knew his prime 'witness' would only need answer to the examining judge, André Delmas. He would also have one of France's top lawyers with him, advising how best to avoid incriminating himself. *Ce n'est pas juste*! There must be something the police could do, a way to counter this diabolical move by the defence. If the Commissioner now reproached himself for not arresting his man when he had the chance – after last night's interrogation at Salon - he could at least console himself with the thought that not even he could have predicted such a brazen manoeuvre.

'I've got it!' Gonzalves banged a hammer-like fist on the desk almost splitting it in half. 'Cartland's suite is brought in conjunction with a single charge, that of murder . . .'

The gangbuster's colleagues looked expectantly towards their leader, the files, papers and telephones they held in their hands momentarily suspended in mid-air.

'And so we shall obtain a warrant to apprehend Mr Cartland for the crime of arson!'

'Bravo Commissioner!'

The detective had called it correctly: Jeremy, his sister and as it would transpire his mother too, were all about to lodge three separate *partie civiles* against persons unknown or 'X' - but only with regards to a charge of murder. In reply to the defence's fiendishly clever move, Gonzalves had conjured up an equally devious counter measure: although it was virtually a no-brainer that whoever had torched the caravan had also committed the murder, it suited Gonzalves' purpose right now to treat them as entirely unconnected crimes. Police could thus continue to directly question Jeremy Cartland. Game on.

Assuming that Lombard would have already preceded him, Gonzalves set out for the Palais of Justice in Aix. His mission: to seek an audience with the Attorney General. The Commissioner preferred the direct approach, man-to-man. Besides, for his ploy to succeed he knew that a certain amount of persuasion and even charm would be required. As to whether or not the police would be able to proceed with a charge of arson was down to the Attorney General's discretion. Gonzalves had to make the case. Rehearsing his argument to himself as he drove, and aware that close of business loomed, the Commissioner steeled himself. Not without pride, this bear of a man did not take too kindly to being outsmarted.

Forty-five minutes after leaving Marseille, Gonzalves arrived outside the imposing neo-classical facade of Aix's Palais de Justice. He was duly received by Marcel Caleb, the Attorney General.

'Let me assure you Commissioner,' said the official lighting his pipe, 'I perfectly understand your dilemma. I appreciate the defence's guile as much as you. But I must also remind you that while some might argue this move by them falls outside the spirit of the rules by which we usually abide, as you must surely know it *is* admissible.'

The Attorney General was chiefly concerned with decorum. Yes, he could, as Gonzalves rightly pointed out, grant the detective permission to pursue a separate charge of arson but not without a degree of reputational damage to both his own office and that of the judicial system more generally. Above all else he did not want to become embroiled in a game of one-upmanship with the defence. It was important to maintain standards, to operate strictly within the parameters laid out by the law.

Gonzalves returned to Marseille disappointed yet sanguine. Deprived of the opportunity to confront their suspect face to face, Krikorian and he could henceforth only ensure Delmas had as much ammunition as possible. Then it would be down to the judge. It was a chance he would rather not take. Delmas had not yet presided over a murder enquiry. Cartland would be his first.

Of the many advantages the *partie civile* granted, breathing space was arguably the most crucial. Now that Delmas would arrange interviews with him on set dates and would be obliged to present evidence to the defence 24 hours in advance, young Cartland had time to prepare himself for any eventualities.

In order to persuade Delmas not to bring charges, Lombard and his fellow lawyers essentially needed to address the anomalies raised by police over the previous two days e.g. *How had the Cartland's axe come to be involved? Why had the prowlers attacked the older Cartland with such ferocity while barely scratching the younger man? Who had set fire to the caravan and why?* And so on. It would certainly help if the defence could supply a plausible explanation of how events had unfolded on the night of 18/19th March. Hence, there would be many intense meetings over the coming days and weeks between Jeremy and his team as they thrashed out possible scenarios.

If the son had not killed his father, who had? Jeremy and his team discussed the matter in detail. Four hypotheses emerged as to the possible identity of the killers:

1. Prowlers, maybe high on drugs.

2. Homicidal maniacs who might have been influenced by *L'Affaire Dominici,* the film of the Drummond murders currently showing in French cinemas.

3. Arabs who might have been provoked to murder had the Arabic-speaking John Cartland insulted them.

4. Smugglers who had concealed drugs inside the caravan and who had come to claim their haul.

Later that Thursday evening, long after the lawyers had departed, the British contingent enjoyed a convivial dinner. Afterwards, the party moved to the apartment's commodious lounge where Mrs Edmonds circulated with the drinks' decanter. Fortified by the knowledge that the *partie civile* had been enacted, Jeremy, Liz and her 'fiancé' felt more settled than at any time over the preceding 72 hours. Thoughts turned homewards, to Brighton, to England. And then the telephone rang. Equanimity was about to turn to anxiety.

Excusing himself, John Edmonds slipped out of the lounge. It was by no means unusual for the Consul to receive calls at all hours of the day – it came with the territory. 'That was the police,' announced Edmonds upon his return to the lounge.

'They're sending over a couple of their men, but I'm not sure why. They'll be here shortly.'

Police officers en route at this time of the evening? There could only be one explanation: Did the police intend to arrest Jeremy here at the official residence of the British Consulate? Had the *partie civile* been somehow invalidated? If, as seemed likely, the police intended to execute a warrant the law stated the process could not start any later than 9pm. Timing was important.

Jeremy sipped his whiskey, one eye cocked on the two lifts over on the other side of the lounge and which opened directly into it in such a way as to remind one of a department store. At a little after 8 o'clock an unmistakable humming noise indicated the imminent arrival of visitors. Out of one of the lifts stepped Krikorian and Gonzalves. John Edmonds greeted the two men in the manner of the professional diplomat he was trained to be.

'Ah, good evening, gentlemen. We have been expecting you,' said Edmonds.

The Commissioners bowed.

'Monsieur le Consul,' began Gonzalves, 'please forgive us for disturbing you, but we are obliged to wait here until we receive further instructions with regards to a certain matter.'

'Of course. Won't you come this way?'

Ever the professional diplomat, Edmonds proceeded to make the introductions. Jeremy acknowledged the visitors with a curt nod of the head. Liz Cartland smiled nervously. While her husband invited the visitors to take their ease on the apartment's plush upholstery, Mrs Edmonds furnished them with tumblers into which she poured whiskey. It was all rather surreal; everybody knew the reason why the commissioners had called, but nobody mentioned it, nor was it alluded to. On the surface the Consul could have been hosting another Anglo-French social event.

Edmonds soon found a reason to slip out into the hallway again. He urgently needed to make a call. While his guests chatted politely but rather stiffly next door, the diplomat updated Sagot, Mitchell-Heggs as well as Lombard's office (The Maitre was otherwise engaged.) Clearly, the way things were headed his British charge was going to require legal counsel before the night was out. Commissioner Gonzalves in particularly bore an air of determination about him. In the time elapsed since his meeting with Caleb that afternoon, it appeared the gangbuster had invoked the highest powers of the constabulary and perhaps some even higher authorities. Indeed, as the policemen made themselves comfortable, a flurry of calls were going back and forwards between Marseille and Aix.

Police had not quite given up hope of bringing a separate charge of arson against Jeremy. On this, the force's Comptroller General agreed with his Chief Commissioner. And there was another avenue to explore: in his role as examining judge, Delmas had it within his power to reject a civil suit thus sending it to appeal. Even if successful the appeal process would take several days to complete - by which time the police would surely have arrested their prime witness and have him safely ensconced behind bars.

As of 8pm on that Thursday evening, Jeremy's fate hung in the balance. Should either Judge Delmas or General Caleb find themselves in sympathy with the Comptroller's arguments, the Brit would find himself in serious trouble.

Again, there are two conflicting accounts of what transpired that evening. According to Paul-Claude Innocenzi's rendition, Jeremy spent those fraught couple of hours scowling at the policemen from a corner of the room, much to Edmond's discomfort. Gonzalves and Krikorian by contrast availed themselves of their host's hospitality, chatting freely and openly on a range of subjects with Ian Smith and the Edmonds. But the journalist's portrayal of events was sharply at odds with Jeremy's recollection who declared Innocenzi's version to be, 'a scurrilous account,' written by 'one of the more odious of the French journalists.' For his part, the teacher-poet recalled a situation wherein the senior detectives, 'were completely out of their depth and were distinctly uncomfortable, like two small schoolboys who have been summoned to the head-master's study, not knowing what to say or where to put their hands.'[1]

At about nine o'clock Jeremy's legal team arrived minus Lombard. In all ten people now sat around the lounge unsure as to what might happen next. Small talk only amplified the awkwardness of the situation. Jeremy and Liz spoke in low voices with Mr Mitchell-Heggs. On the other side of the room, aware of the Brit's status as a *partie civile* and the limitations it imposed upon them, Krikorian and Gonzalves seemed quite oblivious to Jeremy's presence. All very strained.

In the meantime, negotiations between Marseille and Aix dragged on.[2] Finally, a few minutes before ten, Gonzalves took a call from his superior. A minute later he returned into the salon. All eyes on him, the Chief Commissioner took Krikorian aside for a quiet word. He then approached the Edmonds.

'Monsieur et Madame Consul,' said Gonzalves gravely, 'it is time my colleague and I departed. We leave you to your guests. Thank-you for your gracious hospitality tonight.'

With that, the two commissioners saluted the Consul and promptly disappeared into the lift. Jeremy had just had the narrowest of escapes. Somewhere between bemusement and relief, the remaining guests felt the release of pressure as if a blister had just been lanced. The danger had passed - for now. Fortune had been smiling on the young English teacher. Nor would it be the last occasion when the fates or some higher power seemed to intervene to the young man's benefit.

12

Attack, the best form of defence

On Friday morning Lombard collected Liz and Jeremy from La Cadanelle in his distinctive blue Jaguar. It was time to meet the press. Representatives from the major media networks in both the UK and France had been invited to Lombard's Marseille office where they were set to finally meet Jeremy Cartland in the flesh.

After hearing about the bizarre visit of Krikorian and Gonzalves of the previous evening, the lawyer concluded that the commissioners must have had an arrest warrant concealed in their jackets. He could well imagine the disappointment on the detectives' faces. They had left La Cadanelle empty-handed, yet had arrived with such great expectations. That they would attempt such a ploy went to show just how determined the police were to get their man.

Before the conference commenced, Lombard drafted a statement intended for Jeremy to read for radio and TV. The

Brit insisted on making some changes to the script. Lombard agreed. Thus, the dynamic was soon set: it was Jeremy calling the shots, accepting or rejecting advice as he saw fit. If Lombard was a little perturbed by his client's effrontery, he hid it well. He would later remark that never before had he encountered a client with such a forceful character as Mr Jeremy Cartland Esq. – and the Maitre of Marseille counted amongst his clientele, lest we forget, billionaires and even prime ministers. In Salon hospital as well as the town's gendarmerie, the Brit had been a fish out of water, vulnerable and uncertain; equilibrium restored, a rather different Jeremy was emerging – a confident, assertive version who, sister apart, seemed to trust only one other person: himself.

Dressed immaculately in a blue suit and purple tie – Jeremy always was a snappy dresser - the Brit took his seat in front of a media phalanx of cameras and microphones. The only sign that he had been involved in anything amiss was the cluster of scratches on the right side of his forehead and which were healing well. In a steady, clear voice he proceeded to read:

> I, Jeremy Cartland, first wish to pay homage to the French authorities for the care with which they treated me. I affirm that I am innocent. I will do everything in my power to help French justice, whom I trust, discover my father's murderer. This is why I have decided to start a civil action.

The Cartlands then found themselves assailed from all angles. 'I didn't even realise I was a suspect,' Jeremy told journalists from the UK's leading papers - *Guardian, Times, Mirror, Telegraph, Daily Mail* and *Daily Express*. Much to the annoyance of their French colleagues, the British dailies were hogging the attention of this rather photogenic brother and sister. Then again, the British press had been markedly more sympathetic towards the Cartlands than their gallic cousins.

'Were you and your father at loggerheads?'

'Did you drink that night?'

'Did you and your father fight?'

If he stumbled or hesitated Liz Cartland was right there by her brother's side ready to step into the breach. She impressed Bill Hamsher of the *Express* no end. 'What an asset Jeremy Cartland has in Elizabeth,' observed Hamsher. 'She was at his elbow to help him answer the hurricane of questions.'

Following a question about arrangements for their father's funeral, Liz and Jeremy embraced one another and wept. The gentlemen of the press waited respectfully for the Cartlands to compose themselves before continuing with their questions. Somebody asked about Mr Cartland's involvement with intelligence services. The victim's nebulous associations with British intelligence had been first raised on the morning of the murder and, like a bad cold, refused to go away. Another issue rumbling away in the background concerned the nature of the victim's relationship with Edward Heath. After the war Cartland had briefly served as head of the Oxford University Appointments Board, a quango as the name implies which used its weight to secure work opportunities for graduates of the university. Rumour suggested he had used his position to procure for the future prime minister a coveted role in journalism as editor of The *Church Times*.[1]

Jeremy also undertook several radio interviews. To Radio Luxembourg he once more expressed his shock at realising that he was a suspect in his father's murder.

Once the conference had ended, along with Hamsher, Jeremy and Liz took a stroll through Marseille's sunny streets.

With regards to media, the Cartlands knew who their friends were. The idea was to show to all that Jeremy was a free man. It was indeed a symbolic moment, the first time since the tragedy the British teacher had not been chaperoned or directed by officials, medical or judicial. That evening Hamsher would write a highly sympathetic piece about the affair entitled, 'As free as the next man.' The article appeared in Saturday's *Daily Express*. At the time the paper had a readership of around 3 million making it one of Britain's most popular newspapers.

'I am profoundly convinced of my brother's innocence,' the article quoted Liz Cartland as asserting, 'and of course am ready to do all I can to help.' *L'Aurore* carried on its front page that Saturday a headline which read, 'My brother is innocent.'

As a PR exercise the press conference and 'freedom walk' hit the mark. The *Express* front page also carried a tease entitled 'My ordeal by Jeremy Cartland.' The first signs of a strategy had just begun wherein the young British teacher would present himself as the victim of an incompetent and even corrupt French judicial system.

There was just the question of how to spend the week-end. Judge Delmas had scheduled his first interview with Jeremy for Wednesday, 28th March. Although he had only just booked into a hotel in Marseille, prime witness no. 1 decided to hop back over to the UK for a few days. France had become oppressive. It would mean flying back almost immediately, but Jeremy had a pressing need to return home. In what would form part of a sustained and always strident critique of French procedural systems, he had decided to obtain a medical report from an English doctor, a second opinion as regards his physical condition. The sub-text was unmistakable: French systems and the professionals who implemented them could not be trusted. It was a serious charge, one that would nonetheless form a core part of the Englishman's defence strategy. The French system, he would later reflect, 'does not seem to have grown up since the time of Dreyfus.'[2]

By implying French standards were somehow inferior to those in Britain, the defence could achieve several objectives: portray Jeremy as a victim of systemic malfeasance while also diverting the focus of the enquiry onto the competency (and integrity) of police and medical professionals. Rather than Jeremy in the dock, it would be Krikorian or Dr Jouglard having to explain and justify their actions.

If the French media's attitude towards him thus far had been ambiguous, undermining the competency of its institutions was hardly going to endear Jeremy any further. But needs must. As strategists military and non-military both appreciate, attack often is the best form of defence.

Having agreed to return five days hence, Jeremy was cleared to leave France. It was just a case of locating his passport which had been requisitioned by the authorities on the night of the murder. Passport collected, the Brit was free to go. Jeremy, Liz and their journalist friend caught the 20.40 flight from Marseille to Paris. They departed the French capital early the next morning, arriving at Heathrow in time for lunch.

The Cartlands had planned to stay with a family friend in west London. From here Jeremy could keep his appointment with Professor Cameron of London Hospital Medical College who duly carried out a medical examination. Legal, medical and travelling costs were mounting up, but the stakes were high. Salon hospital medical staff might not have been able to identify traces of trauma to the patient's head, but that did not necessarily mean none had been present. Incompetence could not be ruled out. Jeremy indeed had better luck with Cameron.

The professor duly found a large swelling on the back of his patient's head. Conducted almost a week after the assault, promising as they appeared to be, the professor's findings were only ever going to be an exercise in futility. Who knew how and when the swelling had occurred? Commissioned and paid for by their prime suspect, investigators were only ever going to claim such evidence to be inadmissible. Thereafter the professor's report remained private; neither French nor British investigators ever obtained a copy.[3]

While Saturday brought sunshine and showers to London, a heatwave had arrived in Provence. Sightseers crawled all over the clearing where one-week earlier John Cartland had been slain. The RN 572 had never been busier. After they finished their picnics, families strolled around the site. They gazed in silence at the blackened remains of the Cartland caravan - charred bed springs, a single, scorched wheel arch miraculously still intact, looking rather lost. Something powerful was drawing people to this spot, but what exactly? Curiosity? Prurience? It could have been a shrine. For a few weeks in spring 1973 that is precisely what it did become.

For police and journalists who had been working non-stop since the early hours of Monday, the weekend came as welcome respite. It had been a hectic five days. The lull in the enquiry afforded the chance for reflection. Some factions of the French media while not throwing their weight behind Jeremy, were however starting to shift their focus onto the police.

Le Monde was just one newspaper which lamented what it took to be deficiencies with the way the enquiry had been handled. In the immediate aftermath of the crime people had been allowed to trample all over the sight, so claimed the paper. Vital forensic evidence had thus been contaminated or even lost. Jeremy would make a similar claim.[4] It was not the only point of agreement between newspaper and *partie civile*: the paper also complained that the police had only pursued just one line of enquiry, a line which assumed there was but a single suspect: Jeremy Cartland. One week into the enquiry, *Le Monde* was already opining about what it called a 'clumsy investigation' - music to the ears of a defence team hoping to discredit the investigation at every opportunity. The paper then went on to invoke that byword for police ineptitude, the Drummond murders.

Not only did *Le Monde* have reservations about the conduct of the enquiry in terms of competency and lack of progress, it had several other concerns. How, when he had been earmarked as 'witness no.1' by investigators, had Cartland been free to leave France? After all, he was strongly suspected of having committed murder, a capital offence. Permitting the Brit to waltz in and out of France as he pleased seemed to imply a belief that there was no need to detain him. It was an extraordinary privilege to be granted, one that Jeremy was exploiting to his advantage in the surgery of Prof. Cameron.

Had higher powers intervened on his behalf? Writer of the piece James Sarazin detected the hand of the French Interior Ministry. But what struck him most was the omnipotency of British consular officials during the week just past. 'Have you ever,' he asked *Le Monde* readers, 'seen a consul so eager towards one of his fellow citizens struggling with French justice?' Clearly, Sarazin believed the young Brit was benefiting from special attention. Benham and Edmonds would have no doubt disagreed. As a DBS plunged into an especially difficult situation, the consul was simply doing its job, helping him navigate through the minefield in which he now trod. A theme had however been established: the Cartlands had connections.

Not everybody was taking stock this weekend. Up at the Institute of Legal Medicine in Lille, Professor Pierre H Muller and his team of scientists spent the day testing exhibits from the crime scene - clothing and suspected murder weapons. Firstly, two facts were ascertained: John Cartland's blood was of the common A variety, while that of his son belonged to the much rarer B type.

On the night of his murder Cartland senior had been wearing three layers of clothing - testament to the chilliness of the evening. As expected, the large brown patches on his pullovers and floral pyjama bottoms tested positive for blood group A. This type was also detected on the blade of the axe and was spattered on the cushion which had housed the concrete block probably used to fell the victim.

Meanwhile, the much rarer B compound was detected on the kitchen knife. So far, so good. It was also present on the outside of Jeremy's left desert boot in the form of 'two blackish crusts.' More interestingly, three spots of this same B variety were discovered inside Jeremy's right boot. How had they ended up there? According to Jeremy's testimony, upon hearing the noises outside the caravan, along with a pair of trousers, he had also put on this same pair of boots. Yet the discovery of the blood spots on the boot's interior pointed towards a scenario whereby the shoes had not been worn until sometime *after* the attack.

During his interview at Salon police station on Wednesday, Krikorian had asked about these same blood stains. 'I might have put my shoe on again,' Jeremy had replied, 'with my blood-stained hand if it had fallen off.'

If that explanation seemed possible, how to account for what scientists described as an 'indistinct brownish stain 5 cm in diameter' discovered on the victim's pyjama bottoms, just above the knee of the left leg? Initially, Mueller suspected that these marks could have been mud. The professor decided to test the spots nonetheless. The result came back as indeterminate: the spots contained traces of the B antigen found in human blood, the same rare type as Jeremy, but contamination – possibly with a chemical reagent i.e. detergent – meant making a categorical identification was no longer feasible. This antigen is not peculiar to human blood. For example, it can be found in certain species of ape.[5]

Although the picture of what may have occurred on that night of madness one week earlier had all but crystalised, police had still not acquired any evidence that could be classified as conclusive. Detectives also calculated that their prime witness would stick doggedly to the story he had told so far. Thus, their best hope lay in disturbing his composure, giving him enough rope. But Jeremy Cartland was now a civil party. Thanks to Paul Lombard, neither Krikorian nor the pugnacious Gonzalves would have the opportunity to cross examine the witness again. The next time Jeremy would be required to explain himself it would be in front of André Delmas – an entirely different prospect to the gangbuster and Maigret of the south.

13

Intimate convictions

Together with his sister and a family friend, Jeremy flew back to France early on Tuesday, 27th March. There was much preparation to do before the interview with Delmas scheduled for the next day. Snapped breezing through Heathrow with the ever-faithful Liz, the Brit declared himself confident that the matter would soon be resolved. He was determined, he told reporters, to assist the murder enquiry 'until the truth is out.'

In the meantime, team Cartland assembled in the elegant ambience of the Hotel Le Pigeonnet, a luxurious hotel situated a ten-minute drive from Aix-en-Provence's Palais de Justice. Their client's status being that of a *partie civile* meant the defence team now had access to the same police file which the judge would use at Wednesday's hearing. Masters Lombard and Chiappe scrutinised the documents. Marseille's finest legal minds were not impressed.

'Is that all?' snorted Chiappe handing the file back to his

esteemed colleague. 'Why it's nothing! It's less than nothing!'

'My dear Chiappe,' said Lombard with a smile, 'those are my exact sentiments too.'

Was the lawyer's elation justified? The police file it must be said was sorely lacking in actual evidence. Certainly, the enquiry had not been helped by the inferno which had devoured the Cartland caravan, and in whose unforgiving flames who knows how many vital clues might have perished. Essentially, the dossier therefore contained the list of anomalies which had been put to Jeremy during his interviews of the previous week, the explanations to which had been, from the investigator's point of view, either highly implausible or just plain evasive. It was all the police had. Little wonder the defence felt so bullish.

When the team perused the testimony of a certain Arlette Blasco, taken the previous Friday, the day just got better.

Accompanied by her husband and son, Blasco claimed to have arrived at La Barben on the night of the murder at about 0.45am She had noticed two cars, a red Renault 4L and a 'white car.' The 4L's headlights were on and pointing towards the caravan. While her husband pulled the family's green Ford Cortina over to the side of the road and got out to take a closer look at the fire, Mrs Blasco had remained in the vehicle with the couple's young son. What she said next had detectives tearing out their hair. For this attractive woman of Iberian descent had apparently witnessed a key moment in the drama: she had arrived in time to observe the young men move the Cartland's Hillman away from the burning caravan. She had seen two men engaged in this task. One young man was pushing the vehicle from behind. Another was, she recalled, leaning into the car via its front-left door. Fascinated, Mme Blasco had watched their efforts to move the vehicle. The men's gestures and their movements had 'intrigued' her.

Now it was the police's turn to be intrigued. When officers had checked the Hillman shortly after arrival at *Jas de Dane,* its front-left door had been locked. Furthermore, Frederic Delaude and the three young men who had assisted at the scene of the crime swore that they had not opened the door, accessing the car only via its front-right door. Was Madame absolutely sure – perhaps she was mistaken?

> Although you point out to me the importance of this testimony, I am certain that it really was the left-hand front door that the man was leaning through. I also insist on the fact the man was leaning in through the door and not through the open window.[1]

As it was, Mrs Blasco's statement flatly contradicted those of the young men who had assisted at the scene of crime. The defence had its first witness, the testimony of whom appeared to corroborate at least some of their client's story.

Police wasted no time. On Monday they responded by re-interviewing the crime scene witnesses. And so, Delaude along with Lorenzo, Weltman and Chambonnet retold their stories once again. All four men confirmed they had not accessed the Cartland's Hillman via its left front door. They had used the right-front only, the driver's side. Thus, they could not confirm if the left-front door indeed had been locked or not. None of them recalled seeing a red 4L parked at the scene. Joseph Lorenzo also stated he had never seen a green Ford Cortina in the vicinity either.

From the salubrious environs of the Hotel Pigeonnet, Jeremy Cartland had every reason to feel optimistic by the end of play on Tuesday night. Lack of evidence along with Mme

Blasco's beneficial testimony had fortified the 29-year-old's position appreciably. Jeremy would later pay tribute to what he termed Madame Blasco's 'unswerving honesty.'[2] The defence had acquired, or so it must have appeared, yet more ammunition in its burgeoning attack on police methodology.

And these were not the only favourable omens. In the midst of the brouhaha, a related issue had started to evolve – one with the potential to imbue the case with a significance beyond its own confines: *L'Affaire Cartland* was starting to impose itself into politics – more specifically into the diplomatic sphere, that most ambiguous and always delicate realm of political give and take. For a British press never requiring that much incentive to criticise or ridicule its gallic cousins (and vice versa) the Cartland case was proving heaven sent. Just over a week into the investigation and already becoming apparent were some profound differences between the British and French legal methodology in terms of procedure and philosophy, not least in the power invested by French law in the *juge d'instruction*. Could the defence team capitalise on a political environment somewhat delicately poised this spring of 1973? It was worth a try.

Since 1679 British law has been enshrined on the principles of habeas corpus. Under this ancient statute an individual cannot be detained without proof and must be afforded the opportunity to answer charges on a specific date and time. Suspicion alone is not enough to detain a suspect. There must be reason i.e. proof.

In France the system is somewhat different. Here it is not so much a question of proof but of instinct. Whether or not to press charges against an individual in France boils down to what is called *intime conviction*. Personal belief, inner voice, it amounts to the same thing: intuition. Thus, a person can be arrested and charged with a serious crime based on nothing more substantial than a belief albeit the heartfelt belief of an appointed *juge d'instruction*. For those brought up on habeas corpus the French way might seem surprising. Amongst other things it raises issues of subjectivity and bias. There is also the question of fallibility; should the intuition of a single individual - however learned – carry such weight? And yet there is a certain logic at play. In cases where the perpetrator has taken pains to conceal his/her trail (e.g. recourse to arson) and/or where witness testimony may be lacking, whereas in the British system an offender would almost certainly walk free, in France he or she may still be brought to justice thanks to the concept of *intime conviction*. To the (British) mind brought up on the importance of proof, the deficiencies of such a system may seem obvious, but habeas corpus is not itself without blemish. No judicial system can claim infallibility.

With regards to the Cartland affair, the judge charged with trusting his inner voice was the unassuming André Delmas. After a long career spent in provincial obscurity, the 60-year-old had been on the cusp of retirement when the Cartland file had fallen into his lap.

What then of the man who would decide Jeremy's fate? Would he be equal to task? He was said to be both methodical and efficient; he would need to be because the case in front of him was without doubt the biggest of his career. A creature of habit, thrice a-day Delmas would leave his office in the Palais to frequent the nearby Le Madeleine café-bar where he could invariably be found in the same spot sipping his favourite coffee. In his spare time, he kept bees and cultivated roses. Jeremy was less than complimentary. In the Brit's estimation the scooter-riding Delmas was 'a 'lugubrious looking, heavy-jowled individual' with a 'sallow complexion.'

At 2pm Jeremy was summoned. Along with his quartet of lawyers he took a seat in the sparse, washed out room which served as Delmas' office. Also present were an interpreter and, bony fingers poised over the keys of his ancient typewriter, sat the judge's faithful clerk Maurice De Bonfils. Liz Cartland waited in a café across the road with her male friend.

And so, once more Jeremy related his tale. In this account he expanded upon some details of the trip, adding and clarifying others.

One of the most puzzling aspects of the case concerned the provenance of the axe. Neither Gonzalves nor Krikorian could understand why the Cartlands had felt the need to bring an axe on holiday with them. 'Protection' but from who? The question of old scores being settled would explode soon enough, but for now there was another aspect to ponder: precisely how had the axe ended up in Mr Cartland's Hillman? Jeremy retold his tale to the judge: on the night of their departure from the UK his father had duly arrived to collect him from his flat at Highcroft Villas. It was then that he had noticed an unusual item packed in the car: a large chopping axe. Jeremy scoffed at the idea of taking such an item abroad and returned the instrument to his kitchen. When his father sneaked a smaller axe into the car he feigned not to notice.

Ownership of the axe established, what of the origin of the other suspected items used in the murder i.e. knife and pillow case? During his testimony Jeremy listed the items lost in the fire: paraffin stove, hurricane lamp, provisions, candles, spare clothing, sleeping bags, quilts etc. The men had been well prepared for their 3–4-week sojourn. But not *that* prepared. Extensive as this list appeared to be, there was one notable exception: pillows. If the Cartlands had not been using pillows, then ergo pillow cases would have been superfluous; and if that was true some other actor must have brought the pillow case used in the murder to *Jas de Dane*. As for the knife, Jeremy re-iterated his assertion that the one found at the crime scene had not been part of the items which had left Brighton.

Upon listing the clothing lost in the blaze Jeremy mentioned pyjamas, but immediately corrected himself: 'I was mistaken, there were no pyjamas as I was wearing them.' If the judge wondered if one pair of pyjamas would be adequate for a trip which might last four weeks, he didn't say.

Some of the most interesting snippets revolved around the desert boots. When relating how he had slipped on his boots upon being wakened, Jeremy felt it necessary to inform the judge that he had not tied his laces. Further on in his testament he went on to state that:

> At no time, from my leaving the caravan until and including the time when help arrived, did I take off my shoes, I am certain about that point.[3]

This admission once again raised the question of how blood had ended up inside the right boot. Indeed, the issue of boots and whether laces had been tied or not would occupy a fair amount of time over the course of the investigation. For his part, Jeremy would take some pains to clarify that they had been untied when he had left the caravan to check outside; he would also mention socks on more than one occasion – more precisely, the fact that he had not been wearing any under his desert boots on the night of the murder. Anxious to confront the prowlers, socks, it can be allowed, would have been the last thing on his mind. And yet blood spots had been found inside the right boot. The hypothesis that Jeremy had put his boots on after, not before the attack, grew ever more credible.

To the sound of De Bonfils' typewriter snapping away, the testimony continued. Invariably beginning the various stages of his story with the phrase 'to be precise,' Jeremy revealed yet more details of that horrific night:

The caravan had been pale green in colour . . . the Cartlands bought their petrol 'a little before Pélissanne' . . . Jeremy and his father had been 'total strangers' to the area . . . it had been Jeremy's decision to turn off the road at the clearing . . . the Hillman's back doors had remained locked, but not its front doors . . . Cartland senior had fallen asleep between 20.00 and 21.00, Jeremy at about 22.00 . . . Jeremy had used a handkerchief to stem the flow of blood from his abdomen . . .

Delmas listened intently as the teacher recalled the moment he had regained consciousness. Alerted by the flames, Jeremy's first thought had been for his father. He had stumbled over to the caravan calling his name. He recalled the panic upon realising his father was missing. In response, the judge showed the young man a police sketch of the murder location. Taking the pylon as their reference point, officers had catalogued the distance to every conceivable object in the surrounding area: axe, concrete, knife, caravan, car, corpse, tree etc.

'Perhaps you could indicate the precise spot where you awoke on this map?'

Jeremy assessed the map for a few moments. 'Personally, I think some of the details are inaccurate, the position of the tree for example. I see it as being nearer the pylon.' He had a point. The concrete pylon and tree were indeed situated closer to one another than represented on the police sketch. As far as revelations go, this one did not materially alter the facts of the case, but did cast a certain doubt over police competency. An unexpected gift-horse, the defence immediately called for a break in which they could fully assess the map evidence in its entirety. Yet another discrepancy emerged: the relative position of caravan and car. The police drawing showed the former parked at an obtuse angle behind the Hillman, while Jeremy maintained that the vehicles had been parked in a straight line, parallel with the RN 572.

One week after the event there had been plenty of time for the scene of crime to undergo physical change – not least in the shape of souvenir hunters and that Mistral wind. Thus, it was too late to confirm either side's impressions.

Though the issue of the caravan's precise position might have been a quibble, it was one that the defence seized upon – whatever might help call police competency into question. As minor as they were, the defence were clearly trying to make these discrepancies into a point of honour, a cipher almost for whose word could be trusted – that of Jeremy or the police. But there was another reason why the caravan's position had become a bone of contention. Jeremy had originally testified that he had seen the mysterious figure leaning into the Hillman *immediately upon stepping out of the caravan* – an impossibility had the caravan been parked at the obtuse angle as described by police.

'I told him (Delmas)' later wrote Jeremy confirming this part of his testimony, 'I had indeed seen the figure in the car, almost as soon as I had stepped outside (the caravan.)'[4]

However, in his testimony on the day he had the following to say about the moment he left the caravan:

> I went along the left-hand side of the caravan until
> I was level with the tow-bar and I cannot tell you
> exactly when or more precisely where I was when
> I saw, from the front of the caravan and still in line
> with the left-hand side, a person inside the Hillman.

Oddly, this testimony appeared to confirm the details of the police sketch, that the caravan *had* been parked at an obtuse angle. At the very least it contradicted Jeremy's own testimony that he had immediately seen the prowler leaning into the car upon stepping out of the caravan.[5]

Undeterred, the defence composed a letter which accused police of negligence. Once written the letter could be officially submitted to the examining judge. So, while Delmas and De Bonfils waited, Lombard, Chiappe, Mitchell-Heggs and Sagot conferred with Jeremy. Attention was drawn to what it termed three 'serious inaccuracies with the map:' 1) the siting of the tree was incorrect 'to the extent of several metres.' 2) the caravan was 'much more nearly parallel to the road.' 3) the line of bushes 'follows a much sharper convex curve than is shown in the sketch.'

The letter did not end there. The Brit's defenders next complained that their client had not been given a 'detailed' medical examination upon admission to Salon hospital. A non-sequitur is defined as a statement that does not logically follow from what has preceded it and this complaint bore all those hallmarks.

Jeremy, recall, had been treated in the hospital's emergency department for what were presumed to be stab wounds. At the time of his admission (1.20 am) the body of John Cartland had not yet been discovered, let alone a murder investigation launched. The emergency doctor had duly treated and stitched both wounds. He had then gone on to his next patient. Not until 3am did the constable from Salon gendarmerie arrive at Jeremy's bedside. In other words, there had been no reason to subject him to a detailed medical examination upon admission at Salon hospital. There was an undeniable whiff of desperation about this interlude, the letter and the 'evidence' cited within it. From the outside it might have seemed as if the defence was simply trying to find any opportunity to discredit police and medical testimony, manoeuvres of an experienced and razor-sharp defence team.

Even more inexplicably the letter then went on to make a factually incorrect claim. Once in hospital, it asserted, Jeremy had not received a further examination and had consequently sought the help of Professor Cameron. The teacher had in fact been examined by Dr Jouglard on the morning of Tuesday, March 20th. 'She proceeded to make a detailed examination of every inch of my body,' complained Jeremy.[6] He had also undergone endless x-rays while in Salon hospital. For reasons best known to itself the defence appeared to have overlooked these facts.

Factual imprecisions aside, Jeremy seemed delighted at the outcome. The letter had achieved its objective: it had publicly chastised the police. 'Once again,' wrote Jeremy in that inimitable way of his, 'I felt I was dealing with frivolous and naughty little schoolboys, a feeling I originally had while being interrogated at Salon police station.'[7]

Overall, the interview had not progressed the police case. Maitre Chiappe summoned up the defence position thus: 'We are convinced that soon all the light will be shed on a case with multiple aspects, whose strangeness and mystery cannot escape anyone.'

Jeremy and Liz flew back to the UK the next day. However, the matter was far from over. Delmas had scheduled another interview for one week later, Wednesday, 4th of April. Jeremy readily accepted the judge's invitation; no surprise there. He was, after all, helping the police in their efforts to find the killer of his father.

'I never took seriously the business of being a suspect,'

Jeremy told reporters upon his arrival back on home soil.

If he thought interest in the story might have cooled, the teacher was mistaken. Media and public appetite remained unabated. While Jeremy based himself in London, some newspaper people had even decamped to the seaside, to his home town of Brighton. Uppermost in their sights was Mr Cartland's housekeeper, Janet Gibson.

One week until his next interview with Delmas, Jeremy thus had plenty to occupy him. Media intrusion aside, a more troubling proposition loomed on the horizon. Although no formal treaty existed between the UK and France, it was possible, in fact highly likely, that French authorities would apply at some time for an extradition order. In order to deal with this threat Jeremy engaged the services of Michael Relton, a London-based solicitor.[8] Thinking even further ahead, he engaged the services of yet another lawyer, Lionel Bloch. Lawyer no. 6 specialised in libel. Once the case was over and Jeremy had cleared his name, the plan, so it appeared, was to launch defamation suits against certain UK newspapers which had incurred the teacher-poet's wrath. Soon there would be substantial bills to settle. A figure of £100,000 was already being quoted. Retaining a team of six lawyers did not come cheap. Jeremy was going to need every penny he could get.

14

A dish best served exceedingly cold?

While Jeremy and the judge had been locking horns in Aix's imposing Palais de Justice that Wednesday afternoon, unbeknown to either party the Cartland affair was about to take a dramatic twist once more into the area of wartime espionage – a not unwelcome diversion as far as the defence were concerned. Not for the first time fortune seemed to be favouring the young teacher from Brighton.

Right from the start the murder of John Basil Cartland had captured the media's imagination. There was something about the affair that held the interest of editors, journalists and public alike throughout that unforgettable spring and summer of 1973. One aspect of the affair in particularly intrigued: its potential links to previous cases, especially the 1952 murder of the Drummond family. 'Professor killed in way similar to '52 case,' so went the headline in The *New York Times* of 20th March. The *Guardian* also invoked the Drummond case with its front-page story, 'Wealthy Briton Murdered in France.' The spectre of that long ago triple murder would also come to haunt Gonzalves and his colleagues during and after the present case.

Whether summoned up by the media or just existing in the minds of a public who could never completely erase the memory of that grisly crime, Drummond ghosts had been there from the start in Pélissanne, an ominous shadow hanging in the air. Like many others as they motored through France, John and Jerry Cartland had seen the posters along the boulevards announcing the premiere of Claude Bernard-Aubert's newly released film: *L'Affaire Dominici.* Renowned actor Jean Gabin played the title role of Gaston Dominici. A young Gerard Depardieu would also feature. By sheer coincidence, on the morning of the murder the film had arrived for its premiere in Marseille. Bernard-Aubert's reconstruction of the Drummond massacre was one of the year's most eagerly awaited events.

The facts of the Drummond case have been documented time and again. The family had been on a camping holiday when, on the night of 4-5th August 1952, along with their 10-year-old daughter Elizabeth, Sir Jack and Lady Drummond pitched up their Hillman saloon beside the N96 road, a few kilometres from Lurs, a small town situated just over 70 kms to the north of Aix-en-Provence. For reasons only known to themselves, the Drummonds decided to camp by the side of this busy road where lorries hurtled just metres away from their impromptu campsite. One hundred yards away stood La Grande Terre, a farm owned by a family of peasant farmers, the Dominici.

It had been a sultry summer day. In the morning the family planned to set off on the next stage of their holiday. While

Elizabeth slept in the back of the family car that evening, her parents set up a camp-bed next to the vehicle and proceeded to doze in the warm night air. At around 1am tragedy struck. Mr and Mrs Drummond were executed, shot dead in cold blood. Poor Elizabeth, upon realising her parents had been murdered, had run for her life. The assailant gave chase. As she stumbled in the pitch dark, heading in her blind panic towards the nearby River Durance, a bullet zipped past the petrified girl's head grazing her ear. Moments later the ten-year old tripped to the ground. Her pursuer caught up. What happened next has haunted all those involved in the case and many who weren't: seemingly now out of ammunition, the unknown assailant clubbed the terrified girl to death with the rifle's butt as she cowered on the ground.

Ever since the conviction of Gaston Dominici for the murders, controversy had dogged the case. Dominici owned the land upon which the British family had camped. Investigators concluded that the head of the family must have quarrelled with Sir Jack that night – probably as he had returned from checking the fields he farmed. There had been a scuffle. The farmer's gun had gone off. From that moment the fate of Lady Drummond and the couple's daughter had been sealed. But had this irascible old man killed the Drummonds or had one of his sons?[1] Or had the deed been committed by darker forces? The tight-knit Dominici clan, the ferociously proud inhabitants of La Grande Terre, closed ranks and proceeded to lead investigating officers a merry dance as testimonies changed as often as the wind.

After being found guilty of the crimes the 75-year-old Dominici was sentenced to death. Unease with regards to the safety of the conviction growing and with it public sympathy, the sentence was eventually commuted to life. In 1960 De

Gaulle pardoned the illiterate patriarch of La Grande Terre. The Drummond murders remain officially unsolved.

The years went by, but the tragedy that happened on that August night had never been forgotten. Rightly or wrongly, the case became notorious for police inefficiency: Gaston Dominici exonerated, had not the real murderer(s) therefore escaped justice? By 1973, two decades after it had occurred, the incident was still one of France's most notorious crimes. It *still is*.

Brits . . . camping . . . a Hillman car . . . Provence . . . unsolved murder . . . the family had even parked close to an electricity pylon - all that was needed to link Drummond with Cartland. Were there however more than just superficial coincidences linking the two cases? One rumour doing the rounds suggested the two men had known one another during the war. Rumours, they just kept on coming.

On Thursday morning multiple more arrived. These particular rumours, sent to both the Paris office of the *Daily Express* and that of the BBC, arrived in an envelope and had a title: 'Re: The Murder of Mr. John Basil Cartland. Letter to my British Friends.' Dated 26th March the letter was unsigned. One sentence better than any other summarised its theme:

> There may exist a mysterious conspiracy aimed at most of the witnesses of war secrets and secrets of the resistance in territory occupied by the enemy between 1940 and 1945.

To support its thesis, the letter named a series of individuals who had met with what it claimed had been unexplained deaths and all of whom had links with the intelligence services during the second world war: Sir Oliver Duncan's death in

1964 at a clinic in Rome; Michael Lasseter's death in January 1973 outside his home in Cannes. The latter was a 'former collaborator' of the former asserted the letter.

Accordingly, the Drummond family had not been killed by any members of the Dominici clan. The motive lay elsewhere. Sir Jack had been, 'the victim of important war secrets, some of which concern Indo-China.' Never far from the surface, the theme of wartime activities was thus once again pushed to the forefront of the Cartland case. The press couldn't wait to take the story into ever murkier waters: 'Wartime resistance in France linked with Cartland murder,' read The *Times* headline of 29th March.

In a phone call made to the BBC on the same day, the caller – presumably the letter writer – made yet more claims. In 1956 Sir Jack Drummond's secretary Jane Marshall, had also been murdered in France, in the northern seaport of Dieppe. Was there any substance to such claims? Had Sir Jack been involved with the intelligence services?

In certain quarters it had always been rumoured that while he enjoyed a reputation as a nutritionist of international repute, acclaimed for his outstanding work during the second world war, Drummond might have indeed been involved in the murky world of wartime espionage. Rumours had always pointed towards the Special Operations Executive (SOE) the intelligence agency based in London's famous Baker Street and which had played such a pivotal role in sabotaging German operations in France. What bound the two cases together then was a common motif: revenge. Somehow during their previous lives men like John Cartland and Jack Drummond must have made powerful enemies. Now there were scores to be settled, so the theory went. But what could these two well-spoken, upright gentlemen have possibly done to incur such wrath?

Jack Drummond had a background in chemistry. But it was in the field of nutrition where he had gained eminence. During the war he had advised the Ministry of Food where his expertise in such areas as vitamins (especially A & D) had proved invaluable for a nation forced to survive on rations. After the war he travelled to the Netherlands and elsewhere advising on the dietary requirements of undernourished prisoners liberated from camps. By 1952 he held a senior research role with Boots the chemist known back then as the Boots Pure Drug Company. Could someone really have held a grudge against such a man?

For his part, John Cartland had almost certainly worked with De Gaulle's Free France during the second world war. Rumours circulated he had also been connected to the SOE. 'My brother was a British agent with the Resistance,' confirmed the victim's older brother when the story of the mysterious letter broke. Fuelling the revenge motif theory even further, Bryan Cartland also added that his knowledge of his brother's wartime activities in France, 'could throw some light on the case.'

Indeed, when it came to John Cartland, hearsay and rumour were never exactly in short supply. Amongst Cartland's many anecdotes of heroism and bravery one story in particular stood out.

The dead man had always claimed to have played a role in the liberation of Brussels, but in what precise capacity is not known. It was part of the Cartland legend. So, while The Guards Armoured Division swept through Belgium, reaching the capital on Sunday, 3rd September 1944, British agent John Cartland had apparently also been present. Whether by chance or design he found himself at the Gestapo headquarters. And it was in this deserted building, amid the chaos outside on the streets of Brussels, while the city's great buildings burnt, that the young officer stumbled into a room containing dozens upon dozens of files. But these weren't ordinary files. These were top secret files which listed the names of French collaborators. Cartland set them alight. There had been enough bloodshed already he reasoned. What could follow if the files fell into the wrong hands? Only retribution. It was an extraordinary decision to make. If true, if Cartland really had taken it upon himself to torch this incriminating evidence – a junior officer - then here was a possible motive for revenge: he had deprived the Resistance the opportunity of bringing those who had betrayed their country to justice.

The fact that these events alluded to had occurred nearly thirty years prior to Mr Cartland's murder did not deter some from drawing their own conclusions, including the letter writer. The missive went on in a similar vein: Mr Cartland had been in Aix-en-Provence in 1962 where he had known about the supposed assassination of a French agent who, the letter writer claimed, could have revealed the true identity of Drummond's murderer. This agent had been connected to the drug-trafficking 'gangs of Marseille and London' who in turn worked with the mafia . . .

Heavy on supposition light on detail, the letter's author had clearly gleaned information from a variety of sources. It was undeniably true that whoever had composed the letter displayed a certain if rather jumbled grasp of geo-political events and their historical context. Perhaps this is why The *Guardian* found in the letter a 'residue of fresh and credible data.'[2] Today such an individual would run the risk of being labelled as a conspiracy theorist. Maybe so, but in the corridors of power at least some of the claims resonated. Paris became alerted. Pompidou's advisers urged the president to authorise a full review of *L'Affaire Cartland*. Revelations about secret agents, political assassinations and infamous cases such as the Drummond tragedy splashed all over the front pages, the Cartland murder was heading into sensitive territory.

The letter's claims were indeed unsettling, but was there any truth to any of them? A little. 1962 was the year Mr Cartland had been searching for a plot of land in Jouques. He could therefore have been in Aix-en-Provence at this time, likely had been. The claim that he been privy to information about a political assassination was however purely speculative and almost certainly untrue.

Furthermore, research into the deaths of suspected British agents Sir Oliver Duncan and Michael Lasseter drew a blank. The men had indeed died in 1964 and 1973 respectively. But there had been nothing to suggest foul play. Duncan had died in hospital having succumbed to illness; Lasseter's death had been accidental. The informant had also been wrong about the murder of Sir Jack Drummond's secretary. 'Jane Marshall' was in fact a school teacher called Janet Marshall who had been murdered by a vagrant not at Dieppe in 1956 but at Amiens in 1955.[3] Marshall had been killed whilst on a cycling trip of France. The link had probably been made because like the Drummonds, Miss Marshall also lived in Nottingham.

Although a great deal of the information in the letter was unsubstantiated if not wholly incorrect and would soon enough proven to be so, its appeal to team Cartland would have been obvious enough if only as a diversion.

'I regard these letters as important new evidence,' observed Christopher Mitchell-Heggs.

'There could be some truth in it,' commented Jeremy after he initially appeared to have distanced himself from the letter's sensational implications.

However, parts of the jigsaw seemed to be falling into place, at least as far as some minds were concerned. What kind of man packs an axe along with his holiday suitcase? A worried man. A paranoid man. Mr Cartland's chickens were coming home to roost: his past must have finally caught up with him.

But there some serious flaws with these theories: firstly, they were wholly predicated on the belief that the victim had indeed packed the axe. What if he hadn't.? What if John Cartland had been more than happy to voyage to France, a land he loved? Jeremy testified that his father had expressed regret on the night they had driven away from Powis Square: 'I wish I wasn't going.' Apparently, he had been reluctant to leave the comfort of his Brighton home. According to Jeremy, his father would often tell friends and families that he had 'enemies everywhere.' Indeed, there are no shortage of anecdotes that point towards a man haunted by his past. Upon driving into London, the eccentric businessman had once worn a saucepan on his head. Why? to protect himself from a possible attack. If the veracity of these accounts is accepted – that John Cartland did indeed have grave concerns with regards to personal safety - another question arises: were his demons real or imaginary?

Even if Mr Cartland's reservations had any substance, the revenge motif made little sense from a logistical point of view. By what means had the assassin(s) known that John Cartland would be travelling in a caravan around Provence in March of 1973? Beyond the Cartland family circle virtually nobody else would have known about the trip. Apart from pre-arranged meetings in Denia and Marseille there was no itinerary to speak of. Jeremy himself referred to the Cartland's plans as 'vague.' Nor did the Internet or mobile phones exist back then. The last communication from the travellers had arrived in the form of a postcard John Cartland wrote to Janet Gibson on Saturday, 17th March as the little convoy crossed the Spanish-French border. As far as the housekeeper had been aware, her employer was heading next for Marseille to keep his appointment with Monsieur Mont-Reynaud.

The decision to camp out at La Barben had however been made on the spur of the moment. The Cartlands had in fact decided to head that night for Jouques - a decision known only to father and son as indeed was the sudden diversion into the rocky waste ground known as *Jas de Dane*. Unless they had been shadowed all the way through Spain and France, nobody could have possibly known the Cartlands whereabouts on the night of 18/19th March – not even friends and family.

Besides, John Cartland had been visiting this area of France for decades, had owned land since 1963 and had built and sold a villa on that same land. There had been opportunity a-plenty to seek vengeance. As the scene of crime report had noted, the Cartland murder bore none of the hallmarks of pre-meditated assassination which are more often than not characterised by the 'cleanness' of their kills i.e. by bullet. Mr Cartland had been murdered in what amounted to a frenzy. Professional hits by contrast are controlled, calculated. Rarely if ever do they involve multiple murder weapons which, after the crime has been committed, are left strewn over the murder location. That would be careless, unprofessional.

Indeed, it soon emerged the letter had been composed by a certain Henrico Polydeskis. Of Greek origin, the 48-year-old was known to police as a prolific writer of similar types of letters and whom they described as an 'espionage crank.'

However unlikely in reality, the motif of atonement for past actions proved a peculiarly resilient one. Later, while acknowledging much of the letter's content had been 'conjecture,'

Jeremy would remark that, 'it does suggest that my father may have been just the latest victim of people who still have a lot to hide about their past and present activities.'[4]

Echoes of the past would continue to dog the case. Nor had the last been heard of the Drummond family and even more tragedies yet to unfold.

15

She said, he said

Forty-eight hours before Jeremy was due back in Aix, André Delmas assembled the witnesses together. The examining judge had a problem: the testimony of one set of witnesses – Mr and Mrs Blasco - contradicted those of the others. Delmas urgently needed to ascertain the true facts. By bringing the witnesses together face to face so impressions could be challenged and modified if necessary, the judge was hoping to establish a consensus prior to his next confrontation with team Cartland.

Thus at 9.30 am on Monday, 2nd April, the three young men from Beaucaire, Mr and Mrs Blasco, Frederic Delaude and Guy Massieux all sat down in the judge's humble office. They were joined by Sergeant Manson, the officer who first examined the Hillman at the crime scene.

Delmas began by reading back the statements taken by police over the previous weeks. He then invited each witness to augment, clarify or modify their statement if they chose. One aspect of Mme Blasco's account especially perturbed the judge: upon arrival at the crime scene she claimed there had been two vehicles present, namely a garnet-coloured Renault 4L and a 'white car' parked next to it. However, Frederic Delaude, the first witness on the scene, drove a grey Citroen 2CV; the three youths from Beaucaire who had parked alongside him had been driving a white Renault 4L.

M. BLASCO From the place where I was standing I saw again in the direction of Pélissanne, parked out far from the road, one beside the other, a red 4L vehicle and behind this vehicle, partly hidden by the first, another car which with reservation I think was a white 4L.

MME BLASCO I also saw myself, but only when we went past before stopping, two cars parked, a red 4L and another car which I cannot identify exactly.

WELTMAN Personally, I can state that at no time did I see a red car parked. I am certain of that point.

C'BONNET I never saw a red car parked there.

M. BLASCO I am certain that that red car was there and another car; there were only two cars.

LORENZO I cannot precisely place in time the scene that M. and Mme Blasco described, as in any

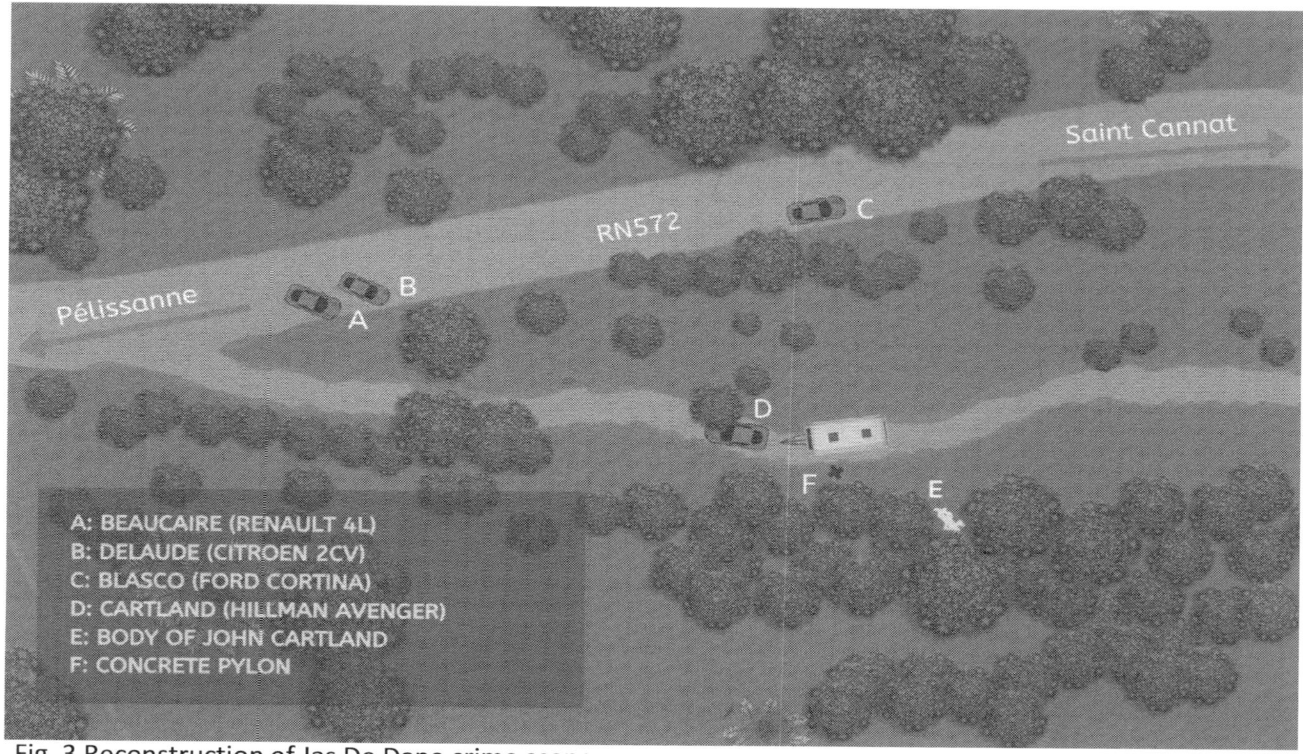

Fig. 3 Reconstruction of Jas De Dane crime scene

case I do not agree on any point; there was no red car.

DELAUDE While at the scene, I did not see any car other than that of the three young men and the two women.[1] However, a little before I left, Mr Massieux, here present arrived in his 403.

As none of the other witnesses had mentioned seeing a red car, Delmas wondered if the Blascos had been mistaken about colour. At 1am it had been dark. The moonlight could easily have distorted colour perception.[2]

The table below sets out the various witnesses in order of their arrival at the scene and the type/colour of car they were driving that night:

Order of arrival	Witness	Car	Colour
1	F. Delaude	Citroen 2CV	Grey
2	Sobanskys x 2	Renault R6	Pale blue
3	Beaucaire x 3	Renault 4L	White
4	Blasco x 3	Ford Cortina	Pale green
5	G Massieux	Peugeot 403	Blue

To date, the owner of a garnet-coloured car had not come forward. Delmas could only conclude there had never been one present at the scene of crime.

As with Krikorian and Gonzalves, the question of whether the Hillman's doors had been locked or unlocked troubled the judge greatly. For his part, Jeremy continued to insist that on the night of the murder he had seen a shadowy figure leaning into the car via its left front door; ergo the door must have been unlocked. It was crucial that Delmas establish the truth of this assertion. If proved to be false – that the Hillman's doors had in fact been locked – then the veracity of Jeremy's prowler story would be seriously in doubt

So, had any of the witnesses locked the left-front door during that hectic evening – possibly via the internal catch? Or perhaps they might have locked the door from the outside? After all, at some time during the night at least two of the witnesses had access to the vehicle's keys.[3]

LORENZO	I confirm, knowing the importance you attach to it, without risk of any error on my part, that I did not touch or manipulate the doors of the car except the right-hand front door.
C'BONNET	I solemnly swear that I never touched any door of the vehicle.
WELTMAN	Even from inside, I confirm I did not unlock even accidentally the left-hand front door
MASSIEUX	I was there when Mr Manson arrived with other military police from the Brigade and noted that the left-hand door was locked.
SGT MANSON	The back doors of the Hillman as well at the left hand front door were locked, as was the boot.

All the witnesses could say is that they had not touched the left front door. It *could* have been unlocked. However, police and Massieux in agreement regarding the integrity of the door meant only one option remained for the defence: imply one of the witnesses *had locked* the door and must have forgotten doing so. As a counter argument it was less than ideal.

Yet more anomalies became apparent when the witnesses described how the Hillman had been moved.

WELTMAN	We concluded that the car was locked, that all doors were locked, and Mr Delaude started to go down to ask the wounded man for the keys. But just before following him I was able to open the right-hand front door of the car which was not locked . . .

Unable to move the vehicle because of its steering lock, Weltman had then gone in search of the keys. This involved walking back down the stony dirt track towards where Delaude and Jeremy waited.[4] In the meantime, Lorenzo and Chambonnet took over.

LORENZO	I sat at the wheel of the car which had still not moved in spite of Weltman's attempt, and thanks to being pushed behind by Chambonnet we were able to move the car, with myself at the wheel, a few metres.
C'BONNET	I pushed the Hillman vehicle from behind while Lorenzo was at the wheel, and Mr Delaude and Weltman were standing at the side of the road.

M. BLASCO	One of the two men bent over the boot at the rear and pushed while another man standing on the left-hand side level with the left hand front door, his body parallel to the left-hand side, also seemed to be pushing.
MME BLASCO	From where our car was parked, I could clearly see the caravan and the Hillman car, and I am more certain than my husband, that I clearly saw a man inside the car or at least leaning inside the car on the left-hand side.
WELTMAN	I went back towards Mr Delaude who was with the wounded man, we got the keys and returned towards the car . . . we noticed that the car, during my short absence, had been moved and we learned that it was Lorenzo who had sat at the wheel while Chambonnet was pushing.
C'BONNET	I pushed the car from behind while Lorenzo was at the wheel, there was no man on the left hand side of the car.
LORENZO	There was no man pushing on the left-hand side.

It was Chambonnet and Lorenzo who had therefore attempted and succeeded in moving the Hillman to safety, that much seemed beyond dispute. Testimony differed not so much in who, but rather how the task had been carried out. Mme Blasco though remained unequivocal: she *had* definitely seen one of the two friends leaning into the Hillman's left-hand front door.

Delmas considered the facts: he knew that while M. Blasco had vacated the family car upon arrival at *Jas de Dane*, his wife had remained in the vehicle. Mme Blasco had thus viewed events from a less than optimal position, that is to say thirty metres from the inferno, her view partially obscured by vegetation. Her impression could not have been helped either by the shadows, smoke and general chaos of the night. Moreover, with car and caravan facing westwards towards Pélissanne, her direct viewpoint had been of the right, not left side of the Cartland's vehicle and caravan. In other words, she could not possibly have seen what was happening on the other side of the car – the left side, the side furthest away – at least not clearly.

Something else didn't quite add up about the testimony of the Blascos. Originally, the couple claimed they had pulled up directly opposite the burning caravan which meant they would have passed the parked (grey) Citroen and (white) Renault 4L on their right before stopping a little further on. 'I also saw myself, but only when we went past before stopping,' testified Mme Blasco, 'two cars parked, a red 4L and another car which I cannot identify.'

Madame had then seen two cars even if their description was at odds with those of their owners. Neither Blasco would swerve from their story: there had been a red 4L and another (white) car parked up although M. Blasco's version now apparently contradicted that of his wife on a key point: 'These cars I state again were seen by me at the side of the road a few dozen metres in *front of me* (my italics) where I was stopped.' Issues of colour and types of car aside, it now appeared that M. Blasco was suggesting the couple had stopped *before* they had driven past the two parked cars. Yet Mme Blasco had clearly stated the couple had not stopped until *after* they had driven past these same vehicles ('we went past before stopping . . .')

What to make of this couple whose testimonies not only contradicted the other witnesses, but now also each other? Just how much could they be trusted? Delmas was perplexed. Maybe the couple had been mistaken – that Sunday they had been out all day, much of it spent travelling back and forth from Aix to Narbonne. Arriving in Pélissanne at almost 1am, it was possible the couple had been fatigued.

Blascos aside, there were one or two other anomalies the judge wished to clarify e.g. the movements of the jerrycan. He could still not figure out how, after Delaude had discarded it, the container had made its way into the footwell of the Hillman. Only one thing was certain: *somebody* had put it in the car. Who and for what reason? Delaude it was who had initially spotted what he deemed a potential hazard:

DELAUDE	I noticed that a plastic container, apparently empty, I don't know if it had its top on or not, was standing near the (gas) bottle. I took it into my hand and threw it away.

A little later, while starting up the vehicle, Lorenzo noticed an item in the footwell:

LORENZO	Weltman gave me the keys of the vehicle . . . I started the engine to do a short reverse. I then noticed that a plastic container which was under my feet was in my way, and I pushed in into the passenger's side.

DELAUDE Subsequently, I was shown the plastic container that was found in the vehicle, and I state that it is exactly the same type as the one that I threw away . . .

WELTMAN I did not put a plastic container in the vehicle whose windows were closed.

C'BONNET I did not put a plastic container in the car.

MASSIEUX Personally, I did not place the plastic container in the Hillman.

WELTMAN At no time did I see Cartland prowling around the burning caravan or car.

LORENZO As Weltman told you, I did not personally see the wounded man move away from the 2CV.

DELAUDE I am absolutely certain that while I was at the scene the only people around the car and the caravan were Mr Weltman, Chambonnet, Lorenzo, and myself. Cartland being, I repeat again, near my car the whole time.

Who then had retrieved the container (jerrycan), taken the trouble to place it in the car and was now reluctant to admit as much? An individual presumably with something to hide.

DELAUDE I say that Cartland never left my vehicle and that is exact, and however to be exactly

> precise, Cartland, at a time I cannot place exactly, leant against one of the trees at the side of the road. He was never at any time near his vehicle.

The judge could not dismiss the possibility that Jeremy had indeed managed to place the container inside the Hillman. If so, what had been his motivation? Delmas could only think of a single reason: as it stood the jerrycan and access to it was the most obvious link to the fire; logic suggested that the prowlers must have used its contents to set the fire. Yet now it seemed that somebody was anxious that a link would not be established between jerrycan and fire. Certainly, none of the other witnesses had a motive for lying about the container, its whereabouts and whether or not they had handled it during the night. As neat as that scenario sounded, there were a couple of logistical considerations: if Jeremy had retrieved it, he would have needed to have been lightening quick; he would have also needed to have been extremely careful not to drip blood into the vehicle.[5] It seemed a long shot.

Overall, it had been a successful morning. Judge Delmas had clarified in his own mind several anomalies. He now had forty-eight hours to prepare for his next interview with Jeremy and his team. In the Blascos, the defence believed it had in its grasp a couple of star witnesses who could corroborate significant portions of their client's testimony. By lunchtime of Monday, 2nd April, Judge André Delmas thought he knew differently.

16

Munitions de Delmas

Jeremy, Liz and a family friend flew back to France on April 3rd. Once again Aix's hotel Le Pigeonnet became an informal HQ for Jeremy's legal representatives and the location from where Lombard and colleagues scrutinised the judge's file as permitted by virtue of their client's *partie civile* status.

In the week since the last interview, police had returned to the murder scene at *Jas de Dane* where they had discovered some pillow cases. They had also re-interviewed Francis Caire. Delmas wanted to ascertain a more precise overview of when and how events had occurred in pursuit of which the farmer's testimony would be invaluable. However, as far as the defence could see there were no smoking guns lurking in the magistrate's file.

At 10am the session began. It was business as usual. From out of what had become a well-rehearsed narrative, one or two additional bits of information did however emerge during the exchanges. For example, at one point Jeremy revealed the caravan's curtains had been yellow and in doing so partially corroborated Mme Chauvet's recollection of a 'pink and yellow' caravan arriving on her forecourt. He also helped to cast further doubt on the Blasco's testimony when stating that: 'There was never a red car with its headlights on.' The mystery of the red car deepened. Delmas found it difficult not to conclude that the Blascos were unreliable witnesses.

A favourite police theory went that alcohol might have sparked a row between the two men which had got out of hand. Quizzed about alcohol consumption, Jeremy confirmed he and his father had drank a small quantity with their meal on the night of the murder. Indeed, a toxicology report would soon show minimal alcohol content in Mr Cartland's blood.

Of more interest were Jeremy's comments about the plastic container/jerrycan. The judge still had no idea how the can had ended up in the Hillman. And as he was waiting for an imminent report on the dregs left behind in it, Delmas invited his interviewee to expand his comments thus far, which Jeremy was happy to do.

The teacher-poet re-iterated the relevant part of his story. Anticipating cold nights ahead in their new caravan, the Cartlands had brought a stove with them on the trip. In Denia, Jeremy filled up a jerrycan with paraffin purchased from a store. The paraffin would be used to power the stove and a hurricane lamp which the travellers had also brought along. Jeremy then explained how, on the evening of Sunday 18th March, he had emptied the contents of the jerrycan into the stove and thereafter taken the empty container outside to place in the Hillman's boot. However, the boot was locked. So instead of going back into the caravan to fetch his keys he had left the container outside, by the gas bottle. 'In any case,' he concluded, 'I should have found the jerrycan next morning beside the cylinder where I had placed it.'

Like the police, Delmas was not entirely satisfied with this explanation. When it would have taken no effort at all to ensure the jerrycan was safely locked away in the car, there must have been some reason why the Englishman had left it outside. Had his indolence been deliberate? The judge sensed there was more to the jerrycan than the Brit was saying – not least its mysterious reappearance inside the Hillman after it had been discarded. For now, he let the matter rest. Soon enough the lab analysis would be available.

It was during this interview that Jeremy expanded upon his father's encounter with an unknown person shortly after their arrival at *Jas de Dane.* The stranger had told Mr Cartland he was on the wrong road for Jouques. Jeremy, busy preparing dinner, had not seen either the individual or his car. Again, Delmas was not convinced. Given the massive amount of publicity the case had generated, why had this individual not come forward?

After lunch Liz Cartland spoke. Naturally, she stressed the good relations that had existed between her brother and father. But it was what she said about Mr Cartland's past which seemed especially worthy of note. Miss Cartland informed the judge that she had always known about her father's role in the Intelligence Service, observing that:

> He had never made the slightest allusion to any danger he might be in or any revenge that he might be afraid of. He did happen to talk to me about people who had been executed by killers but on those occasions he never showed any fear on his own account. In short, he was not afraid of anyone at all.[1]

These comments were hardly commensurate with the picture of John Cartland given so far as man fearful of travelling abroad, a man convinced he had 'enemies everywhere' – a man who allegedly wore saucepans on his head while driving in a nonsensical effort to thwart the assassins' bullet. It certainly didn't sound like a man who had seemed reluctant to leave Brighton on March 12th.

His intimate conviction telling him the answer to the riddle before him lay somewhere in the Cartland family background, Delmas was more than happy for personal matters to come to the fore. Thus, he listened intently when, during her testimony, Ms Cartland mentioned a recent relationship of her brother's with a separated woman. Her father had been a 'little annoyed' about the affair. Not only this, Mr Cartland had apparently been 'afraid of a possible marriage' between Jeremy and this lady. Miss Cartland went on to remark that despite the tension it had caused, the affair had ended amicably.

And so, the session dragged on late into the afternoon. After six and half hours it finally came to an end - 'one of the toughest interrogations of my career,' Paul Lombard would later observe. Although at the end of the interview Delmas had not laid a glove on his British witness, perhaps he had not really wanted to. There would be another interview on April 25th. Was the poker-faced judge saving any aces for what would be the third and possibly final round of this epic psychological battle?

As for Jeremy, he was not impressed. Later, at the Hotel Pigeonnet, the man of the moment held a press conference in which his frustration shone through:

'Even Mr. Plod, from Toytown, could have done a better job,' Jeremy told the press. It was one of many such swipes aimed at the police and which appeared in the following days' papers. The *Daily Express* headlined with 'Jeremy slams French police probe.'

Following the press conference Jeremy gave an exclusive interview to *Paris Match* – the weekly gossip and current affairs magazine and one of France's most widely-read publications. Five-star hotels, air travel and a team of highly paid lawyers – costs were rocketing and Jeremy needed the cash.

Very early the next morning along with Sagot and Mitchell-Heggs, the teacher-poet visited the murder site. It was a pilgrimage he was not looking forward to, or so he claimed. Jeremy had promised some of the friendlier elements in the media he would tip them off about the visit thus presenting an opportunity for them to obtain exclusive pictures, yet none received an invite. 'I did not want anyone but friends to be present,' Jeremy remarked later. Instead, Mitchell-Heggs took photographs. One image of a smoking Jeremy, his right-leg casually resting on the caravan's charred chassis, immaculately attired in suit and tie, was syndicated around the world.

Had the press been present they would surely have had a ringside view of what happened next: team Cartland found not one, but *two* key pieces of evidence.

In amid the ashes of the caravan, Mr Cartland's chamber pot was located. In their many searches of the plot where the caravan had stood, police had somehow missed this vital piece of evidence – a tin can which the victim had used for purposes of urination. The existence of this innocuous little item appeared to contradict the police theory that Mr Cartland had been attacked while *faire ses boissons*. Why would the victim have been urinating outside the caravan if he had a pot to use inside?

And the day was about to get even better. Next, team Cartland located a club or stick which seemed to be stained with blood. At long last the 'hard object' used to strike Jeremy from behind on the night of the murder had been located. Not only had two vital pieces of evidence been found, but the defence's vocal criticism regarding police failings seemed more justified than ever: didn't the discovery of these items demonstrate the true extent of police incompetence? Pity the poor press for they had missed out on a day of revelations.

Jeremy Cartland himself handed in the items to the police. The club was described as '40 cm long and 4 cm in diameter with multiple abrasions and brown stains.' It had been apparently found '10 to 15 cm' from where the axe had also been found i.e. as good as next to it. The chamber pot was described as 'a crushed cylinder.' It had been found next to where Mr Cartland's bed had been. Both items had, in other words, been in the open for several weeks – overlooked by investigating officers and public alike.

When the police had belatedly discovered pillow cases at the murder location, team Cartland had been unimpressed. Reflecting upon this incident a few years later and what he discerned to be the convenience of the discovery, Jeremy would observe that:

> The fact that these exhibits had been found sixteen days after the murder suggests that they were not necessarily present on the site on the night of March 19th.[2]

Had the police planted evidence at the site as this passage seems to imply?

'It's incredible to think,' he told journalists waiting for him at Heathrow airport, 'the police could have missed two obvious clues like this.'

There was much for Delmas to ponder. Upmost in his mind

though were the contradictions in the Blasco testimonies. Both Blascos were insisting that a red car had been present and that they had witnessed an individual accessing the Hillman via its left-front door. In order to clear up any uncertainties once and for all, at 9pm on the night of April 9th - an icy night of high winds - the judge summoned the witnesses to *Jas de Dane*. The shivering witnesses were asked to place their vehicles as per the night of 18-19th March. A substitute caravan and car were also placed in position. And so, in driving wind and rain, Delmas was able to ascertain that from her position in the family Cortina, Mme Blasco could not have had a clear view of what was occurring over in the Hillman. Bushes would have obscured her view.

It was a difficult night in less-than-optimal conditions, but Delmas was satisfied: the Blasco's evidence was not credible. He also observed that the Hillman's interior light did not come on automatically, but had to be switched on and off manually. If Jeremy's version of events was to be believed, the prowlers must have switched the light on upon entering the Hillman, then taken the trouble to switch it off when fleeing the scene. Odd, thought Delmas. Why bother? Meticulous and precise, the examining judge was slowly building his case.

Having listened to Liz Cartland's testimony, Delmas was more certain than ever the answer to the crime would most likely be found in the family's private affairs. And now he had confirmed his suspicions revolving around two key aspects of the case: that a red car had *not* been present on the night of the murder and that the Hillman had *not* been accessed via its left front door.

It was time to test another hypothesis: that the source of light seen by Francis Caire on the night of the murder had come from inside the caravan and not from the Hillman's internal or side-light. At 2.30 pm on the afternoon of 20th April, Delmas met with Krikorian at *Jas de Dane*.

In his latest testimony Caire had confirmed seeing a light shining around midnight on the evening of the murder. The farmer thought it had been that of a car's side-light. This light was 'stationary' and 'white.' Naturally, police wondered if the light might have in fact been the glow from the Cartland's hurricane lamp inside the caravan. If so, the men had likely not been asleep when the alleged prowlers had arrived, but had been up in the caravan. What then had Cartland junior and senior been doing at that late hour? The police hypothesised that father and son had been engaged in a fierce argument. Hence, Delmas needed to establish exactly what Caire could or could not have seen that night.

Stand-in caravan and Hillman once again in place, the police were ready to start their experiment.

Farmer Caire showed officers the exact spot he had stood on that moonlit night, a doorway on the east side of his property. A police photographer took a series of images. From where they stood officers could hardly see the caravan and could not see the Hillman at all, obscured as it was by pine trees. But the farmer had been looking across at the area around midnight – not 3pm in the afternoon. Clearly, the experiment would have to be repeated in darkness.

Thus, officers duly returned at 1am the next morning. Delmas once again stood in the exact spot outside the farm-house indicated by Monsieur Caire. Using a walkie talkie, he communicated with officers over at the clearing who, upon his request, moved a storm lamp to various positions in and around the space which had been occupied by car and caravan. For a few minutes the judge saw nothing but blackness. Then, a flash of light. Then nothing. Then another flash. Delmas spoke with the officers. It transpired the light was coming from a position close to the concrete pylon. Next, Delmas went over to the clearing leaving Krikorian at the farm. After much to-ing and fro-ing, he was able to establish the boundaries of a hypothetical rectangle one metre long and 60 cm high, 1.50 metres off the ground and beyond whose dimensions light could not be seen from the farmhouse. It corresponded to the position where the caravan's right front corner would have been. Focus turned to the car. Could the light Caire saw have been the Hillman's interior light? Apparently not. It soon became clear that while the caravan could be glimpsed from the farm, the vehicle could not. Delmas concluded that the light seen by farmer Caire that night must therefore have been coming from inside the caravan.

Far from being a quiet, peaceful sanctuary where a couple of exhausted travellers had lain their weary heads that Sunday night, the caravan seemed to have been a hive of activity, light not dark. Why then had Jeremy testified that he and his father had been asleep that night? What had the British pair been doing as midnight had fallen?

Myths about John Cartland's trepidation quashed, stories of ghostly cars vanquished and with them unreliable testimonies, Judge Delmas had all the ammunition he now needed to proceed – almost. Before the next interview on April 25th the lab analysis of the jerrycan would be available. He already had the forensic analysis of blood. Was André Delmas' intimate conviction about to be proven correct?

17

Showdown

As April 25th got closer the mood music from France began to unsettle Jeremy's defence team. Talk of arrests and charges being laid on the 29-year-old upon his return to the country swirled around the French media throughout Easter. After assessing the state of the case, Lombard decided the claims were unfounded. Jeremy was cleared to come back to France.

Accompanied by their family friend, the Cartlands jetted off once more for Marseille arriving on the evening of Tuesday, 23rd April. Despite the unmasking of Polydeskis, rumours still circulated about John Cartland's past. Before arriving back in France Jeremy would surely have read the previous day's *Daily Express* story reporting on a new wave of French films taking wartime collaboration for their topic. The article invoked the Drummond and Cartland cases. It also carried comments from a suspected ex-member of the Maquis, Mr X: 'He says in South-West France,' reported the paper, 'any Englishman today is suspected of being an Intelligence man. And that there are people living around Marseilles with enough to hide about their war record to make them ready to kill to protect it.' The revenge motif was proving itself nothing if not durable.

Despite such articles and broad support of the British tabloid press, team Cartland were noticeably nervous in the run up to Wednesday's interview. Now the talk was not just of arrests but of *imminent* arrests.

The day after his son and daughter had departed the UK to meet Delmas for a third and what both parties were hoping would be a final showdown, John Cartland's remains were finally repatriated back to the country of his birth. Jeremy's lawyers had prevented a cremation taking place in France. Instead, the corpse was heading over to Turner Street, home of the London Hospital and where Home Office pathologist Professor James Cameron was due to carry out a belated autopsy.[1] Even at this late stage the defence were hoping to make fresh discoveries, whatever could be done in order to undermine confidence in French procedure.

At 8.40 am Cameron arrived at the hospital's Institute of Pathology to begin work. By and large results mirrored those of the first post-mortem. Indeed, in his report the professor remarked that his examination had 'confirmed most of the findings in the original post-mortem report.'

It was the professor's ancillary remarks that made for arguably much more interesting reading. Police had always suspected that Mr Cartland had been surprised from behind whilst preparing to urinate and/or defecate. Not only had the French autopsy report noted the businessman had a full bladder at the time of his murder, it also observed that his pyjama bottoms had been unfastened – presumably a deliberate act on the part of the victim prior to relieving himself.

For its part, the defence maintained a different version of events: upon hearing his son being attacked John Cartland had rushed to his defence. Armed with the axe he had confronted the prowlers who had proceeded to disarm him prior to launching a vicious and sustained attack with the same axe. However, this theory did not account for how and why Cartland ended up in the thicket. Nor did it explain the reason why the victim had been found in a state of semi undress.

What then, if anything would this fresh autopsy reveal?

'The first blow of the attack,' observed Cameron, 'was in all probability from behind.'[2] To this comment he added: 'There was no definite evidence of a struggle . . . there were no defence wounds.' So much for a life-or-death confrontation. On the contrary, it seemed Cartland senior had indeed been attacked while standing still. Nor were these the only comments that might have made the defence wince. Cameron also went on to observe that he could not confirm any evidence of dragging. In other words, like his French colleagues he thought the victim had been first struck in the same nearby bushes where his corpse would later be discovered, pyjamas rolled down by the ankles. With the exception of the first blow, the others had all been dealt while the victim had been prone. It didn't get much better either. 'In my opinion,' concluded the pathologist, 'there need only have been one assailant, but one cannot be dogmatic.'

The autopsy hadn't quite worked out how the defence had been hoping. Had Cameron's conclusions been available on the day of the hearing, Lombard and his team might have had serious cause for concern.

Fine weather greeted the environs of Bouches-du-Rhône on the morning of Wednesday, 25th April. As the residents of Aix-en-Provence roused themselves from their beds or slept in for an extra half hour, a full-blown council of war was in progress over at the Hotel Le Pigeonnet. Team Cartland were deep in discussion and had been since first light. Papers spread out before them, the air thick with cigarette smoke and the essence of freshly-ground coffee, Jeremy and his team talked strategy. The young teacher wanted a professional opinion about his prospects. Were the rumours correct? Would he be a prisoner of the French state by the end of the day?

'Since you ask, I must be frank,' said Lombard gravely. 'It is very likely the judge will seek an indictment today. I fear we must be prepared for just such an eventuality.'

Jeremy didn't flinch. Thanking his lawyers for their support, he re-affirmed his innocence once again: 'I did not murder my father.' Nevertheless, team Cartland needed a break. Although they could not have known it as they left the hotel in Lombard's Jaguar, the day ahead weighing down on them, in the form of the heavy-jowled, scooter-riding André Delmas their wish might already have been granted.

Judged by the sheer number of reporters hanging around the environs of the Palais de Justice, talk of imminent arrest seemed to have been well-founded. Even the surrounding café bars seemed busier than usual. Dressed in a pearl grey suit and lawyers astride him like a scene from *The Godfather,* Jeremy threaded his way through Place de Verdun, arriving outside the Palais a little before 9am. As he smiled at passers-by, he appeared relaxed, almost carefree. By contrast, his legal team seemed subdued. Lombard and Chiappe had kept something back from their client: according to a tip-off, Delmas had acquired not just one, but three smoking guns.

'Confident, Jeremy?' asked a reporter as the Brit climbed the steps to the courthouse.

'Yes, very.'

Once inside Delmas' first floor office the lawyers took their seats behind their client. It was going to be a long day – perhaps the longest one yet. There was something in the air this sunny Provencal morning, a feeling that today the matter would be settled one way or the other: Jeremy would either walk free or find himself in a prison cell that evening. The atmosphere was, as they say, electric.

'Tell me Mr Cartland,' began the judge offering the Brit a Gauloise as he settled down in his chair, 'have you not been having a joke these past weeks?'

'I'm not sure I understand judge.'

'We have used an interpreter all this time, but you have not required a similar service when speaking to the gentleman of the press. It slows us down considerably would you not agree?'

'Yes, I suppose . . .'

'Then do you agree to waiver, unless for a specific point of clarification of course?'

Much to his counsel's obvious despair Jeremy agreed. He had little choice.

In his many interactions with the French press the Brit had never seemed to require the services of a translator. Thus, there was ample evidence to suggest Jeremy's language skills were much better than he made out - adequate enough to converse with native French speakers.[3] When flagging down Frederic Delaude, for example, the British teacher had spoken in what the press officer described as 'perfectly intelligible French.'[4] If it was a ploy to enable the witness plenty of time to think before answering a question as Delmas suspected, then it was an advantage Jeremy had just lost.

The judge's composure disturbed team Cartland. Delmas had indeed an unmistakable air of equanimity about him this fine morning only possible in those assured of their destiny. At this stage of proceedings, they could only guess as to the nature of his smoking guns.

And so the session began. Soon enough the question of car doors arose. 'A flagrant lie' retorted the judge to Jeremy's claim that the Hillman's front left door had indeed been unlocked. Monsieur Delmas was in no mood to take any prisoners today - or perhaps he *was* . . . When the witness invoked Mme Blasco's testimony in support of his assertion, Delmas could only smile. The examining judge had done his homework. Sat just inches behind his client, Lombard already feared the worst.

Delmas continued to press Jeremy on those same anomalies about which he had spoken innumerable times. Back and forth it went, locked/unlocked doors, caravan fires and axes. The defence lawyers wondered where it was all headed. Thus far the judge had not produced any of his rumoured guns, smoking or otherwise. Eventually the session broke for lunch.

'I would advise the defence,' began Delmas.

'Civil party,' cut in Chiappe.

'I would advise the civil party not to leave the Palais, but if you must I recommend a short lunch break across the road at La Madeleine. We shall reconvene here at 2.30 pm sharp.'

An order cloaked as suggestion, Lombard understood the underlying message alright. The judge wanted the witness to remain within the immediate vicinity of the Palais. Effectively, Jeremy was under house arrest.

Before departing from the elegant confines of one of Aix's most iconic landmarks, Delmas took Lombard aside. What he told the lawyer shocked him to the core: after lunch he intended to confront Jeremy with a testimony from a certain Professor Cameron of London that accused his client of being someone whose word could not be trusted i.e. Jeremy was a liar. Such a testimony could only damage his client's credibility. Lombard knew it was imperative therefore to obtain a swift rebuttal – ideally via telegram. After being reassured by Jeremy that the claim was without substance, Mitchell-Heggs was despatched to call the professor in London.

Meanwhile, across the road at La Madeleine diners were already taking up places on its pretty terrace, basking in warm midday sunshine. Jeremy and his lawyers preferred to take a table inside. There was much to discuss - upmost of which were tactics for the afternoon. Did the judge have any other cards to play? What might they be? On top of all this, the team waited on tenterhooks for a reply from London. It was hardly set to be the most relaxing business lunch ever seen at the popular brasserie. It was about to go from bad to worse.

No sooner had team Cartland settled in their seats browsing through the menu when a party seated themselves at the table opposite, among their number a couple of familiar faces: the Gangbuster and Maigret of the South. The omens were not looking at all good for the young British teacher. Gonzalves and Krikorian politely nodded to Lombard and his party before turning their attention to the menu. What Jeremy must have thought can be imagined. Despite the presence of the police watchdogs, the young teacher ate a hearty meal of smoked ham, green salad and red wine. Team Cartland spoke in hushed tones. By the end of the meal, it had been agreed that there was only one way to respond to Delmas: to come out fighting. Attack, always the best form of defence, *n'est pas*?

If only Professor Cameron would reply to the SOS.

True to its word, the defence team began the afternoon session on the front foot, laying down its own ground rules. Indignant at the treatment meted out to them in the morning, on his feet and in full rhetorical flow, Maitre Chiappe declared that the lawyers would henceforth not tolerate even a minor irregularity in procedure or slightest violation of their client's rights.

The judge appeared to take his lesson well. Now it was time to play his first ace. Defence lawyers settled, satisfied seemingly with their opening gambit, he addressed Jeremy sternly.

'Recently you had the idea of being examined by Professor Cameron, a famous English forensic doctor. Is that correct Mr Cartland?'

'Yes, your honour,' said Jeremy frowning, 'I have consulted with this gentleman. What of it?'

'Do you know what he concluded from his examination? I will tell you: he said your injuries were not consistent with the story you provided.'

'I doubt the professor would have said such a thing.'

'Not only that,' continued Delmas, 'he also warns that you are a fabricator whose word cannot be trusted!'

Even though they had been prepared for it, when the blow had been delivered the accusation still stung. Like a winded prize-fighter, team Cartland took a moment to catch its breath. Recovering first, Lombard sprung out of his chair. 'Your honour, can you kindly tell us from whom you received this information?'

'Certainly. It came to me via Interpol.'

Chiappe next joined Lombard on his feet. The Chairman of the Marseille bar pointed out the relevant passage of article 118 of The Code of Criminal Procedure which stipulates that the civil party must be supplied with documentation 24 hours prior to a hearing. In reply, Delmas invited the defence to submit a written complaint. Chiappe expressed his intention to do just that. As the stakes got higher the atmosphere inside the palace became tetchy, combative and even personal.

'Your honour, this is highly irregular,' shot back Lombard still on his feet. 'How can we be expected to proceed, ambushed as we are? I would like to officially register our unease with this procedure.'

Finally, a message arrived to say Cameron had sent a reply. From his home in Bromley, Kent, the Professor flatly denied referring to Jeremy as a liar whose word could not be trusted: 'It is absolutely inaccurate to say I had said or suggested anything of the sort.' Later that day he would expand this denial in an interview with the media:

> I have not written my report on that examination. The notes are still in my desk and I have not made any statement to anyone. No doctor would say the kind of things I am reported to have said. I am absolutely astounded by it all.

It was not the news Delmas had been expecting. The judge had staked quite a lot on the professor's testimony and now it had been retracted. Transmitted by Interpol - indirectly – had the testimony really been the ace the judge had thought it to be, even if correct? As Cameron himself was quick to point out, he was no psychologist; he was in fact a pathologist and therefore not qualified to make remarks such as had been made - remarks which were, in the final analysis an opinion.

There was nothing else to do but accept the rebuttal. Judge Delmas coloured slightly. He was on the back foot and the defence team knew it.

In the light of this development should not the hearing be suspended? Perhaps, but Delmas was in no mood to be stalled. The lawyers now watched nervously as the magistrate rummaged around in his desk. Moments later he took out a document. His second ace was Professor Muller's report in which the haematologist had noted the presence of a staining on the left leg of John Cartland's pyjamas – unidentifiable matter which just so happened to share certain haematological features with the dead man's son. How did the witness account for this phenomenon?

'It is possible,' began Jeremy choosing his words carefully, 'with the knife they attacked me, the prowlers used this same knife on my father later. This could explain the presence of my blood, if it is indeed blood.'

The look on Delmas' face upon hearing this explanation told its own story. Alert to every nuance of verbal and non-verbal communication as the safari guide is to the rhythm of the jungle, Paul Lombard rose once again to his feet.

'Judge, we respectfully request that Dr Jouglard's comments are also committed to the record, that is to say her opinion that the stains could have in fact been mud.'

Delmas had no choice but to acquiesce. Due to degradation caused by an agent unknown there was no way of proving the stains were human blood even if a scientist as renowned as Muller thought as much. Suspicion though was not proof. Never mind, the *juge d'instruction* had another report nestling in his desk – a chemical analysis of the fuel from the jerrycan, analysis of which had returned some unusual results: firstly, this oil was candy-pink in colour whereas paraffin or kerosene presents as a low viscosity, colourless liquid. Further testing had detected the presence of petroleum. The pink liquid was in fact a compound of kerosene and gasoline of a type of fuel used in the aviation industry. Research revealed such a substance to be not commercially available in Spain. There was only one possible conclusion: the mixture found in the Cartland's jerrycan had not in fact been purchased in Denia.

'Now Mr Cartland, perhaps you would care to explain this,' said the judge taking out the report from his drawer and wafting it triumphantly in the air. 'It is a chemical report regarding the composition of the oil found in the jerrycan.'

Fearing another surprise, the lawyers sprung to their feet in unison, four musketeers coming to the aid of their stricken client. *Another invalid document! What about article 118! What about procedure! Outrageous! Invalid! Time to annul the hearing!*

By nature a reserved man, Delmas was visibly shaken by the protests. The evident fury of some of the most eminent legal minds in the Republic seemed to spook the magistrate. About to enter unchartered territory and discretion always the better part of valour, the veteran official baulked. Somehow the judge had contrived to place himself into a cul-de-sac escape from which could be found only one way.

Delmas took a moment to collect himself. What would happen next? For Jeremy and his defenders, hanging upon his every word, seconds seemed like an eternity.

'You will be pleased to hear,' said Delmas addressing the witness in his most sombre voice, 'that there will be no charges advanced against you. You may leave the court.'

At six o'clock a beaming Jeremy appeared on the steps of the Palais flanked by his lawyers. A large crowd of journalists flocked around him. 'I have been cleared,' he grinned as his sister sobbed into his shoulder. 'The magistrate says there is no case for me to answer. I am free to go home. It is overwhelming.' The Brit also revealed he intended to initiate a summons against the police accusing them of 'producing false evidence to pervert the course of justice.' The timing could not have been better. For just as the teacher-poet was making this announcement the former head of Marseille's vice squad,

Germain Bezert, was facing charges for corruption.

At the end of a day during which his future had hung by a thread for the greater part thereof, Jeremy Cartland had won through. The ginger-bearded teacher emerged into the early evening air a free man. Looking back on this momentous occasion many years later Paul Lombard had lost none of his admiration for his client's resolve when writing: 'We probably witnessed that day one of the finest examples of composure that man can give.'[5]

As the Cartlands headed back to their hotel to celebrate with champagne, the contrast with André Delmas could not have been more acute. 'I made a mistake,' said a dejected and weary sixty-year-old upon leaving the court house.

In this, his last case before retirement, he had indeed made several costly mistakes, most of them elementary. His worst mistake had surely been not exploiting the professor's conclusion that Jeremy's wounds were not consistent with his account of the attack. It would not have required much work from this point to raise the possibility of staging, an even shorter step thereafter to arriving at questions of self-inflicted wounds and deceit. Delmas had never needed to produce a statement explicitly accusing the witness of lying. Cameron had practically implied as much. The uncomfortable truth was that the professor had rebutted a claim the authorities need never have relied upon. Perhaps, when all was said and done, the biggest mistake had been the appointment of a judge inexperienced in handling cases of such magnitude.

Notwithstanding the fact that the case had been annulled on a technicality, the British press had a field day. A Thursday *Daily Mail* editorial declared that, 'The French police have acted unforgivably. They have shown incompetence,' Jeremy's allies at The *Daily Express* ran a story in which the infamous young man claimed police had actually shown him the prison cell prepared for him!

Within the next 24 hours New Scotland Yard would deny ever sending a report authored by Professor James Cameron to Interpol. That only left a single possibility: Interpol, more precisely a person(s) unknown within the St Cloud head-quartered operation, had invented the allegation. The phrase 'frame-up' began to circulate widely: police must have invented what they assumed to be an incriminating statement prior to attributing it to the eminent pathologist. If so, it had been a blunder of quite epic proportions. Did police really believe they would get away with such a transparent ruse? Given the risks involved and an at best variable pay-off, had it really been worth falsifying a witness statement? The provenance of the Professor's statement was and still remains a mystery. As far as the civil party was concerned it was a mystery heaven sent.

If Jeremy let off some steam that night at the Hotel Le Pigeonnet, it was not without justification. The ultimate poker player, his had been the coolest head in Aix that day. 'What really brought me through was a faith in the truth,' he would later observe. 'I knew I had nothing to hide.'[6] Questioned whether his client would be prepared to return for a fourth time to take part in a re-enactment at the crime scene at some future date, Mitchell-Heggs agreed but only on the condition that the police would provide a written guarantee that Jeremy would not be arrested. It would be his client's choice.

A day that had begun ominously - the threat of prison hanging over him - had ended in triumph for Jeremy. As he sipped champagne that evening in company with his support network, ebullient, relieved, recharged, though it might have felt like closure, the end of a tumultuous road, these were sentiments that might not necessarily have been shared by Judge Delmas and a couple of police commissioners known as Jack Palance and the Maigret of the South none of whom would have felt like raising a toast that night.

18

The colour pink

There was no shortage of offers for Jeremy's story upon his triumphant return to London. Broadsheets as well as tabloids competed furiously for an exclusive insight into what had become known as the teacher-poet's 'ordeal.' After careful consideration he chose to open his heart to the *Sunday Times* in a hefty article published on 29th April.

In what *Le Monde* referred to as a 'bitter and sarcastic tone,' in the article Jeremy revealed the ordeal he had suffered at the hands of the French system. His list of grievances was long: police had not searched for any other suspects; nor had they secured the site of the murder; Jeremy had been interviewed for several hours without refreshment; he had incurred substantial debts defending himself etc. One of his chief complaints lay with how the police had applied psychological pressure throughout the interviews; at one point an officer had urged him to confess to his father's murder: 'You know that one day you must make your peace with God. Would you not like to make peace with man first? Tell us how you did it.' Yet another officer had urged him to confess citing the story of Cain and Abel – fratricide rather than parricide – but who was counting?

Especial vitriol was reserved for what Jeremy ascribed as the 'monstrous attitude' of the French press. For example, that neither he nor his sister had collapsed in public was interpreted as a sign of their 'coolness' – yet another example of the media's unsympathetic portrayal of the Cartland children. According to Jeremy then his ordeal had been caused by a mixture of police incompetency and French media antipathy. It could never have happened in England.

The vast majority of journalists writing about the case agreed that the aspiring writer had indeed been treated abysmally. Some of them, such as the barrister Fenton Bresler, perceptively remarked how his status as a British subject had played a major role in the outcome. 'He is lucky,' began Bresler:

> He had eminent lawyers to help him. Through taking out a mortgage on his house, he managed to find nearly £10,000 legal costs necessary to vindicate his innocence. But if he were a Frenchman and the alleged crime was not a near-international incident but just another cynically humdrum murder, the examination might well have been far less protracted, far less probing. He could have spent much of the time in jail. And he could by now have been arrested and charged with murder.[1]

It was generally agreed that by dint of his nationality, the Brit had avoided some of the harsher aspects of the French judicial process. But was it the only factor? The Cartland connection to Ted Heath was again alluded to this time in a *Paris Match* article which claimed Jeremy was sometimes, 'received by Prime Minister Heath, an old friend of his father's.'[2] Nor had the press forgotten about the attendance of Vice Consul Benham in the days following the murder. Special favours? The plot thickened.

Despite what appeared to be overwhelming public support, Jeremy still had cause for concern. A third party reported that Lombard and Chiappe had not been impressed with the party held at Le Pigeonnet which had followed the dismissal of the case. The lawyers judged such celebrations premature. This pair of wily old heads knew that from the authorities' point of view the case had merely been suspended while police re-orientated. Their instincts proved sound. Before any hangovers had even begun to clear, Delmas announced his intention to stage a reconstruction of the crime on May 17th, the next date when a full moon was expected similar to that of the murder night. Naturally, Jeremy's presence would be required. The Brit was still witness no. 1, at least in the eyes of the French police. As such there was still the distinct possibility of an extradition request being made at some point. Jeremy was not out of the woods, not by a long way.

When Krikorian and Gonzalves were despatched on 'secret' missions overseas during the second week of May it was a reminder that as far as the French were concerned the case was indeed far from over. No doubt irritated by Jeremy's constant and strident criticism, upon issuing the rogatories, Judge Delmas took the unusual step of adding a statement which referred to the detectives as 'men of integrity.' Krikorian was headed north to Britain, Gonzalves south towards Spain's Costa del Sol.

Grey clouds and drizzle greeted Krikorian as he touched down at Heathrow. Despite the gloomy May weather, the press turned out in numbers to greet the 'Maigret of the South.' The Commissioner's arrival had been anticipated for some days. Surprised to be a figure of interest to press photographers, the detective shielded his face at the airport, a celebrity desperate to avoid the paparazzi. The trip had already caused an embarrassing moment when he had set off the alarms while going through airport security. Krikorian had brought the large kitchen knife used in the attack in a plastic bag! Some awkward explanations followed. Once the formalities had been concluded, Detective Chief Inspector Ronald Page escorted the Frenchman to New Scotland Yard where a press conference had been arranged. At 6pm he told the press that his mission in the UK was to discover more about the Cartland family; no, he confirmed, he would not be speaking to Jeremy or Liz Cartland but he did intend travelling to Brighton. He was keen, he announced, to check the victim's wartime records - whatever it took to enable police to establish, 'who might have wanted to kill John Cartland.'

Means, motive and opportunity, applying this basic trinity of detection methodology to their prime witness detectives thought two of three components were watertight. Jeremy had had both means (access to the axe) and the opportunity (alone with his father on the night of the murder). There was just the question of motive to be established. It was the reason behind Commissioner Krikorian's UK sojourn.

Meanwhile, Lombard and associates had an appointment at the French Ministry of Justice. Suffice to say their client's denouncements and vocal attacks on the French judicial system had not been appreciated in Paris or elsewhere for that matter. The teacher's accusations were becoming irksome.

From his point of view, Jeremy's offensive was working well enough: French justice and its procedures were being scorned and mocked all over the British media as inadequate, flawed, unfit for purpose. Moreover, those working within the system were incompetent and quite possibly corrupt. In representing their British client then Lombard and co were attacking the very system in which they worked and in which they presumably had at least some degree of faith. In a statement the defence team agreed, 'that it is incorrect, and therefore unjust, to assert that the guarantees offered by French law, in particular with regard to the right of defence, are not sufficient to effectively ensure the protection of freedoms while allowing the search for the truth.' With this statement Jeremy's French lawyers were re-affirming their belief in their own judicial system – an extraordinary turn of events.

While their British counterparts kept track of the enigmatic French detective, journalists the other side of the channel were following up leads of their own. Language student Renee Ripert had lodged with Mr Cartland at his Brighton home during Xmas 1972. Could she shed any light on the family's domestic affairs? Her recollections painted a rather different picture of Cartland's home life than hitherto given.

The student revealed that during her stay she had noticed her host had not celebrated festivities with his children that Christmas; on Christmas Eve he had helped out at the retirement home in which he had a share. Always loose with his tongue, during her stay with him, Cartland had apparently told her that he did not agree with his daughter's marriage plans. Miss Ripert did reveal however that the headmaster had given her the impression of 'being on good terms with his children.' In the same breath though she also remarked that the kindly Mr Cartland never spoke about his son, Jeremy, 'who I never met during the time I stayed there.'[3] This insight appeared to contradict Jeremy's assertion that since returning to Brighton in September 1972 he and his father had enjoyed a close relationship: 'I had been lunching with him every day,' claimed Jeremy, 'and spending a good deal of time with him.'[4]

Over in England, Krikorian had found his way to the Georgian city of Bath. When Liz Cartland had mentioned her brother's affair with a married woman Delmas' ears had immediately pricked up. John Cartland had supposedly been 'annoyed' at his son's indiscretion but the judge wondered if it might have caused a more profound rupture within the Cartland family circle than the young lady had intimated.

He wasn't the only one on the trail of what the press chose to call a 'mystery blonde.' A pack of bloodhounds, the media now had the scent of what it hoped was a story of family intrigue in its finely-tuned nostrils. It didn't take the hacks long to track down the pretty wife of a Somerset headteacher, beating Krikorian by a matter of days.

'We both knew Jeremy and his father,' said the bespectacled young woman from behind the door of a fine converted mill house just outside the picturesque village of Chew Magna, fifteen miles to the west of Bath. 'But I shall be quite astonished if the detective comes here.'

Nonetheless, on a dreary afternoon in May the Marseille sleuth stood outside the gates of the same handsome property deep in rural Somerset which the press had just visited. He too was hoping to gain an audience with the mistress of the house, a certain Mrs L, wife to the headmaster of The Downs Preparatory School in nearby Wraxall, a lady described as a 'good friend' of Jeremy's. However, the lady of the house was under no obligation to speak to the detective. Krikorian's authority did not extend nearly as far as Somersetshire.

Waiting around the hedgerows like a forlorn lover, Krikorian had plenty of time to reflect on what he knew: Mrs L had denied suggestions of a relationship with Jeremy when the press had called. She'd merely said that the young teacher had been a 'popular' figure at The Downs School. This was not entirely true as the Commissioner knew; Liz Cartland had already testified as much. That the petite Mrs L had lied to the media was not especially surprising: she'd been taken by surprise, literally doorstepped and heaven knows how she must have felt to see her image splashed across the front pages of the tabloids. Her affair with a member of her husband's teaching staff could have little if anything to do with the murder of John Cartland. Or could it? Judged by what he had seen and heard so far sensitivities around the affair were still raw.

The day wore on. Still no sign of the occupiers. After what felt like several hours hanging around, the Maigret of the south admitted defeat.

Next, the cop headed south towards Brighton. If anybody knew the real John Cartland – if anybody could hazard a guess at who might want him dead – then it was surely the deceased man's housekeeper, Janet Gibson. Accompanying Krikorian was Claude Jeal, a bilingual New Scotland Yard inspector who, with his precocious baldness and auburn beard, looked a dead ringer for . . . Jeremy Cartland.

In a distinctive Scots' brogue Miss Gibson told the Anglo-French detectives that relations between Cartland senior and junior had always been 'friendly.' She also testified to never having known the two men quarrel. During an interview which lasted three hours, the housekeeper went on to affirm that her employer had 'not been very happy' about his son's romance with the married woman, but that the affair had ended amicably a couple of months before the murder in January 1973. The housekeeper did not recognise the kitchen knife when presented with it nor did she recognise the axe depicted in police photographs. So that was that. Krikorian left the seaside town not much wiser than when he had arrived.

While his colleague battled not only English weather and reserve but also the vagaries of its cuisine, two thousand kilometres south of Brighton, Emile Gonzalves had arrived on Spain's Costa Blanca. His mission was rather less complicated than that of Krikorian. The chief commissioner was primarily concerned with paraffin – specifically he wished to trace the provenance of the strange pink oil discovered in the jerrycan.

At Alicante police station, Gonzalves met Nicholas Lyon. The ex-pat had been summoned to attend an interview with the detective.

'What was the relationship like between Mr Cartland and his son?' asked the policeman taking a seat opposite the British born adventurer who had spent the majority of his life farming in Kenya.

'They had a normal father and son relationship as far as I could tell.'

Mr Lyon then outlined the circumstances which had led the Cartlands to arrive in Denia to collect the caravan. He also recalled that on a previous visit John Cartland had spoken fondly about his son, expressing the hope that one day he would take over the running of the language school business. As with Miss Gibson, when presented with (a photograph of) the kitchen knife he was unable to make a positive identification. Lyon thought he had possessed some French knives at some point, but could not be any more precise.

From here local police escorted the Englishman, his wife and the French detective to Denia.

'I must say I was shocked to hear that Mr Cartland had been murdered,' said Lyon on the journey back to his home. 'Have you any idea at all who could have done such a thing?'

'I am convinced Jeremy Cartland murdered his father,' said Gonzalves.

Lyon was visibly moved. 'I just can't believe it. I was with them on the day they left Denia. I took Jeremy into town to buy some oil. Why? I don't understand.'

'Can you take me to this store later?'

'Yes, of course.'

Back at the Lyon's villa it was established that the couple did not currently possess any French-style kitchen knives. Nobody had yet been able to identify the knife used on Jeremy. So where had it been acquired? Gonzalves knew the model was manufactured in France; he also knew it was almost exclusively sold in the UK. If Jeremy was the culprit, could he have bought the knife prior to departing for the trip? In the days before PayPal and the widespread use of debit cards it would be impossible to prove one way or the other. All too easy back in the 1970s to make a cash purchase without leaving behind any kind of trail, paper or otherwise. The gangbuster had arrived at a dead end.

Gonzalves next turned his attention to paraffin. On the short drive to the centre of Denia, Lyon recalled how he had driven Jeremy along the same route shortly before he and his father had departed for the Las Rotas campsite, that Friday, 16th March. Jeremy had been carrying a plastic can. Before taking his leave, the young teacher had sought his host's advice with regards to where to buy oil for the caravan's heater and lamp. Lyon then related how he had recommended a place in town whereupon Jeremy had readily accepted his host's offer of a lift. Having arrived at a store the proprietor had filled the can with what Lyon described as 'colourless liquid.' The detective raised an eyebrow: *colourless* liquid?

The two men arrived at Denia's bustling town. Lyon parked his car and together they strolled along Calle Loretto, a narrow pedestrianised back street home to a bakery, a hairdressing salon and where dogs dozed in the drowsy midday sun. Eventually they reached a store on the corner selling household goods and appliances. Once inside the cool, dark interior the shop's owner confirmed to the French detective that the only paraffin sold by him was indeed colourless. What about a pink oil? Did he not stock any alternatives? The vendor shook his head. In Spain paraffin was produced by Campsa, the national fuel company. Just one type of paraffin was sold throughout the whole of the country.

The Commissioner thanked Lyon for his assistance and headed back to France with his findings. There was only one conclusion to be drawn: to the paraffin bought in Denia had been added petroleum thereby producing a much more volatile substance.

Though the gangbuster spent several days in the region - a trip back to his Spanish roots - it seems he might have forgotten to clarify a vital discrepancy in witness testimonies: the actual colour of the Sprite Musketeer caravan Lyon had sold to the eccentric Brighton academic.[5] Mme Chauvet had insisted the caravan that rolled up on the forecourt of the Total garage on that windy Sunday afternoon had been pink and yellow. Jeremy himself had mentioned yellow curtains. But he also maintained the colour was pale green. On this point, he appeared to be on firm ground: Sprite caravans of this period were invariably painted sage green and white – a sort of home colour for the East London company which manufactured Sprites and other models. Pale pink, beige and blue models were much rarer to come by. Did not Gonzalves check this crucial detail with the caravan's former owner? Strangely, of all the many articles written about the case, the question of the caravan's livery was never mentioned.

It is possible that Mme Chauvet had been mistaken. Could the hazy sunshine have played tricks with the old lady's eyes to the extent she had mistaken the colours? On the other hand, it is also possible that Nikko Lyon had in fact sold one of the rarer pink Sprite models.

The issue of caravan colour remains yet another unresolved mystery in a case rich in unanswered questions.

19

John n' Jerry: 'Diabolical fermentations?'

Following Krikorian's visit to the UK, more than ever focus now shifted to the relationship between Cartland senior and his only son. Talk was no longer all about rash acts committed in wartime Brussels or the Drummonds or of vengeance. Nor was it even about night-time prowlers. The media had itself a new angle: a family psychodrama within whose hidden depths might be found the key to unlocking the mystery of John Cartland's brutal murder.

Paris Match had already told its readers the solution to the Pélissanne riddle likely would be found in Brighton. 'It is an English crime,' writer Jean Marvier quoted a police officer as saying. Sure enough, from the time Cartland's mutilated corpse had been discovered amid the wild herbs and flowers of La Barben, it was impossible not to feel that the French had wanted to disown the case, wash their hands off it, send it straight back across the English Channel.

Like mothers and daughters, relationships between fathers and sons can be equally fraught, subject to ebbs and flows. In the same *Paris Match* interview Jeremy had apparently declared that 'Father was weird.' Though it might have been meant as a throwaway comment, to a French readership puzzled by what it took to be the young man's cool reserve to his father's murder, it smacked rather more of indifference. The French media had expected grief. What it got instead was Anglo Saxon composure. 'Stubborn' was a word used on more than one occasion to describe the teacher's facial features.

What then was the true nature of the relationship between Jerry and John? Were the two men just a pair of good friends who enjoyed each other's company so much they had gone on a month's long camping trip together? Or was there something else going on beneath the surface?

While others doggedly pursued stories of collaborators and even tales of hidden wartime treasure, the *Paris Match* article had been one of the first to broach domestic matters, to suggest the real clues might lie not in the pine forests of Provence but in and around the pebbly beaches of Sussex.

Initially, Jeremy had been happy to cooperate with the magazine. He'd spoken with its journalists on the evening of his second interview with Delmas while he and Liz were dining at Le Pigeonnet; he'd even supplied pictures of his late father from the family album. In one image a baby Jeremy sits next to a proud father dressed in military garb, shorts and puttees, which placed it around 1944-45. Other photographs depicted Cartland on safari in exotic, faraway places in far-off times. Upon publication Jeremy would denounce the article.[1] The article's writer had certainly painted an idealised picture of Brighton. Elsewhere he made reference to his subject's prowess with women, painting him as somewhat of a louche playboy while making a point of referring to what he termed 'Jerry's turbulent temper.'

What exactly did Marvier mean? Was the journalist privy to private information about his subject's character?

Those close to him invariably described Jeremy's character as mild, gentle even. Hadn't Liz Cartland told Delmas that her brother was 'even-tempered?' Testimony from witnesses such as Nikko Lyons and Mont-Reynaud seemed to confirm this view of the teacher-poet.

A former pupil has a somewhat different memory of the man who taught him at the Downs school: 'He took me for English and Games,' recalls the student who would himself become a successful teacher and school rugby coach after a career initially spent with the Metropolitan police. 'On one occasion I remember playing hockey. I clipped Jeremy's heels during the game. When I looked up, he had his stick raised above his head as if to strike me. His eyes were bulging. Another time I scored a try during a game of rugby. Jeremy was furious and flung me up against the post by my shirt. I must have been 12-years old at the time.'

'I remember him being rather fierce with Lara, his dog,' recalls another former student. 'He had quite a temper on him, now I remember, and we were pretty scared of him. But we lived in fear of a number of staff. The headmaster was terrifying, and the possibility of being beaten was always high up in one's mind.' The same student vividly recalls the dashing figure the teacher cut on the school's rugby field: 'I remember his bearing in his kit being somewhat contrived: shirt out, socks down, raffish.'

Marvier ended his article with a rather curious allusion to Jack the Ripper. Outward respectability can hide the darkest of interior motives counsels the author moving presciently towards his conclusion wherein he confesses to being haunted by visions of:

> A perverse England behind the flowery curtains of the reassuring cottages of Brighton, incubating monstrous complexes, diabolical fermentations, under Oxford varnish or Victorian Puritanism.

In a nod to the inscrutable nature of the case, Marvier chose to call his article 'The Enigmatic Jeremy Cartland.' Perhaps it was a rather deliberately hyperbolic parody of Albion and her prissy mannerisms, but there was surely some truth in its implications: repression is a real enough phenomenon. Once unleashed it can be deadly.

Speculation mounted. Journalists started to dig deeper. The Cartland family found itself thrust into the media spotlight. It didn't take long for more information to leak out concerning the dead man's background and what seemed to be his always complex relationships with those around him, children as well as wives.

When Cartland's first wife divorced him in the early 1950s it seems to have taken him completely by surprise. And yet the relationship had been on rocky ground for some time evident enough in the fact that while her husband had latterly taken a post in Dubai, Mrs Cartland had remained at their Eastbourne home. The story goes that upon his return to the UK Cartland unexpectedly burst in on his wife in the middle of a garden party, every inch the jilted husband, furious and disbelieving. The marriage was over. Thus, Jeremy and his sister had lost one father, but upon their mother's remarriage would gain another. Crucially, John Cartland would miss a great deal of his children's formative years. That first marriage – the way it ended – left a bitter taste in the mouth of the globetrotting academic. By all accounts the rejection really did seem to have taken him by surprise.

As the years went by Cartland seems to have masked the brooding, morose side to his character behind a ruddy, jovial exterior He was gregarious, travelled widely and yet deep down may indeed never have recovered from that early humiliation whereby he had lost not only a wife, but possibly a son and daughter too. When marrying for the second time in 1955 Cartland confided in his son that he had been overcome by dread at the registry office: 'What have I done?' he supposedly asked himself. Life was going forwards, but John Cartland might have preferred it to go backwards. And so, he drifted on. His third divorce in the late 1960s coincided with a period of unprecedented social change in the UK and wider world. In less than a decade society had altered beyond recognition. For a man like John Cartland, brought up on the immutability inherent in both public school and colonial life, it must have felt like the world around him was changing much more quickly than he would have liked.

'He would never admit he was disillusioned with life,' confirmed the elusive Janet Gibson in a rare interview, 'but this was a world in which he was ill at ease.' The housekeeper also revealed how her employer liked to spend winter evenings in his study thumbing through photograph albums, a catalyst for him to, 'talk to me for hours on end about his days in India, the Middle East and Africa.'[2]

Staunchly conservative in his political beliefs, it was never going to be easy for a man like John Cartland to accept the mores of the times. In one interview his daughter had referred to her father's politics as 'bizarre.' If that seems judgemental then it is important to appreciate that the Cartland children had both come of age during the decade known as the 'swinging sixties,' a period which had spawned the Beatles, free love and the contraceptive pill. It was also the decade of student protest. Jeremy himself had been in Paris just prior to the May 1968 protests. Radicalism was all the rage.

An insight into John Cartland's views emerged in a series of journal entries. One day he had hoped to publish a book which would chart his remarkable life while providing a space for him to espouse his rather unique brand of philosophy. When Jean Marvier had alluded in his article to 'Oxford varnish' and 'Victorian Puritanism' he had been much closer to cracking the enigma that was Worcester College graduate John Basil Cartland than he might have realised. Some of the business-man's ideas did have a distinctly outmoded feel to them:

> It seems to me an immeasurable advantage for a boy to be brought up perhaps in a hard, world and move into an easier one than vice versa, and that an environment and strict discipline is the best preparation for life and the greatest kindness which a boy can receive.

So how would a father of a lost, idealised Edwardian age, brought up on principles of deference and stability cope with a couple of young liberated adults whom he would have seen only intermittently after his divorce from their mother?

How did the Cartland patriarch cope? Marguerite Wheeler, Jeremy's 75-year-old maternal grandmother, told the media that Cartland senior and junior had grown closer during Jeremy's days at teacher training college in Chelsea. Here they discovered a shared sense of humour. Like his father, Jeremy loved literature; they also enjoyed travel and had an especial fondness for all things French. According to Ms Wheeler these weren't the only things the pair had in common:

'Their relationship became rather like brother to brother, rather than father to son. After all, John Cartland was a great womaniser too.' A chip off the old block then, *Paris Match* had got *this much* right.

Ms Wheeler was not the only person to notice the warm and affectionate relations between the two men. Cartland's business partner Jacques Mont-Reynaud recalled how, when in each other's company, Jerry and John resembled a couple of chums rather than father and son. It was 'unthinkable' that they would come to blows said Mont-Reynaud – 'under normal conditions.' 'Jeremy was devoted to his father,' added Ms Wheeler. 'He loved him. He is just not capable of murder — or, even losing his temper.'

They might have been at the opposite end of the spectrum in terms of politics, yet at one time there does appear to have been genuine affection between the two men. For his part, the older man retained a certain pride in his 'wild' son as illustrated in the following anecdote first published in 'The Enigmatic Jeremy Cartland' article and therefore almost certainly sourced from Jeremy himself. It concerned a bizarre proposal supposedly once made by the older man. At one time it seems the fledgling poet had become involved with a rather profligate young woman. It was a situation that worried his notoriously parsimonious father to such an extent he offered him a choice. Papa Cartland would buy his ladykilling son a Rolls Royce, but there was a snag: he could not have the car *and* the girl; he would have to choose one or the other. Much to his father's delight, Jeremy chose the car. A girl he could get any time; a Rolls Royce on the other hand . . . [3]

That was then. Somehow, in some way, things had changed in the interim. After talking to friends and family of the deceased man, journalist Alain Cass shed yet more light on the affair when speaking of (Cartland's) 'increasingly strained relationship with his children.' According to Cass, things had not been right for some time – four years. If so, then recent events could only have helped increase any alienation.

Well into their twenties, Jeremy and Liz had of late been involved in adult relationships neither of which apparently met with their father's approval. Cartland had yet another facet to his character, or so it appears: that of the strict, overbearing patriarch. Jeremy's relationship with the wife of his employer at the Downs School seems to have caused somewhat of a scandal in and around the leafy suburbs of Somerset where he had taught the past three years. Living on site amid the school's lush, green pastures must have been a dream role for a young teacher, but it also meant a degree of intrusion into private matters. It couldn't last and so in the summer of 1972 Jeremy resigned his post.

At some point he and Mrs L fled to Golspie, a small village in the Scottish Highlands where his mother now lived. Subsequently, the couple had co-habited in Brighton. Although often cited as proof of the closeness between Cartland senior and junior, Jeremy's return to Sussex in September 1972 may have had less to do with a desire to succeed his father in the language school and more to do with necessity. Rather, he had nowhere else to go.

The affair had officially ended in January 1973. The precise role Mr Cartland played in bringing about its closure has always been unclear but at its height in June 1972 – coinciding with Jeremy's resignation - the older man had walked into the office of his solicitor to alter his last will and testament. Janet Gibson had been named as the sole beneficiary. Upon her employer's demise, the housekeeper would inherit an estate which included the splendid Georgian townhouse at Powis Square. The will noted that 'ample provision' had already been made for the Cartland children; Jeremy and Liz already owned property bequeathed from their father from a transaction made in 1967.

'I wish the said Janet Gibson,' read the text of the will, 'to allow my children to have such small items of personal effects as they may desire but without imposing upon the said Janet Gibson.'

Did Cartland object to his children's choice of partners to such an extent to consider disinheritance? (Krikorian thought so. A full house, the detective now had a motive along with opportunity and means.) It is entirely possible that these relationships of his children triggered something deep within John Cartland, a visceral objection to what might be termed 'improper behaviour.' In his later years, he would often rail against the injustice of life – especially the collapse of his first marriage to Joan Wheeler who had gone on to marry an associate. His amorous interludes had, it seemed, always ended in unhappiness and it is just possible he wanted to protect his offspring from making similarly bad choices. Take his second marriage which ended after the middle-aged academic had embarked on a year-long affair with a German au pair employed by himself and his headmistress wife. As a result of these and other experiences, he seemed to have developed an almost evangelical aversion to relations of any description but especially those of the illicit variety.

Viewed this way, perhaps Mr Cartland's objections were to be expected. If both his children were involved in 'illicit affairs' then for a forthright man such as he, expressing his reservations would have been entirely commensurate with his role of father – his duty even. Sense of duty was, after all, one of the defining qualities of gentlemen. It was this sense of duty that probably inspired a typically extravagant gesture which came to the attention of Alain Cass during his research:

'His taste for love,' impishly wrote Cass, 'didn't prevent him in the last year, writing to his son and daughter warning them against the evils of extra-marital relationships.'[4]

Ever the paradox, here was Cartland warning his children to do as he said, not as he himself did. All of this points towards tensions. If his children objected to their father's proclamations about their personal lives then it is perhaps understandable; after all, Jeremy and Liz were no longer children and John Cartland was not exactly the most ideal model to take advice from where affairs of the heart were concerned. If, as seems likely, old Cartland had issued or hinted at ultimatums that summer of '72 as evidenced by the redrawing of his will, clearly he had meant them. Come spring of 1973 relations twixt father and son appear to have cooled considerably.

And then came the camping trip, an opportunity to set things right perhaps? Crime writer Dick Kirby seemed to think so. He devoted a chapter of his book, *Scotland Yard's Murder Squad* to the affair. According to Kirby, the trip to the continent had been arranged, at least in part, to enable the two men chance to 'patch up' their differences.

Had the trip indeed been planned as a way of bringing father and son together after recent disagreements? Neither Jeremy nor his sister had mentioned this as a reason for the trip. According to their version of events, the two men enjoyed one another's company and had happily set out for a business-cum-holiday trip round the continent.

'To tell the truth,' recalls an old rugger-playing friend of Jeremy's, 'I was rather surprised that he went on that camping trip to France with his father. I never thought they were that close. Jeremy never spoke about his dad.'

If the voyage had been engineered to bring about reconciliation, who had proposed the venture?' I know the trip was instigated by John,' continues the friend, 'and it might have been an attempt to rebuild bridges.' According to someone who knew Jeremy well, John Cartland it was who had proposed the trip – possibly as a means to heal a broken relationship. The two men would return from France with a renewed sense of respect.

That was the view of an outsider. On the other hand, the family viewed the trip as nothing extraordinary – just the penchant of a father and son who enjoyed the outdoors and had decided to combine adventure with business.

20

Flirting with Madame Guillotine

In the week leading up to the reconstruction the investigation took yet another new twist. Together with a third person, on the night of May 11th, Alain Weltman and Joseph Lorenzo were arrested on suspicion of car theft in their home town of Beaucaire. Clearly, the young men who had assisted Jeremy on the night of the murder were no angels. They might even be devils. A new and potentially significant line of enquiry had just opened up: could the car thieves have been involved in John Cartland's murder? Gonzalves headed straight over to Beaucaire.

It was a couple of ashen-faced young men who met a particularly stern looking 'Jack Palance' upon his arrival at the local police station. Yes, the pair admitted they did occasionally take a car for joyriding purposes, but murder? *Not possible! Unimaginable!* Weltman and Lorenzo had always maintained they had been carousing in Salon's bowling bar on the night of the murder. There must be someone who would remember them.

While a couple of anxious young bucks paced their holding cells, Marseille's gangbuster went off to check alibis. Fortunately for them one of the young men had ordered an unusual drink that Sunday night – a mint beer. Even after several weeks waitresses vividly recalled serving this odd brew. From here they were able to identify Weltman by his limp. And they distinctly remembered shooing the rowdy friends off when the bar had been shutting at 12.30 am. Gonzalves did some calculations: if the Beaucaire boys had left the bar at closing time as the waitresses were saying, the very earliest they could have arrived at *Jas de Dane* would have been between 12.45-12.50 am by which time Delaude, and shortly after him, the Sobanskys had all arrived at the scene of crime. The time frame simply did not stack up. No doubt owing to the defence's criticism that Jeremy had been the only suspect, police duly searched the young men's homes, drawing a blank. The tearaways were released from custody promising never to cross Gonzalves' path again.

Attention now focused on May 17th, the day of the reconstruction. Delmas had arranged for all the witnesses to meet yet again - in the afternoon for a rehearsal and then later in the evening when the moon was expected to be shining as brightly as it had on the evening of Sunday, 18th March. But what about the prime witness? Would he accept the summons?

Although Jeremy declared himself more than willing to take part, his legal team remained split. While their French counterparts were happy for their client to attend, Mitchell-Heggs and Relton considered it a courtesy fraught with danger. According to the French judicial system, there were still strong presumptions of guilt against the young man's name in regards to a capital offence. What was to prevent Delmas charging and arresting Jeremy during, or more likely, after the staging? But Lombard was not at all convinced. If the civil party declined the invitation to assist the judge it could only be interpreted one way: that Jeremy had something to hide. Lombard wanted to call the authorities' bluff: for Jeremy to present himself and by doing so dare Delmas to take action. The lawyer was gambling that while laying charges in his client's absence would be a no-brainer, it would be nigh on impossible in the presence of a dutiful civil party so anxious to assist the enquiry he had flown all the way over from the UK.

Discussions went on right up to the wire. From his London office, Michael Relton sought assurances that should Jeremy attend it would be in the capacity of a witness. Meanwhile, just one day before the reconstruction, Lombard was locked into discussion with Mitchell-Heggs in his Paris office. The British lawman was convinced Jeremy would be arrested once on French soil. The Maitre of Marseille disagreed, but even he started to wonder:

'What if I was wrong?' wrote Lombard in his memoirs. 'What if the re-enactment brought something unexpected to the prosecution? What if Jeremy hadn't told me the whole truth?'[1]

Only days previously the Aix appeal court had ruled the April 25th hearing null and void. Even though he had categorically denied making them, Professor Cameron's alleged remarks doubting Jeremy's honesty would have still been on the record but could now be erased. Not only this, but by virtue of the fact it too had been introduced without proper notice, the evidence of the pink oil and mysterious blood stain had also been ruled as inadmissible. With this in mind, Lombard felt his client's position had improved significantly. The re-enactment then would be a chance for the British teacher to draw a line under the affair, the actions of an innocent man – at least in the eyes of the world. Lawyerly discussions went on. In the end, the British and French faction could not agree on the best course of action. For his part, Jeremy listened carefully to the pros and cons. Ultimately, it would be his decision whether or not to answer Delmas' call. There was much thinking to do.

Agence France Presse reported the situation thus: 'The number one witness in the case continues to confer with his lawyers, who are preparing, it seems, to advise their client not to return to France. They fear, indeed, a possible indictment of the son of the murdered professor.'

To stay or go? Late on Wednesday evening it was still not clear if Jeremy would be returning to Aix. Flight reservations had been made on Thursday's 10.35 am London-Paris flight and on a further transfer that would arrive in Marseille just after 1pm giving enough time to make it to *Jas de Dane* in time for the scheduled 3pm start of the reconstruction. Further, a suite of rooms had been booked at Le Pigeonnet – one in the name of 'Jeremy Bryan Cartland.' The teacher-poet was keeping his options open. It all depended on obtaining assurances as he explained in a statement: 'I will come if I am considered as a civil party or as a witness and not as an accused.' The audacity of a prime witness setting the judicial agenda impressed some, staggered others.

By Thursday morning the actors in the drama were readying themselves for what promised to be a frantic day ahead. Team Cartland were negotiating hard with an obdurate Delmas. The Judge however remained impervious to the defence's pleas:

'Your honour, all we ask is that our client be allowed to attend the reconstruction without prejudice.'

Delmas was unmoved. 'I remind you gentlemen that our task today is to simply establish basic facts. Obviously, we will be unable to achieve this objective without the assistance of Mr Cartland.'

'Then can we take it there will be no indictment?'

'No masters, you cannot.'

The defence team was asking the impossible and must have known it. Convened to progress the enquiry, as Delmas was at some pains to point out he could not rule out the possibility of an indictment *before* the reconstruction had even taken place. New evidence might emerge. Even so, Mitchell-Heggs suspected a warrant had already been issued. Stalemate. Having caught an early morning flight from Paris, Lombard joined his fellow lawyers to petition Delmas. But even he could not obtain an assurance.

Meanwhile, at Heathrow airport along with Michael Relton, Jeremy waited for the telephone call which would either clear him to travel to France or advise him to stay put. The clock was ticking. With minutes to spare before flight BE-084 was due to depart the call came through:

'Stay where you are!' advised Christopher Mitchell-Heggs' urgent voice. 'We haven't been able to obtain an assurance. I repeat: stay where you are. Do not take the flight!' Jeremy got the message. He and Relton left the airport for the solicitor's Putney office. The reconstruction would go ahead without its prime witness.

Outside Aix's Palais de Justice an army of journalists waited for news too. The car park was swamped by television and radio equipment. It seemed as if the whole of France was waiting to know what the bearded Englishman would do on this bright, windy morning. Some had already anticipated even more than this. For example, a BBC film crew were already filming outside Marseille's notorious Baumettes prison in the expectation that once indicted Jeremy would be transferred there at some time during the day.

Though he had expected as much, informed that his witness no. 1 would be remaining in the UK, Delmas grimaced. The judge expressed his confusion. When he had always signalled that he would gladly take part in a reconstruction – whatever it took to assist the hunt for his father's killers - why had Jeremy changed his mind? According to Lombard, his client had 'concerns.' He was concerned about the police file and prejudicial media coverage. Furthermore, as a result of his experiences over the past few weeks the Brit was mentally and physically exhausted and in no fit state to make the journey.

'In view of my client's absence,' said Lombard smoothly, 'I humbly request that the reconstruction is postponed to a later date when he may be able to attend.'

'Impossible!' thundered Delmas. 'Everything is arranged: the witnesses, equipment, caravan hire. It's too late.'

'My dear judge don't think I do not sympathise with you, I do. But what is the point of proceeding with a production without its chief actor?'

The lawyer had a point, but Delmas could not be shifted. 'I think you are aware master as much as I am that should your client fail to attend the reconstruction, justice will . . . draw its own conclusion.'

Lombard winced. Damned if he did, damned if he didn't, a no-show by Jeremy would, as the lawyer had always feared, be interpreted as a sign of guilt. The only solution was to have the event cancelled, but however hard he pressed him, Delmas refused. At 3 o'clock the first part of the reconstruction would go ahead as planned. In the meantime, the two sides slipped over to La Madeleine for lunch. Here Gonzalves and Krikorian mingled with Lombard and Liz Cartland, who had flown in that morning ahead of her brother. For a moment it might have been a gathering of acquaintances, allies even.

As 3pm approached an eerie silence fell over Aix's historic city centre. Everybody so it seemed had decamped the 20 or so miles to the unassuming clearing known as *Jas de Dane* and the exodus had left the bars and bistros bereft of all but a few indifferent customers. There was only the mistral, whistling down the city's thoroughfares.

At the clearing activity was brisk. Police had cordoned off the RN 572 at both ends. With just minutes left before the re-enactment was due to begin, Delmas was directing both civilians and officers in preparation for what should have been a rehearsal prior to the main event scheduled for 11.20 pm. What, with the amount of cameras, wires and extras hanging around it might have been a film set. The Hillman and a hired caravan were positioned according to the instructions of the witnesses – Caire, Delaude, the Blascos and a Beaucaire trio anxious to avoid Gonzalves. A little distance away the media pack kicked its heels. Finally, everything and everybody was in place. It was time to begin, almost. Team Cartland had yet to arrive. The good judge checked his watch.

Eventually, Lombard's familiar blue Jaguar rolled up, but neither the defence nor Miss Cartland stayed long – a gesture presumably conceived to delegitimise the event. Only Chiappe remained in situ.

A police officer assumed the role of Jeremy Cartland, but that didn't fool anybody: the matinee and with it main event later that evening were over almost before they had begun. What next? With the Mistral blowing gustily through the pine and oak trees, Delmas disappeared into the caravan. Not long after he appeared with a document. Released from their pen, journalists swarmed round the judge as he prepared to read a statement. In sombre voice, and in what The *Sydney Morning Herald* called a 'macabre ceremony,' Delmas announced that the absentee was to be formally charged with the murder of his father, John Basil Cartland and that an arrest warrant had been issued to that effect.

News spread quickly. Through Relton, Jeremy immediately issued a statement:

'I am astonished at this grotesque turn of events and the issue of a warrant for my arrest . . . I only feel a sense of despair, shared by my family, that now it may be that the murderers of my father will never be found. I am confident that once the whole truth about the conduct of their investigation is revealed, it will be shown that appalling irregularity, inefficiency, bias and precipitate action have characterised the whole enquiry into the case by the French authorities.'

As of Thursday night the teacher-poet found himself in an unprecedented as well as precarious position. Dating from 1876, a treaty between England and France agreed that each country undertook to surrender individuals charged with crimes on the territory of the other. It was just a case of setting diplomatic channels in motion. Ultimately Bow Street magistrates would consider any evidence presented to them by their French counterparts and if deciding it constituted a prima facie case against him, Jeremy would be detained in Brixton prison for 15 days pending an appeal. Thereafter he ran the risk of being extradited back to France to stand trial.

Liz Cartland wasted no time lodging an appeal. To André Delmas she presented a dossier containing a list of twenty alleged errors committed by investigators.

In London, Jeremy endured a torrid week-end. Would he be arrested on Monday morning prior to a hearing in front of Bow

Street magistrates? If French authorities were indeed looking to extradite the young teacher back to France, then the week-end of 19-20th May could be his last as a free man for some considerable time.

When The *Daily Express* caught up with the teacher in Putney the following Monday it was a subdued Jeremy who posed for pictures besides the River Thames. The article painted a bleak picture. 'He came along the Thames towpath,' began its first paragraph, 'with a smile and an outstretched hand—a man on Interpol's wanted list all over Europe, Jeremy Cartland. A man, although he wouldn't mention it, with the guillotine on his mind.' Dressed casually in jacket and jeans and smoking his favourite brand of French cigarettes, the teacher-poet seemed resigned to his fate. He was, he said, enjoying what might be his last day of freedom.

'I don't really know what is going to happen,' he told the paper's Michael Brown. 'I will just surrender myself to the warrant when Scotland Yard say they want me. It could be tomorrow; I just don't know.'[2]

A pivotal moment had arrived in the anatomy of the affair. If the situation seemed hopeless on that chilly, May morning there was however more than a glimmer of hope: French authorities might eventually hand the case over to their British counterparts and probably would do just that. Should this happen, rather than a route which could lead to extradition and a date with Mme Guillotine, the case would be referred to the UK's Director of Public Prosecutions, Sir Norman Skelhorn QC. Jeremy and his legal team were hoping and praying that the French authorities would indeed wish to extricate them-selves from a case that could only cause further difficulties, not least in the diplomatic realm. The very last thing the Republic needed was an incarcerated British subject launching attacks on its justice system on a regular basis. Cries of 'unfair trial' they could already hear.

When Delmas was quoted as saying the affair was now a matter for the English authorities it seemed Jeremy's prayers might once again have been answered.

21

Entente uncordial

While Jeremy waited for the long arm of the Yard to 'feel his collar,' his many supporters began to campaign furiously on his behalf. Family members wrote to papers expressing anger and frustration at his treatment; in Brighton, students of the language school staged a series of protests. Jeremy meanwhile started to petition MPs. As well as his local member of parliament he wrote to Alex Lyon, the Labour member for York, who had been identified via a family friend as a potentially sympathetic ally.

Meanwhile back in Aix, Monsieur and Madame Blasco had once again resurfaced. Admitting to being 'bowled over' by the charge of parricide brought against the Brit, the couple had spoken with journalists at the popular *Le Provençal* newspaper. In a breathless report, the paper ran an interview with the couple. The Blascos retold their story – they had seen two men pushing the Hillman etc.[1] However, rather than leaning into the vehicle's left-front door, Mme Blasco claimed she had seen one of the men actually *opening* the door . . .

There was just one other additional detail absent from the couple's original statement:

PROVENCAL	Did you recognise among the witnesses at the re-enactment either of the two men you saw pushing the Hillman?
MME BLASCO	Absolutely not. We recognized in the two men present, neither Mr. Delaude nor any of the three Beaucairois.[2]
PROVENCAL	Could you estimate the age of the two men you saw?
MME BLASCO	The darker was about forty, the blond one younger, about thirty.

How the police rolled their eyes, how Delmas shook his head. The 'mysterious' men, as they already knew, were none other than 22-year-old blond Michel Chambonnet and the 19-year-old darker-haired Joseph Lorenzo both of whom had been attempting to push the Hillman clear of the burning caravan. 'Nice gesture of the prowlers,' remarked one cop drily, 'to save the car of the man they had just axed to death . . .'

Be that as it may, the press on both sides of the English Channel picked up on what was essentially a non-story and ran with it. *Witnesses had seen the murderers! How could the case progress or even conclude when important eye-witness testimony had been overlooked?* The *Times* was one of several newspapers to give the story prominent coverage. 'The evidence that he and his wife have given,' reported the paper referring to the Blascos, 'tends to confirm the explanation that Mr Jeremy Cartland has given of what happened when his father was killed with an axe.'[3] The *Guardian* reported that Jeremy's lawyers were seeking an 'urgent meeting' with the couple.

The news buoyed Jeremy. In a radio interview with France-Inter he pressed home what must have been an unexpected advantage: 'I told you I was innocent! Why haven't we heard from this couple again? Nothing is regular in this case.'

With the media reporting on 'new' witness statements and Jeremy's advocates becoming ever more vociferous, little wonder the pressure eventually paid off. On May 22nd, Alex Lyon brought the matter to the House of Commons where he asked an in absentia Prime Minister:

'Whether he will raise with President Pompidou in his forthcoming discussions the treatment of a British subject, Jeremy Cartland, by the French police?'

'My right honourable friend is in Paris now,' replied Chancellor of the Exchequer, Anthony Barber MP on Mr Heath's behalf. 'I have received no full account of his discussions with President Pompidou, but I have no reason to believe that he was proposing to raise this matter with the president.'[4]

At the very moment the case was being discussed at the French Ministry of Justice, talks which reputedly involved the president himself, British Prime Minister Ted Heath, an old, old comrade of John Basil Cartland ('twas said) happened to be in Paris for talks with the same Mr Pompidou. Was the Cartland case raised? Not *officially* it seems. But if Heath had raised the subject, he would not have been the first nor the last leader in such a position to make polite enquiries into matters of current interest. After all, *L'Affaire Cartland* was virtually unavoidable in the weeks running up to summer, both at home and abroad.

As the evenings became lighter and warmer, Jeremy spent the early part of summer in a state of limbo. The good news was that extradition now looked a distant if not wholly improbable prospect and with it the threat of languishing in a French jail while awaiting trial, the fate of a certain Edouard Dega. After being imprisoned for 16 months without trial on suspicion of fraud, the former accountant had undertaken a hunger strike in April 1972. By all accounts the 51-year-old had come perilously close to death. Thanks to the furore which followed a high-profile media campaign, eventually Dega had been granted bail.

Living a transient life between friends and relatives in London and occasional visits to Brighton, Jeremy felt he could not afford to relax. A new development could happen at any moment; hence he kept in daily contact with Michael Relton in nearby Putney.

And so, he waited. A trip to Oxfordshire to hear further accounts of his father's secret service exploits yielded nothing new and so the wait continued. Though it appeared nothing was happening, at Aix's Palais de Justice, a team of sixteen were in fact busily translating the 2,000-page police file. As far as Jeremy was concerned this was welcome news. And sure enough, by the start of July there had been unconfirmed reports that the French authorities would not be seeking extradition. Meanwhile, The Cartland file, as it would become known – a copy of the original French language version - had been sent from the clerk of court in Aix to the Ministry of Justice where a final decision would be made. Along with his family and friends, Jeremy was more than hopeful.

When it became clear that French Prime Minister Pierre Messmer was personally reviewing the case, team Cartland's tactics appeared to be vindicated. Incessant lobbying had indeed ensured the case had found its way to the highest political echelons in both France and at home in the UK. Unbecoming as it might first have appeared, the defence's sustained assault on French procedure – and by extension its integrity - had eventually succeeded in investing much more significance in the case than merited. Because in some subtle, ill-defined way, thanks largely to the media, the case had somehow come to symbolise something way beyond its own remit. It was all about cumulative effect. Forcing the affair into the political and diplomatic realms had always been the objective.

The *Entente Cordiale* pact between France and Great Britain had been signed in 1904. Since that auspicious date there had been some wobbles, but relations between the two countries were usually considered warm, friendly even. In January 1973 Britain had even become a member of the EEC. However, the path towards European unity had been a long and at times fractious one.

Fearing what its influence might be once admitted, a decade earlier General de Gaulle had blocked Britain's entry and had it not been for the efforts of a certain arch-Europhile named Ted Heath, arguably that would have been that for some time. Hence, as of summer 1973 the UK and France stood tentatively on the brink of a new age of co-operation. However, commentators had already noted how the Cartland case had highlighted a raft of profound, seemingly irreconcilable disparities - philosophical as well as procedural - between the judicial systems of two great rivals who had just joined together as part of a 'common market' of shared interests and standards. Could such profound disparities ever be overcome? Would yet more emerge?

It just so happened then that *L'Affaire Cartland* had occurred at a delicate moment in the evolution of relations between two age old European rivals. And the charges levied didn't get any more serious: a British national murdered on French soil was bad enough, but for the victim's son to then accuse the French authorities of not only gross incompetency but also of having framed him for the murder upped the tempo considerably. It could never have happened in Britain. Why? Presumably due to higher standards, superior morals. Along with his advisors the British teacher was impugning not only the reputation of French police but the country's wider values too, or so it appeared.

As a microcosm of what some observers had always felt was an intrinsic incompatibility between the two countries, in its own way the Cartland murder had acted as a catalyst. It had certainly succeeded in putting hitherto unresolved tensions under a frenetic media microscope.

Only recently *Le Monde* had accused the pro-Cartland British media of 'Francophobia.' The paper had also castigated as 'nationalistic' papers which supplied a platform for Jeremy and his supporter's always strident critiques of French justice and its police. Nobody was suggesting this tit-for-tat battle playing out amongst the media of each country could derail progress, but such manoeuvres were hardly geared to help consolidate Anglo-French relations. Here was an irritation that all parties could have done without. Little wonder the case was under review in the splendid setting of Hôtel Matignon, official residence of the French Prime Minister.

In an article about the current state of play, The *Times* observed how the relentless criticism by team Cartland had indeed likely influenced the outcome of the matter: much 'heat' had been raised by the criticisms said the paper. Such were sensitivities each side of the channel, the French government had 'no wish to add fuel to the flames.' Given the circumstances surrounding the murder (a burning caravan) the metaphors might have been better chosen, but there was no denying that the pressure appeared to be paying off: extradition now looked a distant prospect. Section 9 of the Offences against the Person Act (1861) decreed that should a subject of Her Majesty suffer murder in a foreign country, the perpetrator could be brought to trial in England. The Cartland file was almost certainly destined to cross the channel.

What, if anything, could be done in the meantime? In order to discredit the file ahead of its arrival, aided by Michael Relton, Jeremy continued to launch blistering attacks on the police who had created it – what is known in warfare as pre-emptive strikes. Lawyer and client directed as much pressure as possible down political avenues mainly in the shape of Alex Lyon MP, who in turn petitioned the Home Secretary. In Paris, Mitchell-Heggs visited the Ministry of Justice. The onslaught was impressive, as was Jeremy's legal bill.

Diplomatic rumblings continued until Monday, 9th July when the French Ministry of Justice officially confirmed it would not be seeking extradition. According to a spokesman, from this point onwards the Ministry desired the case to be handled 'according to British law as if the crime had been committed on British soil.' Two days later the dossier arrived with the Director of Public Prosecutions. Delmas, Krikorian and Gonzalves had seen the last of the Brighton school teacher. The Cartland murder had become a British case. In response, Michael Relton issued a statement whose theme would not have been unfamiliar:

'Mr Cartland is greatly relieved that they (French police) are not to pursue the extradition order because he felt that he would not get a fair trial in France and might not get a fair crack of the whip by the French press. He is confident that the truth of his innocence will be accepted in Britain. He has always maintained his innocence in this case.'

It was now up to Sir Anthony Skelhorn QC, Director of Public Prosecutions, to decide if there was a case to answer and if so, to thereafter seek the permission of the Attorney General to authorise British police to commence a new investigation. Skelhorn considered the evidence before him. After assessing the file, he decided there was indeed a case to answer. Pipe-smoking Chief Superintendent Ronald Page of New Scotland Yard would now assume control of the enquiry aided by Detective Sergeant John Troon. Page immediately set to work. He and his team assessed the mountain of paperwork before them. Writing later about his hopes and expectations at this time Jeremy would express himself puzzled that rather than closing down the enquiry with immediate effect, the Scotland Yard detective appeared to be taking the matter seriously:

'I naively believed that a statement would soon be issued clearing my name, saying the French investigation was a complete farrago of nonsense, and that they should be ashamed to call themselves policemen.'[5]

But Page and his team had been keeping abreast of the affair for some time and however much it irked certain parties, had work to do. As recently as June, officers had been alerted to the reading of Mr Cartland's will which had confirmed that Janet Gibson, his trusted housekeeper, stood to inherent an estate valued at over £300,000 in today's money. Executor Frederick Scales seemed eager to downplay the legacy. Scales reminded interested parties that six years previously the dead man had presented his children with what the lawyer seemed to be suggesting was an advance of their inheritance. Jeremy and Liz had each received a house from their father. They had also received a cash sum from the sale of other properties. With regards to the properties, what he failed to add was that these gifts had been proffered *before* the alleged souring in relations between the Cartlands had occurred and therefore the opportunity to rescind had long since passed. By his actions the previous summer Cartland had ensured that what was left of his estate did not pass to his immediate family – that was the salient point. And anyway £300k was a substantial amount of money by anyone's standards and the Scottish housekeeper duly expressed her gratitude.

'She deserves it,' remarked Jeremy. 'Janet was very good to my father.' Scotland Yard took note. That the young teacher could accept what was his disinheritance with such apparent equanimity further alerted officers. Somehow, it didn't add up. Jeremy claimed to have run up debts of some £200,000 fighting the case and was in fact desperately short of money.

No doubt there was a very good reason why neither of the Cartland children attended Mr Cartland's deferred cremation at the London Cemetery that summer, but it must be said the optics did not look too good. Detectives must have been just as perplexed as the casual observer. The dead man's ashes were placed in the family grave – according to Jeremy without either his son or daughter's permission.[6]

Scotland Yard's Murder Squad then were set to follow in the footsteps of their French counterparts. Effectively they would be starting the investigation anew. Language and culture aside, Page and his five-man squad faced an uphill task: as the French investigative team had soon discovered the difficulty might not necessarily lie in 'solving' the case, but rather in accommodating the priorities of two key agencies, media and political. The British media had long since decided that the young teacher had been the victim of gallic bungling and had become fixated with his 'ordeal.' With its victim (Jeremy) and villains (French police) this was just the type of story cherished by journalists. Altering a narrative so firmly established is not so easily done. For instance, the British media had so far ignored the news that the kitchen knife used on Jeremy, while manufactured in France (Thiers), had been found to be almost exclusively sold in the UK. It didn't fit the preferred narrative. Meanwhile, the Blasco's tendentious testimony had received coverage which as well as generous had always been credulous; it *did fit* the narrative.

If the media possessed enough influence to steer the case in its favoured direction, it was nothing compared to that wielded at the very top of the political pyramid. For both British and French political establishments, the case had become nothing more than an inconvenience. If left to run its natural course, there was every possibility the affair would conclude in a highly publicised trial in which Anglo-French relations might possibly be tested to breaking point. Nobody really wanted that, did they? As Page, Troon and colleagues got to grips with what was an exceptionally weighty dossier, combing through hundreds of pages of witness statements, forensic reports and photographs, there were those in high places who couldn't wait for the whole affair to be over.

22

End of the beginning

Despite Jeremy's incredulity, New Scotland Yard arrived in Aix towards the end of July. 'I arrive here with an open mind and without prejudices,' declared Chief Supt. Page in a press conference. The British Attorney General, he added diplomatically, had been 'very impressed by the excellent documents in the case prepared by Messrs. Krikorian and Gonzalves, the two French policemen.'

It was high summer in Provence. Hot, dry days preceded humid nights. Fishes out of water, the London detectives were set to spend a great portion of their time in France holed up in hotel rooms and lobbies, much of it checking through endless reams of witness statements. Early in their sojourn yet more witnesses emerged.

On the day of the murder, a couple claimed they had been out driving in Pélissanne when at some point they had found themselves travelling behind a caravan.[1] Between their own

Renault 4L and the caravan had been a 'large black Citroen.' As this vehicle did not attempt to overtake the caravan in front, the couple sensed the vehicle was, to use their own term, 'shadowing' it. When the Hillman and Sprite turned off the road at *Jas de Dane* the Citroen had followed suit. Phlegmatic as ever, Maitre Lombard duly recorded this sensational account. Did these late, late witnesses hold the key to the affair? It got better: when the couple drove back along the RN 572 later that evening – at 11pm – the Citroen was *still there*, parked close by to the Cartland's temporary campsite. Had not Mr Cartland spoken to a stranger(s) parked nearby the site shortly after arrival at the clearing?

Despite the highly questionable nature of this testimony, it didn't prevent Michael Relton from seizing upon it. The lawyer flew off to France to interview the new witnesses. But there was a snag: the couple had been conducting an adulterous affair so they claimed, and were anxious to keep their names out of the press. Apparently, it was the reason why they had left it so late in the day to come forward.[2]

Questions soon arose with regards to the veracity of this account. Was this another couple, who, like the Blascos had heard all about the young Brit's 'ordeal' at the hands of *Les flics*[3] and were also anxious to assist – even if that meant inventing false stories? Jeremy himself had never mentioned a 'black Citroen' yet according to the witnesses the vehicle had trailed closely behind the Cartlands through Pélissanne and onwards to *Jas de Dane* - a further two kilometres away. What, with the Hillman and the Sprite followed by the large black Citroen and the couple's 4L behind that, it must have been an especially slow train of four vehicles crawling through town that afternoon, but nobody else seemed to have seen it. Moreover, if the story was to be believed, the mysterious car must have been parked at a crime scene for at least 4 hours yet nobody else reported its presence. Needless to say, neither Citroen nor its occupant(s) came forward or were ever traced thereafter. Whether through misplaced empathy or a genuine mistake, Page and Troon had acquired another piece of jigsaw to consider. Yet another witness would emerge even later in the day - Gerald Sparrow of whom more in due course.

Sleeves rolled up and shirts dampened with sweat, by early August the six members of the Murder Squad had found their way to *Jas de Dane*. Here they replicated Delmas' experiments when the judge had tried to ascertain the precise location of the light farmer Caire had seen on the night of the murder. In all, New Scotland Yard spent six weeks in the south of France.

Page and his small team returned to the UK with a stack of paperwork. The month of October was spent sifting through the documents and liaising with the office of the Director of Public Prosecution.

All Jeremy could do was wait. Friends and family continued to bombard the media with letters expressing their outrage over the manner of his treatment; first by the French authorities and latterly by their English counterparts whom they implied were taking much more time to complete their enquiries than was necessary. Summer 1973 was turning into a nightmare for the aspiring writer. Work was all but impossible. Things became so bad Jeremy started to hallucinate. One day he received a visit from a 'Mr Bregonzi' and a female associate with 'blue-rinsed hair, a beaky nose' and large pair of glasses which kept sliding down her nose. Yet another figment of the imagination, one afternoon a hawk also dropped by his flat, coming to rest on a lectern which began to collapse, 'turning into wobbling rubber like a Dali soft watch melting on the rocks.'

In his more lucid moments Jeremy continued to apply as much pressure as possible, he and Relton writing letters of complaint to Scotland Yard and Alex Lyon MP, who in turn continued to petition Home Secretary, Robert Carr. Naturally, he was anxious to know what progress had been made and the likelihood of his standing trial for murder. On top of his mental tortures he had, he said, lost weight. He wanted to get it all over, to return to normality. The letters ended up with Sir Peter Rawlinson, the Attorney General who wrote back assuring Jeremy that once essential forensic tests had been conducted the case would swiftly conclude. It all depended on the scientists who were carrying out tests on various crime scene exhibits.

This delay meant that Jeremy had still not been called in by Scotland Yard for interview. The teacher let it be known he was willing to sit down with Page and his team at their convenience. As far as Jeremy was concerned, the sooner he met detectives the sooner the case could be closed and his name cleared.

Finally, on October 16th, Page handed the file to Skelhorn and the DPP settled down to assess the merits of the case. The weeks went by. 'The agony continues,' said Michael Relton in a pointed reference to the protracted nature of an investigation that had been in progress over six months from its first inception in Salon. According to his lawyer, Jeremy was now suffering from several complaints such as nervous tension and insomnia.

Nothing was straightforward in this case though. As if to prove the point Page and Troon returned to France towards the end of November where they remained for a further two weeks and from where they arrived back armed with several additional witness statements. 'It's alright for some,' cynically remarked certain observers. As for Jeremy it merely prolonged the agony. 'I almost wish New Scotland Yard would charge me with this murder,' he announced to the media, 'so I could say publicly and in open court, I am innocent.'

It wasn't until late in December that Jeremy received the call from Scotland Yard. Plans to embark to Golspie for a vacation were put on hold as, on December 21st, he and Relton walked through the doors of the world's most famous police force for an interview that would either make or break him. A lift took them up to the Chief Superintendent's office. Relton thought the signs were promising: had police intended to charge his client likely the interview would have been conducted not at the Yard but in the more formal setting of a police station interview room.

Were police merely going through the formalities? It had started to look that way. Jeremy seated himself opposite Page. DS Troon prepared to take notes.

Forensic tests had detected a very faint blood stain on the back of the corded trousers worn by Jeremy on the night of the murder and which had presumably been overlooked by Lille.[4] The sample matched John Cartland's blood group. Jeremy though remained unperturbed. The murderer(s) must have been covered in his father's blood, he explained, and thus would have left traces of it everywhere. Easy therefore to come into contact with it. As simple as this explanation sounded there was a problem: the spot of blood had been miniscule, only found after advanced forensic analysis. If Mr Cartland's blood had indeed been smeared here, there and everywhere and his son had indeed come into contact with it while wandering around the site, dazed and confused, it might be expected to have been present on Jeremy's person in somewhat larger quantities than at the level of the microscopic. If the complete absence of his father's blood about his person could be interpreted in the teacher's favour, just as its presence would logically condemn him, what to say about a spot so feint it could not be seen by the naked eye? Would such a revelation suggest innocence, guilt or neither?

Judging by how unproblematically the Yard appears to have accepted this unsubstantiated explanation, perhaps the outcome never had really been in doubt. Jeremy even took a moment to muse over what the French reaction to discovering his father's blood on his person might have been: 'conclusive proof of my guilt.'

For the most part the interview was a rerun of those which had taken place in France, a familiar script and one in which Jeremy was well rehearsed. His main concern was consistency; after such a long period of time had elapsed since his first interviews, police he feared might try to catch him out on 'minor errors of memory.'

Like his predecessors, Page focused a fair amount of attention on the question of locked and unlocked car doors. In response, Jeremy turned to his main witness:

> Since Madame Blasco's statement that she had seen the car door open destroyed the French police 'theory' that it had been locked all the time, I found it very disturbing and was very surprised to discover that Page apparently regarded this as a key piece of evidence.[5]

Typically, the defence strategy relied heavily on quibbling over points that had little or no significance in the determination of guilt. For example, at one point Page apparently produced a notebook of Jeremy's in which were scribbled a series of notes, 'Exhumation,' 'Death of Lizzie,' 'Guilt.' The detective wanted to know what the notes referred to. According to Jeremy, they related to the pre-Raphaelite painter Dante Gabriel Rossetti and his feelings over the death of his wife Lizzie – a subject he was considering for the topic of a play.

The slow-witted police had decided the notes amounted to incriminating evidence against the poet-teacher, but why is not at all clear. There was, after all, no mention of 'father' or 'John Cartland' in the notes. If 'Lizzie' equated to Liz Cartland then she was very much alive.[6] Therefore, it is impossible to know what if any importance Page attached to such notes.

'I gave Page a brief lecture on English Literature history,' remarked Jeremy. 'One does not expect a policeman to have a great knowledge of literature or culture,' he continued 'but I found it alarming to see how prepared he was to interpret any piece of evidence to my disadvantage.' Upon conclusion of the lecture Jeremy realised his role as 'educator to the police forces of western Europe' was not yet over. British police appeared to require as much education, if not more, than their French counterparts.[7]

And so it went on. By the end of the interview Chief Supt. Page joined a host of other figures which included Delmas and Krikorian, who (according to Jeremy) did not truly believe in his guilt and never had. Seven and a half hours after it had started, the interview concluded. No charges or arrests forthcoming, Jeremy headed over to Euston station to catch the Inverness train. His ordeal was surely over.

The case was indeed officially dropped on Thursday, January 3rd as Jeremy enjoyed new year festivities in Scotland. According to the DPP there had been 'insufficient evidence' in order to initiate criminal proceedings. For a case containing some 2,000 documents from the original French investigation – a figure augmented by several hundred more pages resulting from the Yard's enquiry – it was a nothing if not bizarre summation. Evidence was in fact plentiful. Quality was a different matter altogether and a matter for a jury.

Chief Supt. Page and his team had in fact collated a whole stack of fairly damning testimonies from friends and associates of the Cartlands. Witnesses revealed how Jeremy had fantasised about killing his father. Detectives heard too disturbing stories about the young teacher's mental health manifest in what were described as 'nightmares.' On one such occasion he was said to have woken late at night in the grounds of the Downs school holding an axe; another time he woke from an episode holding a knife with which he was threatening a flatmate. The Murder Squad also obtained a quantity of letters written by Jeremy which revealed more about this darker side to his personality.[8]

All this effort counted for naught though. Not only had the DPP decided there was insufficient evidence to proceed to court, the decision was also taken to seal the Cartland dossier from public view until 2045. Skelhorn, it appeared, had no appetite for his decision to be subject to further scrutiny . . .

As for Jeremy, relief was mixed with concern. As pointed out by legal commentators, the phrase 'insufficient evidence' could easily be interpreted in such a way as to imply that he had in fact committed the crime only police had not been able to prove it, a subtle distinction. A judgement of insufficient evidence does not of course imply innocence nor is it meant to. Here then was potential millstone around his client's neck Michael Relton was keen to remove.

Reliable as ever, Alex Lyon joined the fight. The MP for York wrote to the Attorney General reminding him that Jeremy's account of events had always been 'consistent and credible.' He also somewhat melodramatically asked the AG to consider the ramifications in the light of the UK's European Community membership: with more Brits than ever expected to cross the channel they could so easily find themselves on the wrong side of French law, under suspicion for little or nothing as happened to Jeremy. In reply, the Attorney General reaffirmed the judgement. Halfway between guilt and innocence, it was an especially unsatisfactory verdict which failed to satisfy supporters or detractors.

What or perhaps more to the point *who* had prevented the case proceeding to court? In his memoirs Paul Lombard provides a tantalising clue. When he was agonising whether to return to France for the re-enactment of May 17th, it transpired that Jeremy had been advised not to return by an individual who, according to the Marseille lawyer, at that time 'occupied in Great Britain a considerable post.'[9] Clearly, the young teacher had been tipped off, but by whom? Had he decided to attend that day at Delmas' behest there can be little doubt arrest and trial would have followed. With parricide attracting a sentence of execution via guillotine in the France of that era, the decision to remain in the UK might therefore just have been a life-saver; it almost certainly saved what would have been a long and very protracted diplomatic wrangle that could only have damaged Anglo-French relations, perhaps irreparably.

As to the identity of the secret adviser, had not *Paris Match* mentioned Jeremy was a not infrequent caller on his father's old friend, Mr Ted Heath? Whether out of loyalty to old friends or to protect a project dear to his heart, could the British Prime Minister have intervened on the young teacher's behalf both at this juncture and again later in the affair - at the point Sir Norman Skelhorn made his final and somewhat puzzling judgement?

Having accumulated £200,000 worth of debts during the past year, Jeremy expressed his intention to reclaim some of that amount by suing the French police. For whatever reasons this course of action never materialised.

And so, the story finally dropped off the radar. From time to time, it would pop up in newspapers, but its days as a front-page story were over. Eventually, the former English master returned home to Brighton where, easily identifiable via his trademark ginger beard and that precocious pate, he had acquired a certain infamy. People knew who he was and all about the terrible crime he had been accused. Driving his Renault estate accompanied as ever by Lara, Jeremy Cartland became a familiar face in the Prestonville area of the city. Whispers, glances, nudges, he took it all in his stride.

Late in 1974 The *Observer* caught up with him at his home at Highcroft Villas, what it described as a 'ramshackle' terrace.[10] Far from a contented individual, the paper found a man agitated, unable to move on with life. Nor had his obsession towards the French police cooled as evident in his description of their methods ('a 'mixture of Kafka and Alice in Wonderland.') Heavily in debt, the poet-teacher was absorbed now in pursuits of a creative nature. On the cusp of becoming a professional writer, he was fulfilling a lifetime ambition.

Nonetheless, some aspects of the affair still rankled. When recalling the reaction in the French media to his lack of emotion following the murder, Jeremy took the opportunity to explain himself: 'I don't even lose my temper on the rugby field.'[11] Moving on was proving easier said than done.

The *Observer* left a man seemingly trapped in purgatory, the only possible escape from which seemed obvious: a book; a book in whose pages Jeremy could set the record straight once and for all.

23

The Cartland File

The years 1974 to 1976 saw Jeremy as good as disappear from the wider public view. Three years or so after the case the world had moved on as it always does. In and around the streets of his home town however the former teacher would still be recognised and was still capable of setting tongues a-wagging despite the passage of time. *Did he, or didn't he?* A whiff of notoriety hung around his broad shoulders, but idle gossip he maintained did not concern him. His family and friends believed in him and that's what mattered.

At the beginning of the long, hot summer of 1976 journalist Geoffrey Levy paid a visit to the Sussex coast to catch up with a man whose name had not so long ago been as widely known as any celebrity of the time.[1] He found a changed man. Gone, albeit temporarily, was the beard; the eyes were 'ringed' and he had lost even more hair. Levy thought his interviewee looked a decade older than his thirty-two years. Judged by his appearance it was clear to the journalist that over the past few years Jeremy had experienced all the vicissitudes fate could throw his way and more still.

Just one phrase occupied his subject's thoughts: 'insufficient evidence.' As predicted, these two words had done just as much – perhaps more damage – than any prison sentence might have. Levy titled his interview 'I don't mind if the world thinks I killed my father.' A tale of woe unfolded.

In order to clear his mountain of debts Jeremy had been forced to sell a house he owned in Eastbourne which had belonged to his grandmother. To make matters worse, he still owed several thousand pounds to his French lawyers. Finding employment however had proved nigh on impossible he complained. 'Cartland' was a name that came with enough baggage to deter prospective employers. In order to alleviate some of the financial pressure, the ex-teacher had eventually been forced to share accommodation with his sister and her husband at . . . Powis Square. Besides no. 11 Powis Square it seems Mr Cartland had owned the house opposite, no. 13, so perhaps it was here at 'Brighton House' where the meeting took place.

Work on Jeremy's account of the murder was, after many false starts, finally progressing. From his study at the top of the house he worked assiduously on the manuscript that would soon enough become *The Cartland File*, his ambition of becoming a successful writer within grasp. In the meantime, he continued to play rugby in the claret and blue hoops of Hove (where he would remain well into the 1980s serving in a number of roles.) He also played cricket. Lately he had joined a social-sports club, the Late Niters, a band of like-minded fellows who played hard and partied even harder. Sometimes he could be found enjoying a beer in and around Brighton's bohemian area known as the Lanes – a shortish walk from Powis Square. Other than that, there were his dogs. But most of all he craved a literary career, always had.

Overall, the article paints a melancholic picture of Jeremy and his life at this period. Levy encountered that day a wistful, unfulfilled man still stigmatised by the judgement of the DPP and whose life as a result had changed in ways he could never have predicted. The interview ended with the journalist in reflective mood. True, life seemed bleak but recognition had finally come for the poet-teacher – of a sort. 'One cannot help feeling that however wretched the circumstances,' concluded Levy, 'the alternative celebrity foisted on him . . . is not entirely unwelcome.'[2]

After being rejected by larger publishers, a company local to Brighton, Linkline, published *The Cartland File* in January 1978. At last Jeremy had a platform from which to tell his extraordinary story in the way he wanted.

On first reading the impression is one of a man wronged – wronged by the police, media and abused ultimately by a flawed justice system. This was the impression left upon at least one reviewer. 'His book is full of the pain, anger and disillusionment of the entrapped,' observed Richard Whittington-Egan writing in the literary journal *Contemporary Review*. Perusing Jeremy's account of his ordeal would, cautioned the reviewer, leave the reader 'coldly fascinated.'[3]

Though variously scathing, bitter and sarcastic, the authorial tone of *The Cartland File* is for the most part one of profound indignation. Whether real or affected the book's author presents a portrait of himself as someone genuinely mystified that he should have been suspected of his father's murder. Incredulity is thus the order of the day. While readers such as Whittington-Egan found themselves moved, the book's tone, alternating between self-indignation and sarcasm, might not so readily convince other readers. If French police focused attention on the young English teacher it was because, as they readily admitted, the presumption of guilt against him had been especially strong. Jeremy's explanations never convinced Gonzalves nor any of the other French investigators.

According to Jeremy however key figures such as Page and Krikorian never really had believed in his guilt. But was it true? Did investigators think him innocent? Here then is just one example of the many anomalies that emerge, albeit inadvertently, from *The Cartland File*.

When reflecting on his encounters with Delmas the author makes the startling observation that the judge himself did not think him guilty of the crime and what is more told him so. Delmas, thought Jeremy, was therefore more than a little relieved when the case stalled during their April 25th interview. By introducing Prof. Cameron's testimony in which he had supposedly labelled the British teacher untrustworthy, the writer wonders if this was a deliberate attempt by the examining judge to sabotage the case, 'so that he would not have to arrest a man whom he really believed to be innocent.' Jeremy goes on: 'Had he (Delmas) not, on more than one occasion, told me that he personally thought I was innocent?'

Meanwhile, Paul Lombard had an entirely different view of an official he knew and respected:[4] 'From the start,' wrote Lombard, 'his (Delmas') religion was made. For him, Jeremy Cartland was guilty and everything had to be done so that this culpable received the punishment he deserved.'[5] Of course at the time of the case, it is possible that the canny judge might have been 'playing both sides' as the old adage goes, even if it would have represented for an examining judge behaviour of the most irregular kind possible. Perhaps, but a year later the recently-retired judge spoke of the Cartland affair in the November 5th edition of *France-Soir.* When asked to comment about the British teacher with whom he had duelled so often the previous year, 'I remain,' he observed, 'deeply convinced of his guilt.'

The Cartland File is peppered with such inconsistencies the effect of which, at times, is to blur the margins between fact and fiction. Often, it's a seemingly unimportant off the cuff remark that on reflection appears not to tally with existing knowledge.

For example, when questioned why he had chosen to camp out at *Jas de Dane* by Delmas rather than a nearby campsite, Jeremy writes that, 'as total strangers to the area, we had absolutely no way of knowing of the existence of such a camp site.'[6] The phrase 'total strangers' immediately jars. As already remarked, Cartland senior had business contacts spread throughout the Marseille-Aix area; he had owned land in the region since the early 1960s to where he had been a regular visitor over the past decade. Not only this but as a result of his war service he'd spent much time in the south of France. *Total* strangers? It sounded almost as if this couple of fluent French speakers had never set foot in this area of France before. Perhaps the writer might have helped his cause more by claiming they had never driven on that *particular section* of the RN 572 before, if indeed it were true.

If that claim seemed a stretch too far, what to make of the writer's exploits on the rugby field? No sooner had he returned home than Jeremy was turning out for Hove RUFC in his customary fly-half position; one picture captured him leaving the field after a match against Eastbourne in the autumn of '73. Back at Salon hospital he had complained about a pain in his shoulder. 'To this day,' he wrote in 1977, 'I still suffer from the injury to my right shoulder, being unable to raise my arm above shoulder-height without pain.'[7]

The anomalies come thick and fast, but *only* for those with a reasonably sound knowledge of the case. Through no fault of their own readers in the mould of Mr Whittington-Egan might miss the nuances, have neither time nor inclination to verify information before them.

One such example concerns the question of how the Cartlands ended up taking an axe with them on holiday. In his interview of 28th March Jeremy offered an explanation. To recap: when his father had turned up to collect him from Highcroft Villas, he noticed a large axe in the Hillman's boot. Mr Cartland said he needed it to defend himself at which Jeremy had scoffed. 'It was I who took the large axe to my home, and my father told me in that case we would take the small axe which was at my home.'[8] In *The Cartland File* this key moment is retold rather differently. While packing the car Jeremy looked up to notice his father 'stealthily sneaking' the smaller axe into the Hillman. 'Looking around to make sure he was unseen,' continues the author, 'he slipped it into the boot where the large felling axe had been.'[9] Hence there are two very different versions of how the axe ended up travelling to France.[10]

Previously, in his interviews of 19th and 20th March, Jeremy had not mentioned how the murder weapon came to be in the caravan. 'I can tell you we brought this axe from England in the boot of our car,' is his only comment when shown the axe on 20th March. There is no mention at all about his father's fears for his safety, or how he supposedly smuggled the item into the Hillman.

This reluctance to expand, to offer little more than the sketchiest of details, is a feature of Jeremy's many interviews.

More often than not his discourse feels tentative, the testimony of an individual treading carefully.

Sometimes, it's the various accusations of corruption which catch the eye. Now the French police had its issues in this area and its interrogation techniques sometimes left quite a lot to be desired, but Jeremy had benefitted from the full protection of the British consulate prior to becoming a *partie civile.*[11] As noted by several commentators he had received a level of privilege unusual for an individual designated as witness no. 1. Still, when there is no readily available explanation, when the facts appear to contradict the narrator's story – which they frequently do – as if in desperation, *The Cartland File* can veer into conspiracy territory.

Take for instance the bloodied kitchen knife assumed to have been used to stab a writer who wonders, 'if it got there at some other than when I was stabbed.'[12] Had police planted the knife? The author's suspicions that police may have also planted pillows and feathers at *Jas de Dane* has already been remarked upon. Having had blood taken at Salon hospital he later 'wonders' where his blood might have been 'sprinkled.'

Jeremy seems to be suggesting he was the victim of a cynical and highly elaborate set-up, that where evidence could not be obtained police simply fabricated it. He had been chosen, so he claims, to be a 'scapegoat.' Late on in the book the author outlines his belief that the French police knew or suspected from the outset the identity of his father's killers. There had been a cover-up. Thus, Krikorian, Ettori, Gonzalves, Delmas and Page are weighed up and found to be either corrupt, inept or both. A feature of the book is indeed the sheer number of ad hominem attacks on its prominent characters, especially police and judiciary.

Similarly, confronted by testimony that does not support

his version of events, the writer invariably responds by attempting to discredit the individual. For example, the Beaucaire youths are dismissed as 'car thieves.' Sometimes it's a person's motivation which is questioned. Madame Chauvet's account is one such example. Did the Cartlands stop at Mme Chauvet's garage on Allée de Craponee or not on that fateful afternoon? Jeremy never could quite make up his mind; to have admitted as much would have granted the old lady credibility – seemingly the last thing the civil party had wanted or the present author wants.

In this passage he relates what occurred *immediately after* the stop for petrol:

> As it neared seven o'clock in the evening, my father began to grow tired. He had been studying the map for the last few miles as we kept an eye out for a particular road that would enable us to by-pass the town of Aix-en-Provence.[13] We drove through the village of Pélissanne, on the *Route Nationale* 572, and were almost certain we had missed the turning.[14]

Imagine for a moment this account is true; if Mr Cartland had indeed been poring over maps 'for the last few miles' the petrol stop must have therefore occurred some distance before Pélissanne, in or around the town of Salon which is located 5 kilometres (3 miles) away. It's a supposition which raises an interesting question: fuel obtained, why branch off the RN 572 to divert into Pélissanne only to drive through the village and re-join the same road a few minutes later? Logically, they could and should have bypassed the village. Dragging a caravan through its narrow streets would have made little if any sense, especially for a father and son anxious to avoid certain places presumably because of the caravan they towed. Nor does Jeremy supply a reason for the detour. The Cartlands didn't stop in the village for supplies or such like.

It's not clear either which 'turning' the caravanners feared they had missed in order to bypass Aix, which itself is located some 40 kilometres (25 miles) south-east of Salon.[15] By taking the RN 572 the Cartlands were in fact right on track to achieve their objective: bypass Aix en route to Jouques.[16] This they could have done at the village of Célony or a little further on at the larger junction at Les Plâtrières (N 296).

Elsewhere in the book the author suggests Mme Chauvet might have confused the Cartlands with other travellers. If so, there must have been two British-registered caravans circulating round Pélissanne that day both of whose occupants were male, one younger and one older, but no women or children – an unusual composition and quite a coincidence if so. There might however have been another reason why the pump attendant had testified speculates the author: Madame might have been 'enjoying a bit of publicity.'[17]

Space prevents a detailed analysis of the many anomalies to emerge in *The Cartland File*. One further contradiction is however worth pursuing and it concerns Jeremy's account of the alleged blind-side attack on the murder night.

Why, after such a violent attack, had there been no cuts, bruises or swelling to the point of impact - Jeremy's skull? Simply because the young man did not bruise easily. As proof the author describes an occasion while playing cricket. Attempting to catch a ball he had been hit square on the forehead, but had not bruised. An injury to his head while playing rugby also failed to register any marks. The teacher-poet had a head made of granite. Yet had not Professor

Cameron found a large swelling on the back of his head during their private consultation? And was it not Jeremy himself who found a bloodied club at *Jas de Dane* – the elusive weapon apparently used to attack him? Once again, the author seems unsure of a key aspect of his story – in this instance whether he does indeed have the capacity to bruise/bleed.

Five years after the event has the author forgotten some of the details? Victims of traumatic events have been known to ''blank out' stressful events – so-called hidden memories.

Or is there something else at play here, a phenomenon well-known to those in the judicial and psychological fields. When a story is true, despite the number of times it is told, it will invariably display internal consistency; the facts will not alter. By contrast, a false tale may struggle to achieve the same degree of consistency and will almost certainly be much more difficult to replicate - more so when further questioning will invariably necessitate further explanation and the addition of even more details.[18]

Eventually, retelling a story replete with things that did not or could not have happened becomes burdensome, all too easy to contradict oneself or forget fabricated details. One way to mitigate this risk is to minimise the information relayed from the outset: play deaf, dumb and blind. Better still feign unconsciousness. All well and good, but interrogation will invariably compel the witness to create, conceal or modify ever more elements thus increasing the risk of exposure. For example, when Delmas pressed Jeremy to be precise regarding the spot where he had woken upon regaining consciousness, he confesses that he became 'quite exasperated.'[19] Did investigators know something Jeremy didn't? Pressed on matters he felt less than certain about, that had not been fully synthesised into the master script, his unease at such moments becomes manifest. Was his discomfort due to hidden memory complex or because of feeling threatened by such probing?

As a further illustration, consider the issue of footwear. Did the teacher wear his boots during the attack on himself and his father? It's a question that clearly interests police. As such it requires a very cautious approach. Once again, the question arises: is the author's apparent hesitancy caused by digging up painful memories, or is this an individual struggling to formulate a sequence of events which is both cogent and consistent?

In his interview of March 20th Jeremy revealed that upon hearing noises outside the caravan he had put on his shoes 'without socks.' For a witness whose watchword was always vagueness it was an interesting detail upon which to focus. Why include this particular piece of information? Socks – the question of whether they had been worn or not – presumably held some sort of significance for the teacher. On 28th March a new detail is added about the young man's footwear on the night of the murder: he did not tie his boots up. This is the same interview in which he asserted that he had not taken the boots off at any point during the night.[20] By now police were pressing very hard to know how those three spots of blood had come to be inside the right-boot.

Shoes on or shoes off, Jeremy appeared to be hedging his bets: *Yes, I did wear my boots, but because I didn't tie the laces they might have come off at some point. If so, this explains the presence of blood in the right boot.* Becoming ever more elaborate as time went on, explanations were having to be refined to concur with emerging forensic evidence. More often than not this renders them a little less than convincing.

By the time of *The Cartland File* this nagging issue still appears to be unresolved in the writer's mind. Thus, on the very first page of the book the writer is careful to tell the reader that, 'I stepped into my shoes . . . without bothering to tie the laces.' Later in the book the point is re-iterated: 'my shoes were untied at the time of the attack.' Had a boot inadvertently slipped off, continues the author, he would have put it back on with a hand 'dripping with blood.' However, if blood had indeed dripped into the shoe in anything like the manner described (a 'hand dripping with blood') likely it would have been found in greater quantities than just three small spots; the inside (and outside) of the shoe would have probably been soaked in blood.

If the writer's focus on shoes and whether his laces were tied or not seems out of proportion to other aspects of the investigation, that's because it was an issue investigators dwelt upon. Trivial this matter was not. And so, against his better instincts Jeremy is drawn into explanation whereas as every gambler appreciates sometimes it is better to stick rather than keep on twisting.

Look what happens when Jeremy recalls the moment his father supposedly bumped into a stranger upon arrival at *Jas de Dane:* a hitherto never revealed detail is added: 'I just met someone,' he (Mr Cartland) said. 'And they've confirmed our suspicions. We are on the wrong road and we'll have to go back a few miles in the morning to find the right one.'[21] Long since safe in his Brighton study, the author appears to be somewhat confused about precisely what happened that day. The Cartlands already *were* on the right road – that is if they were indeed headed for Jouques. Possibly, this episode could have been another example of the author's impaired mental function – another delusion similar to those experienced at the time of the murder.

It's not all one-way traffic. Some of the author's complaints about the media ring all too true. The young teacher found himself at the centre of a storm in spring and summer of 1973 faced with a profession that wanted a story and would stop at nothing to get it. No doubt his privacy and that of his family was breached many times and a whole chapter of the book is devoted to criticism of the media. However, passages that describe physical attacks on his sister by French police seem hyperbolic. And while it is true police did make some hasty judgements early on, the book's strident anti-police tone is a trowel loaded to tipping point, disdainful to the point of deep, visceral hatred.

How then to sum up *The Cartland File*? Somewhere between fact and fiction, the book stands as a curious artefact. Has its author reached a point where he believes all that he says or is this a book written by an individual still traumatised by those horrific events? It would help explain some if not all of the contradictions and lapses.

According to its creator, it's a book he never wanted to write. Financial pressures forced his hand. It is to the writer's credit that original medical, police and witness testimony is included within the book's appendices, without any of which the present book could never have been written.

24

Murder triangles

The Cartland case might have been officially over – unsolved in the eyes of the law - but as with the Drummond affair one aspect would prove to be peculiarly resilient, resurfacing over the subsequent decades on a regular basis: the secret service motif. Had Mr Cartland been taken out by vengeful assassins after all? From the media point of view, it was a theory packed with suspense - just the type of angle beloved by editors seeking to spice up copy, to sell newspapers. *Cartland the spy! Cartland assassinated!* Stories wrote themselves, but was there any truth in any of them?

Even as the DPP had been assessing the Cartland dossier that Autumn of 1973, the ever-dependable *Daily Express* had unearthed yet another witness who told a remarkable story.[1] A retired judge living in Brighton, Gerald Sparrow claimed he had met the late Mr Cartland at a dinner party four years previously. After coffee, the businessman had taken the judge to one side. Cartland produced a bundle of about 15 typed pages which had been heavily corrected in ink.

'What do you think about this?' he asked his fellow guest. Do you think this would make a good book?'

Strangers until that evening, a bemused Sparrow read the documents with growing fascination. What the judge had in his hands was an autobiography which charted not only the author's roles with British intelligence in Vichy France, but his involvement in the Algerian war of the 1950s. Cartland had also produced a list of enemies. According to Mr Sparrow, he made special mention of the Algerian National Liberation Front (FLN) which under its leader Ahmed Ben Bella had fought for and won independence from Gaullist France.

'He was in real dread of his life from enemies who had sworn to take revenge on him,' recalled the judge. 'If necessary, I am ready to tell these facts under oath to a court of law.'

At evening's end, Sparrow watched this intriguing character act in an odd manner. Upon leaving the house, Cartland made a point of scanning the surrounding streets as if he suspected somebody might be lying in wait. 'Here was a man,' remarked Sparrow, 'whose life was permeated with a very real and lasting fear.' It was the paper itself that cast some doubt on parts of this story. During this period of the Algerian war (1954-56) it pointed out that Mr Cartland had supposedly been teaching in Kuwait – cover so he had always claimed for intelligence work. It also reminded readers of the dead man's fondness for telling stories. Perhaps he was not the only one who could spin a yarn.[2]

Nonetheless, viewing the case as part of a wider pattern of nefarious events began to gather traction as the 1970s progressed. British nationals were dying on French soil and not from natural causes. It was The *Daily Mail* which introduced its readers to a concept it termed 'The Murder Triangle' of south east France. The most familiar part of the triangle was its southern edge known as the French Riviera famous for its climate and the chic resorts which hug its Mediterranean coastline. Brits had been holidaying in the region for decades. Many had made permanent moves to the area literary giants such as Somerset Maugham, Aldous Huxley and Graham Greene had called home. Paradise had however turned into the stuff of nightmares - at least for some. It had started with the Drummond case and not looked back.

In the years to come other newspapers would also draw attention to what appeared to be the disproportionate number of British nationals who had met their ends on French soil of whom the Drummond family and John Basil Cartland had been just two examples. As recently as 1999 in an article entitled 'Fear stalks a rural paradise: 25 British deaths . . . only two solved,' *The Independent* charted the unusually high number of murders and suspicious deaths of Britons in France.

According to one author, the death of Michael Lasseter in Cannes in 1973 was one of the first in a series which could have been linked to subterfuge. Including Lasseter, Roger Louis Bianchini counted six more deaths of British nationals which had occurred in the years 1973-78 between Marseille in the west of the region and Menton in the east and which had either been murder or suspicious in nature.

As already noted, the official enquiry into Lasseter's death had returned a verdict of accidental death. The retired 71-year-old British army officer had been found lying in the road opposite Cannes' Alexandra Palace where he had lived alone in an apartment since the death of his wife some years earlier. Death had occurred as a result of a deep wound to the occipital region of the skull - the same injury inflicted upon John

Cartland. The tall, still-dashing officer had been returning home from dinner on the night of 29th January and was just metres away from the Palace's private car park where he habitually left his car when disaster struck. According to police, he had had a seizure. Rather than continuing into the car park entrance Lasseter had stepped out of the vehicle whereupon he had suffered yet another seizure. From here it appears he fell backwards onto the pavement, hitting his head on the kerb. A terrible accident.

However, the presence of injuries to the victim's knee and hands as well as the discovery of a blood stain on the handle of the car, aroused Bianchini's suspicions. Further, police didn't wait to close the enquiry down; it was sealed within 48 hours. Bianchini speculated that the ex-intelligence officer might have actually been accosted while approaching the car park. Had he been forced out of the vehicle at this point? Could the head injury have resulted from an accident as police suggested or had assassins unknown been waiting for Lasseter to return home that evening?

In *The Cartland File* Jeremy mentions that prior to his death Lasseter had been attempting to get his war diaries published and had 'become a familiar face in the offices of French publishers.' Were certain actors determined to prevent him publishing his memoirs whatever the cost? Officially, the case is closed.

The second death in this sequence would have been that of John Cartland in March 1973. Two and a half years would elapse until death number three – the murder of Courtney Prentice. Squadron Leader Prentice had been a pioneer of aviation and had enjoyed a career in the RAF in its Special Duties Branch. In October 1975 he had arrived in Menton to visit his wife. Having left the caravan in which he arrived at the stretch of seafront known as Garavan, it appears he was subsequently asked to move it elsewhere. Before setting off to do as requested, he confided some worrying information to his wife: since his arrival in Menton Prentice believed the driver of a green Triumph car had been watching him. According to Mrs Prentice, her husband had been exceptionally nervous the last time they had spoken, tense, not himself. He'd even taken the precaution of making a note of the Triumph's registration.

On Thursday, October 16th, the sprightly 76-year-old set off to relocate his caravan. He had mentioned moving it across the border to a campsite in San Remo and was expected back sometime on Friday afternoon. But Mr Prentice did not return. The next day a frantic Ethel Prentice reported her husband missing. And so, the weekend of 18-19th October came and went with still no sign of the Suffolk flying ace. Out walking along the Porte de France on Monday, Mrs Prentice was shocked to discover that the caravan had in fact not moved from its position on the seafront and approached tentatively. Inside, a scene of horror greeted her: Courtney Prentice had been beaten around the head and left to die. Judged by the disarray inside the caravan, he had clearly put a struggle for his life, but had succumbed to horrific injuries.

Led by a certain Emile Gonzalves, police concluded that two assailants had attacked the victim. No valuables appeared to have been taken from the caravan. Mr Prentice had been dead for several days. Investigators were more than a little puzzled: Prentice's caravan parked on one of the town's busiest roads, it seemed odd that the perpetrators had escaped detection. Nobody reported anything untoward viz the caravan or its owner. Had Mr Prentice known his attackers then? Police hypothesised that the ex-officer may have indeed recognised his killers and had invited them into the caravan. What then of the Triumph? Registration plates proving to be false, its driver was never traced and the murder remains unsolved.

Another two years passed without incident until the double murder in 1977 of the Brodericks. Like the Drummonds twenty-five years previously, Sidney and Avis Broderick were shot dead while sleeping in their car – in this case while parked in a remote beauty spot three miles off the Col du Canadel, a steep climb affording spectacular views over the St Tropez region of the Côte d'Azur. The couple had been holidaying in the area for years. When they could not find a suitable hotel, they would use sleeping bags and happily camp out in their car, a course of action that brought them even closer to the land they adored.

On the evening of the attack they had dined in the town of Lavandou from where, according to eye witnesses, the couple had been trailed by another guest driving a blue Volkswagen – possibly all the way back to the same forest track where they had spent the last couple of nights. A little after 2am on 8th August an assailant blasted 65-year-old Mr Broderick with three bullets while he slept in the front of the couple's blue Ford Cortina. How Mrs Broderick must have felt as she awoke on the back seat to the sound of gun fire can only be imagined; next the assassin turned the gun on her. The couple's papers were taken but little else. Jewellery and a substantial cash sum (£1500) remained hidden under the car seats.

Motive thus remained a mystery: was it a crime motivated merely by hatred for tourists or another reason? Unlike other cases there seemed to be no apparent secret service connection. Had the Brodericks simply been in the wrong place at the wrong time?

Nine months after the Broderick murders another couple met violent deaths at the hands of an unknown assassin(s). Mr and Mrs Maurice Moss lived in the village of Mougins just north of St Tropez. At some point over the week-end of May 27 and 28, 1978 the couple were shot in the head by two blasts from a double-barrelled hunting rifle. Again, the perpetrators had not stolen valuables, but had taken the contents of a safe. Mr Moss had been a biochemical engineer rumours suggested that he may have been working on secret designs.

According to information passed to Bianchini, with the exception of Moss, the victims of this series of murders had one thing in common: links to MI6. Meanwhile, Drummond, Cartland, Prentice and Broderick, so the informant claimed, had been so-called 'sleepers' – transient agents able to accept assignments at short notice on behalf of British intelligence. Specifically, they had been victims of the Cold War played out between western and Russian agencies during this era of heightened tension.

Cold War machinations is a line of enquiry pursued by James Ferguson in *The Vitamin Murders* - his investigation into the Drummond murders. The author makes a convincing case that in his capacity as Head of Research at Boots, Sir Jack Drummond had been in France that summer of '52 for purposes other than relaxation. The former nutritionist might have been on a spying mission. Not far from the busy N96 road where the family had chosen to camp stood a chemical factory located at Château-Arnoux-Saint-Auban. According to Ferguson, the plant specialised in the production of compounds used in chemical warfare - the largest of its kind in Europe at that time. Drummond had been in the vicinity to find out more. If so, it might explain why the family had chosen to park by the side of the busy N96 that balmy August evening.

However, even had Drummond been using the camping trip to cloak his true intentions – elaborate as such a ploy seems - it does not follow that the murder of the professor and his family was as a consequence of intrigue linked to the Cold War. The Drummonds may simply have had the misfortune to camp out close to where a ticking time bomb named Dominici just so happened to live. Sir Jack could have been involved in industrial espionage *and* fallen victim to the rage of a psychopath quite separately. Ferguson does however mange to quash one theory: Drummond had not been involved with the Special Operations Executive after all - a fact established when, towards the end of his research, the author meets the aging SOE agent Francis Cammaerts who confirms as much.

As proof of the endurance of the secret service motif it has even been floated in relation to the Jeremy Bamber saga. Imprisoned for the 1986 murders of five family members in order to inherit half-a-million pounds, Bamber claimed that his adoptive father Neville had in fact been murdered by spies. The former British intelligence officer joined a list comprising some familiar names: Sir Jack Drummond, Sir Oliver Duncan, Michael Lasseter and John Cartland.

Bamber's legal team prepared an appeal arguing that the five cases were linked in 'a campaign of murder against former British intelligence officers.' Lawyers claimed that each of the victims had served with Mr Neville in Egypt and Palestine after the Second World War.

There is often a grain of truth with theories such as these. John Cartland had seen service in and around the Blue Nile, that much is certain. As to whether there was a link with Mr Neville is unknown. It is possible – likely even - the two men, along with thousands of others, did serve in Egypt around the same period.

'They all died in mysterious circumstances and nobody has been brought to justice,' remarked Bamber's legal team. 'It is far too coincidental that over a period of 30 years all of these people linked to each other were murdered mysteriously.'

As with all Bamber's appeals to date this one also failed. If nothing else it illustrates the power of the secret service motif as a catch-all, a way to make the inexplicable explicable. In a world where random killings inspire fear is there not a certain comfort to be taken from organised killings, that however warped, there may at least be rudimentary 'logic' behind acts of murder? Of course, there might be a less exotic explanation for the spate of murders which occurred within the 'murder triangle' during these years: coincidence.

Drawn by its benevolent climate and rustic charm, Britons have been flocking to the South of France for decades, many of them elderly. To the opportunist such people might appear to be especially vulnerable 'soft targets.' In the cases presented it is true that some of the victims made choices which put them in potentially dangerous situations e.g. Drummond, Broderick and, though likely no fault of his own, John Cartland. For others they might have indeed been in the wrong place at the wrong time, victims of circumstance e.g. Lasseter, Prentice.

But it doesn't end there. As noted by The *Independent,* since the end of the 70s several more British nationals have met with violent ends on French soil – all of them unconnected to the security services – thus further weakening espionage or revenge theories espoused by some writers and lawyers. Moreover, when taken as a percentage of the sheer quantity of British residents and visitors to the area, numbers regarding death/murder become statistically insignificant.

The so-called 'murder triangle' is an area of France extremely popular with the British; it also happens to be home to an army of itinerant workers, drifters and chancers who eke out their livings on the back of the tourist trade. By the early

70s Marseille had become known as the heroin capital of the world. Working with contacts in Turkey and Munich the city's drug gangs ran a highly efficient racket which exported heroin worth £2 billion to the USA alone.[3] Balmy climate aside, the Cote d'Azur is in fact a place notorious for criminal activity, always has been.

Truth it is oft said is stranger than fiction. At times however it can be far less exciting to the point of being mundane.

25

Mythologies

After publication of *The Cartland File* in 1978, the BBC soon made an approach to its author: would he grant permission for a drama to be made of the events described in the book? Jeremy said yes – provided he could oversee the script. The BBC agreed and two years later had produced a one-hour film based upon the book.

Known in the trade as drama-doc, 'The Cartland Murder' would be the fifth instalment of a BBC series entitled *Escape* billed as 'Six celebrated bids for freedom, in dramatic reconstruction.' Other episodes featured reconstructions of Lord Lucan's escape from justice and Kim Philby's flight to Moscow. A few days before 'The Cartland Murder' aired Jeremy received a preview copy of the film. He was not pleased with the results and wasted no time communicating his reservations to the BBC. Whatever his concerns, they did not appear to be shared by certain TV critics:

'The French police and judicial system which gave him months of torment,' wrote James Murray in his preview for The *Daily Express,* 'emerge as unscrupulous, sinister manipulators who were determined to pin the killing on him despite the lack of evidence.' The theme of police malfeasance so apparent, it seems that the programme had faithfully reproduced *The Cartland File*'s major theme.

And so, at 9pm on a Friday evening in October 1980, some 3 million viewers tuned into to episode five of *Escape*. What they witnessed by all accounts was an accurate portrayal of events as described in the film's original source. Although the copy of the programme lodged with the British Film Institute has disappeared, a flavour of its approach can still be gleaned from Richard Deacon's book of the series also entitled *Escape!.*

Deacon's account is basically a precis of Jeremy's book. As such its content is predictable enough. Added to this partisan base must be the author's own bias which shines through on virtually every page. For example, when discussing the issue of Jeremy's wounds, he has this to say about the police (and Prof Cameron's) theory that they were in fact self-inflicted: 'Few sane and well-balanced people would have inflicted such injuries on themselves even to cover up their own crime, and Jeremy was certainly perfectly sane.' He goes on to observe that, 'There was no obvious motive for Jeremy to have killed his father.'[1] Later on in his essay, Deacon states that Jeremy's claim that thieves had broken into the left-hand front door of the Hillman were 'upheld by Madame Arlette Blasco.'

As the text continues gaps in Deacon's knowledge become ever more apparent though the anecdote concerning Rossetti *is* included along with that report of a 'large black Citroen.' However, regarding speculation that the Cartlands had argued over a woman, the author confidently asserts that 'no evidence was produced to support the allegation.' Based on a single source - *The Cartland* File - the essay marches boldly on. Sometimes embellishments creep in absent even from the original source. So, when dismissing the case, Delmas, the reader learns, had apparently 'beamed down at Jeremy Cartland.'

If the text of *Escape!* is anything to judge by, Jeremy could have few if any problems with its small screen realisation. Credulous is the word that springs most readily to mind yet the former teacher seemed far from satisfied. In fact, he was sufficiently aggrieved to seek legal advice. In April 1983 the case duly reached the High Court.

Mr Charles Gray told the court that upon watching the film his client had been 'appalled.' Its content he went on to argue had been defamatory, that is to say had implied that Jeremy might have indeed murdered his father. Despite the fact it had been originally used by the DPP and stood as the official judgement, Gray also objected to the film's use of the phrase 'insufficient evidence' and all it implied. Counsel for the BBC, David Eady QC, denied the accusations countering that even if the film's language could have been termed defamatory it was true in substance and fact. 'The fundamental assumption of the film,' stressed Eady, 'is of his (Cartland's) innocence.' Thereafter, he reminded the court that the film's content had been closely based on the text of *The Cartland File*.

In his evidence, Jeremy alleged the BBC had never sent him the final script of the programme as agreed and thus had duped him. He then complained that John Rowe – the actor playing himself – 'looked as if he had something to hide.' Overall, the production implied, he argued, that he might have indeed killed his father. Hardly surprising on the morning after the broadcast he had received abusive phone calls, or so he claimed. One anonymous caller had called him a 'murderer.'

Jeremy won the case with an 11-1 majority verdict. The court awarded him £50,000 in damages, equivalent to £150,000 in 2021. He was, he declared, relieved but would have preferred that the BBC had apologised earlier thereby avoiding the need for litigation.

The irony – seemingly lost on the prosecution and it seems the jury too – is the fact that 'The Cartland Murder' is indeed wholly based on *The Cartland File*; this much is clear from reading Deacon's essay in *Escape!* Events are exactly as those depicted in the book - from midnight prowlers, Jeremy being knocked out, right through to police intimidation and incompetency. There is not even the merest whiff of scepticism evident. Its tone is always one of strong pro-Jeremy advocacy – the basis of the BBC defence. Hence, when the jury sat down to watch a private screening of the film what they in fact observed would have been a condensed version of *The Cartland File.* Notwithstanding, the jury decided that the same film implied Jeremy might have been guilty.

As the years went by the Cartland case would sometimes find its way into the pages of various books on crime and unsolved murder cases. With the exception of Dirk Kirby's *Scotland Yard's Murder Squad* (2020) the presentation was and it seems always will be similar to that of *Escape!* Jeremy had suffered a great injustice at the hands of French police.

Published in 1987, *Unsolved Murders and Mysteries* is an anthology of essays contributed by various crime writers and experts. As with *Escape!* the tone of the essay dealing with the Cartland affair is wholly credulous, evident in its title: 'The ordeal of Jeremy Cartland.' All that publicity wherein Jeremy bitterly complained about his treatment at the hands of the French police had certainly paid off – handsomely so. For in some ways the murder of John Cartland, apparent here and elsewhere, has become almost an adjunct to the real story: the mistreatment of Jeremy and a miscarriage of justice. The Cartland narrative has been established, one acceptable to authors and writers who forever recycle its elements until it attains an almost mythological status.

What marks 'The Ordeal of Jeremy Cartland' out from similar accounts is its sheer number of errors, an indictment of how facts can be lost and how false narratives can so easily replace them. A few samples: upon hearing the prowlers the author writes that Jeremy 'sat upright and saw that his father was not in the caravan.' When describing the moment M. Delaude noticed the flames, he asserts that the press attaché stopped his car and ran over to the flames where he: 'saw a sight out of a nightmare: a young man lay slumped near the caravan, blood oozing from stab wounds.' It continues: 'Beside him (Mr Cartland) lay the murder weapon: a bloodstained axe' swiftly followed with, 'Examination of the dead man revealed that he had put up a fierce fight for his life.' And so forth.[2]

To put the icing on an especially erratic account, the essay ends with its author posing yet more questions: 'Who was driving the black Citroen? And who were the two men seen near the Cartland's caravan?'[3]

Do facts matter? As with the author's previous book *Unnatural Death, Unsolved Murders and Mysteries* sold in substantial numbers upon publication. Not many readers would have known about the true facts of the Cartland case, and so the myth further cements itself. In his preview of *Escape!* a reviewer for The *Times* remarked that, 'Mr Cartland's story is a remarkable one, a puzzle from which some vital pieces have permanently gone missing.' Or perhaps they had been there all the time just waiting to be discovered.

As for Jeremy himself, he spent the rest of his days in Preston, an urban rectangle bordered by Preston Park on its east side and Hove Green and Brighton Open Air Theatre to the west. Those media reports that did mention him in later years referred to him as a writer and it seems he may have written novels under a pseudonym though this is unverified. But his true vocation was poetry. Along with like-minded people he devoted much energy to projects such as Salatticum Poets, a poetry performance group he formed with John Carder Bush, brother of the singer Kate and mind map creator Tony Buzan. A single slim, rare volume of their work survives, *Riding Lights*.

Perhaps Jeremy's best-known poem, included in several anthologies, was 'The Frog Prince,' of which the following is a portion:

> I remember the agony in each tissue:
> the ripping of webs, the rasp of eyelids,
> choking on a tightening pharynx.
> Blood howled through throbbing muscles,
> bones scored cramps into the limbs,
> a burning wind seared my skin to dryness.

The years went by. What became of the man whose face and name had been, for a brief moment, rarely off the front page of the papers? Nothing *that* extraordinary.

Occasionally he might be found at Brighton racecourse, a ten-minute drive from the heart of Preston. Journalists at the *Brighton Argus* might sometimes mention his attendance at this function or that. One couple remember meeting him at an art show where a painting of 11 Powis Square was among the works exhibited and with whom he politely chatted in that softly spoken voice of his. With their mix of sport and socialising there were always the Late Niter events to look forward to and the camaraderie of Hove RUFC to be enjoyed. As far as the spotlight was concerned, his time had come to an end. Like his father before him, Jeremy never did attain the acclaim his talents might otherwise have warranted. Had it not been for events on that long ago night, life could have turned out very differently.

In later life he organised and ran book groups from a local community centre where attendees would discuss literary works, some of them local to the area such as Graham Greene's *Brighton Rock*. As he shared his enthusiasm for literature, he could once more have been the same sartorially elegant, hip young teacher who had taught at the Downs school all those years ago, whose pet dog Lara would faithfully sit in her master's classroom and one of whose favourite pupils had been Hugo Weaving, the actor who would go on to star in *Lord of the Rings* and *The Matrix*.

Charming and personable, by all accounts he was a popular and respected member of the community. Indeed, he seems to have devoted much of his time and energy to helping others. *That* Jeremy, the one who had set off for France on a cold, dark March evening in 1973 might have been an altogether different person.

In a portrait which exhibits more than just a superficial understanding of its subject, one anonymous social media contributor visualises him during this period of his life in the following way:

'As Jeremy Cartland crosses the road from Regency Square and makes his way down to the beach, crunching pebbles underfoot and looking up at the murmation of starlings, evening joggers and children's chatter, one wonders what secrets lay beneath that calm, distinguished exterior as he takes care not to soil his blue pinstripe suit and black brogues, maybe a little worse for wear but a staple of his wardrobe, as he gains inspiration for his latest poetry anthology.'

Not only does this brief sketch appear to exhibit intimate knowledge of the milieu in which Jeremy lived, with its theme of the poet seeking inspiration it presents a suitably romantic picture of its subject. Yet even here, it's the hint of a disquiet soul that abides.

When Jeremy died suddenly in June 2014 thoughts of that long ago murder had been all but forgotten. Time as well as people had moved on since that merry-go-round of high drama in the spring and summer of '73. One paper did however remember him.

'A Falstaffian figure in many ways,' so read the obituary notice in The *Times*, 'he was often to be seen with a flagon of "large" beer in hand, holding court among his followers and admirers.'[4] Indeed, the nearby Chimney House pub was a favourite haunt. Even if tinged with a touch of romantic licence, the portrayal of a gregarious, larger-than-life character may be close enough to the truth and one can't help but feel it captures at least one aspect of the man – a yearning perhaps for recognition as well as companionship. 'Wherever the poet Jeremy Cartland appeared,' the notice continues in the same vein, 'he seemed to become involved in a fascinating or outrageous situation from which only his extreme ingenuity could extricate him.'

And so are legends born. Jeremy Cartland spent the last years of his life amid the whitewashed villas of Prestonville, safe and secure living an unremarkable life in middle class suburbia, but whether fully at peace with himself or not, it is impossible to say.

Postscript: Imagining a murder

It is not uncommon for the biographer to warm to his or her subject even among those who chronicle the lives of the unloved or controversial. Hence, I am able to freely admit that during the course of writing this book I have become rather attached to Jeremy, though I never met him, nor never shall. We'd have got on rather well, he and me I like to think: literature, writing, French culture and cinema, teaching (TEFL), sport, dogs and not forgetting ale, our venn diagrams cross continually. Heck, I even admire that waspish humour that some might misread or fail to appreciate.

Yet despite this awakened sense of empathy, any personal feelings must be put aside. This is because having come this far it seems appropriate to weigh up the evidence and perhaps even reach some conclusions, if only tentatively. Thus, I have no hesitation in declaring Jeremy as one of three actors possibly culpable in the murder of his father. The other two candidates can therefore only be:

- Political assassins seeking redress in relation to the Mr Cartland's wartime or cold war activities

- Opportunist thieves who just so happened to spot the British-registered caravan/car parked off the main highway

Which of these three actors committed the crime, which had the means, motive and opportunity? With the aid of what clues remain – witness testimonies, maps, crime scene reports etc. – it is possible to reconstruct some, if not all, of the events of that tragic day. Expect more questions than answers.

Finally, an opportunity presents to exorcise the demons that haunted a ten-year-old's dreams all those years ago in the shape of a caravan that burned ferociously in the forest of the night for reasons unfathomable - to do so by imagining a murder long forgotten which occurred once upon a moonlit Provence night . . .

The first image is impressionistic: a father and son towing their newly acquired caravan along a dusky highway, windows open, the Mistral fanning their faces, cooling the car's hot interior. Sitting in the passenger seat, his shirtless torso pressing into the sticky seat, John Cartland - man of a thousand stories. Next to him Jeremy driving, calm, impassive. That's how it always starts for me, father and son heading out of northern Spain into south-west France on a dusky, somnolent afternoon.

If police theories were correct, one of these two men had something dreadful in mind, conjecture that leads to an almost unthinkable supposition: the entire escapade might have been planned. By the time the travellers arrived at *Jas de Dane* that windy day the charade would have therefore been edging inexorably towards a final, bloody crescendo. Is that what happened? From Brighton to La Barben, had this whole unsavoury affair been orchestrated?

But what if Krikorian, Gonzalves *et al* had been wrong? After all, John Cartland was a man with a somewhat colourful past. From covert activities with British intelligence through sudden wealth acquired in mysterious and rather fortuitous circumstances, the victim had a background for which the term 'murky' could have been invented.

If Cartland's death had indeed been an assassination, revenge of a nefarious, underground organisation still active in 1970s France, it's just possible the British teachers were the victims of a complex revenge plot. A vehicle must have been shadowing the British teachers for several days - presumably since their departure from the Lyons' home in Denia though neither of the Hillman's occupants appear to have noticed its presence. It must certainly have been right behind the British visitors as they detoured through the village of Pélissanne before stopping at the rocky clearing on the edge of La Barben. Had not a pair of illicit lovers observed a 'large black Citroen' do just that – follow the Cartlands into *Jas de Dane*? The assassins must have then waited for nightfall. Were these the individuals to whom John Cartland supposedly chatted upon arrival at the clearing – the same individuals who would butcher him later that night?

So many questions about that day remain unresolved; but one thing is certain: John Cartland was not a happy man that afternoon. As far as he'd been concerned, he should have been headed southwards down to Marseille as arranged with Mont-

Reynaud. Jeremy though had other ideas. He wanted to head easterly, to Jouques. Tension, misunderstanding, it probably happened somewhere along the Arles to Pélissanne road, the moment the truce between these two complex characters began to unravel, the moment hostilities once again resumed between an estranged father and son.

Wherever it occurred, by the time the travellers rolled up onto the forecourt of the Total garage the atmosphere inside the car had deteriorated enough for the pump attendant to notice. Bad karma exuded from the Hillman Avenger. Augusta Chauvet felt and saw it.

Pitching his new caravan in Jouques was not at all what Cartland senior had in mind. What had Jeremy said about this strip of land in *The Cartland File*? That it was: 'not a place at which we were ever likely to stay. The caravan could easily fall prey to vandalism once it was left unattended there.'[1] And yet there he was proposing they pitch up at this same village! John Cartland would not have been impressed. Not the sort of man to be thwarted, I sense he would have made his feelings plain. How dare Jeremy take it upon himself to change their plans![2] Always fragile, the truce which had held since departing Brighton had indeed finally broken down with both parties now feeling themselves aggrieved.

As well as angered Cartland senior must have been dismayed at this sudden nosedive in relations between himself and Jeremy. He had, after all, allegedly proposed the trip with reconciliation in mind. Spending time abroad with his only son was supposed to recapture the easy mood of similar voyages when the teenage Jeremy had happily accompanied his father to the Manzargues district of Marseille where Cartland senior kept a caravan in the early 1960s. The invitation had come out of the blue and no doubt Jeremy had been surprised by his father's suggestion. A trip to the continent, just the two of them camping out like old times? He accepted. Perhaps it had been John Cartland's turn to be surprised.

Back on that windy garage forecourt all was not well inside the Hillman. Transaction complete, Chauvet had been expecting the British customers to drive off, but instead car and caravan remained stationary for several minutes. I imagine a heated discussion taking place. I'm certain Mr Cartland was asking - instructing his son - to head back to the junction they had left just minutes earlier which would deliver them onto the A7 route south. It was only 5.30 pm. They could be in Marseille within an hour. But Jeremy was adamant: he wanted to press on to Jouques, also an hour away. Either way the men would be sleeping in the trailer that night. Diverting down to Marseille would therefore have served no useful purpose – at least from Jeremy's viewpoint.

The meeting with Mont-Reynaud and the proposal to pitch the caravan at Marseille – these details are not mentioned once by Jeremy in any of his police statements or indeed in any part of *The Cartland File.* As omissions go it must be said these seem to be especially glaring ones. Perhaps he thought them details not worth mentioning. Maybe so, but the way Jeremy tells it the reader could be forgiven for thinking the Cartlands *had always intended pitching up at Jouques.*

Observed by Chauvet, car and caravan suddenly darted out into the road. An oncoming car swerved. It was getting pretty tense inside the Hillman. What, with the irascibility of Mr Cartland and Jeremy silently brooding, the atmosphere in the car thereafter can't have been pleasant.

Jeremy would later state that he and his father had been lost. This might explain the frosty atmosphere between the two men witnessed by the pump attendant; tempers can fray in stressful situations and few things are quite as stressful as getting lost in a foreign country. And yet . . . Aix-en-Provence and its environs familiar to both men but especially the older of the two, the chances of Mr Cartland getting lost would have been remote. And that's not all. Why does Jeremy tell readers of *The Cartland File* that his father had been checking maps as the pair of them had left the Total garage? That's a scenario I struggle with. Sure, maps would have been required for the Spanish leg of the trip. But when it came to travelling east to Jouques, the men knew *exactly* where they were going. Far from being lost, they were headed in precisely the right direction. When Jeremy testified he and his father had been 'total strangers' in the area it can only have been a memory lapse; in all probability the two men had oft travelled along this very stretch of the RN 572, knew the locality, felt at home amongst its ancient villages and olive groves.

Jas de Dane would have now only been a couple of kilometres away. John Cartland could do little else but accept the situation much as it angered him. When Jeremy suddenly pulled off the road at La Barben, the older man must have been rather confused and perhaps even hopeful: maybe they weren't going to Jouques after all.

Despite what the Marseille police might have thought, travellers did camp out on this patch of ground. Perhaps the British teaching duo had themselves seen a caravan pitched up one evening as they had driven past coming from or going to Jouques. Or perhaps Cartland junior assumed there would be plenty of places to pitch up for the night off this somewhat nondescript road. Either way, if the premeditation theory is accepted, for one of the two British travellers the RN 572 had always been the ultimate destination, the end of the road.

At the very least Mr Cartland must have been puzzled. Why

had his son taken it upon himself to change their schedule and with it sour the trip? Just one week earlier he'd left Powis Square in an optimistic frame of mind. If that tenacious duo of French police commissioners Krikorian and Gonzalves had been correct, aside from the conical cypress trees, olive fields and the essence of rosemary, thyme and pine there had been something else lingering in the air throughout the trip, and especially on that Provencal afternoon of sunlit mellowness: resentment, bitterness.

Upon arrival at *Jas de Dane* the tension between the two men must have been palpable. John Cartland had been brought to this place expressly against his wishes. Did he insist they turn back for Marseille in the morning? Rather than to preserve Jeremy's items in the Hillman as the police theorised, might this explain why the Cartlands turned car and caravan through 180 degrees? Was it a gesture of appeasement to temporarily placate a furious father? The caravan was in fact going nowhere, neither to Jouques nor Marseille. If the police theory is true, it had reached its final destination.

It is true that for French and later British investigators the murder of John Cartland only ever had but one explanation: patricide. Similarly, theories revolving around assassins and thieves were dismissed as highly improbable if not wholly unfeasible. Why might that have been? Well, it also true that had assassins or thieves committed the crime, they dissolved into the night air as quickly and as unobtrusively as they had emerged. Even the police sniffer dog failed to pick up a trail. Given this reality, it's easy to see why French police honed in on the strapping English poet. He was there.

Oh yes, Krikorian and Gonzalves thought they knew what had happened between the hours of 1900 and midnight at the crime location that crisp, moonlit night. Furthermore, this pair of high-flyers never did receive satisfactory answers to their long list of anomalies. Take the issue of weapons.

For the murder detective tying a suspect to the weapons used in a crime is a crucial aspect of their trade. Axe, concrete slab and knife, here were a set of implements nothing if not diverse. This somewhat eclectic range of weapons duly alerted investigators to the possibility of design. Whoever had committed this crime, swapping between concrete, axe and knife during what had been a frenzied attack, had clearly planned their moves in advance. But why? With a blade measuring some 15 inches the kitchen knife, wrought from sharp and deadly steel, would have easily taken care of the caravan's two occupants – and anyone else who had the misfortune to cross its path. If interchanging weapons had been done to prevent cross contamination – as seemed likely – detectives naturally wondered why random killers would take such precautions. What did it matter to *them*?

So, from where did these items originate? Police were faced with yet more conundrums: the provenance of the axe was clear enough while the concrete slab presumably had been sourced from the clearing, but what of the pillow case - where had it come from? The Cartland's caravan? It seemed a reasonable enough hypothesis. If, like the pillow case, the inclusion of the axe was some kind of double-bluff intended to confuse or even tease, this was audacity of a rare and special type.

On top of all this was the provenance of the French knife used in the assault. Could it have come from the Lyons' kitchen? Links to Jeremy seemed obvious, almost *too* obvious. After all, what kind of criminal uses weapons bearing their own signature? An inexperienced one certainly. Or perhaps one whose confidence in themselves far outstrips their actual capabilities, an individual brimful of chutzpah who harbours nothing but contempt for law enforcement agents?

Ah yes, the axe. If detectives were right and this fearsome implement had been brought to France for a purpose other than protection, likely it was Jeremy who, if anyone, had used a pretext in order to bring it along – a reversal of how events unfold in *The Cartland File.* Chillingly, this fits rather neatly with the pre-meditation hypothesis. Conceivably, Cartland senior might never have known there was an axe in the boot of the Avenger. Detectives concluded that he hadn't been afraid of going to France; he had no reason to be. Besides, he wasn't the one planning to camp out in rural isolation. As far as the older Cartland knew, the caravan would be pitched up in Marseille that Sunday evening. The next day he and Jeremy would be in San Remo, the rest of their nights spent in hotels.

Amid the speculation one aspect does seem undeniable and that is the needle between father and son leading up to the trip and on the day of the murder itself. Yes, but homicide is a different matter altogether. Ok, John and Jerry might have had their differences that day, but *murder* . . .

Detectives always maintained at some point during the evening relations between the caravanners worsened. If so, shortly after their arrival at *Jas de Dane* it is easy to imagine this disgruntled father and son sitting down to eat what must have been a very awkward dinner. Bad blood simmering, they would then have got ready for bed. It can't have been easy, not within the cramped confines of the Sprite. Police assumed a drunken brawl had broken out. Forensic tests though would later reveal next to no alcohol in the victim's blood.

Whatever sparked it, police were certain that a little while later the friction boiled over into physical confrontation. In this scenario the conversation might well have turned to Mrs

L, quite possibly becoming heated. Mr Cartland couldn't have realised it, but the affair he had played a role in bringing to an end and which he thought had ceased for good in January, was still going on. Jeremy had been serious about the petite headmaster's wife. She was no passing fancy. At one point she'd even brought her two children to stay with Jeremy in Brighton before returning once more to her husband in Somerset.

Mr Cartland would have been no pushover. In his youth he had boxed for Oxford and at that moment in time had been an angry man. The confrontation must have spilled outside the caravan, father and son brawling on the stone-ridden ground a couple of moonlit silhouettes. The commotion alerted farmer Caire's dogs. Sensing peril, they started to yap.

Both men may have ended up with cuts and grazes. No quarter would had been given. Months, possibly years of rage could have been unleashed in those few minutes. I imagine Cartland, shaken and a little bloodied, returning into the caravan to seek a handkerchief. As was his habit, shortly afterwards he must have decided he needed the toilet and perhaps he took a toilet roll out to the little thicket which lay directly opposite the caravan door, just six metres away.

French detectives never wavered from their *faire des boissons* theory. Circumstantial evidence indeed points only one way: to a surprise attack. Investigators hypothesised that Jeremy must have been biding his time, lying awake on his bunk, one eye half-cocked. If their hypothesis is correct, he must have calculated his father would leave the caravan at some point to make a final toilet visit.

That's one scenario. There are others: had the perpetrator been prowlers or assassins, these nebulous figures must have been somewhere in the vicinity of the campsite, lurking in the shadows, fresh from assaulting Jeremy. Like his son moments before him, the older man stepped outside to confront he knew not what. There was no sign of Jeremy, just the silvery silence of a Provence night. Despite the rancour, the old man must surely have been concerned about the fate of his son who had seemingly disappeared into the wilderness. Now in imminent danger himself, it seems this knowledge did not prevent the businessman from ambling over to the thicket whereupon the prowlers caught up with him. Or perhaps he had run for his life, stumbling blindly over to the thicket.

Another scenario – the one favoured by the defence team - has Mr Cartland, axe in hand, engaging in combat with his assailants. Is this what disturbed Caire's dogs? The problem here is that the corpse exhibited no signs of having been dragged. Indeed, forensic analysis strongly indicated that the unfortunate man had almost certainly been first struck whilst standing in the thicket – likely as he prepared to urinate and/or defecate.

Whoever attacked Mr Cartland – thief, assassin or kin, he or she would have tiptoed over to the thicket, stealthily placing the concrete slab inside the pillow case as they picked their way through the stones and debris in their path. It was a cool, cloudless Provencal night. Decades after it occurred, I find myself reliving those final seconds over and over again in my imagination, as if the anger which fuelled the act still persists in a twilight place between then and now.

It seems John Cartland was just about to relieve himself when the blow was struck. Given the necessity for the assailant to launch the attack sideways to the target, the last earthly impression this brilliant and eccentric man may have had was of a face glimpsed in the moon's shadowy half-light – a face unknown or perhaps one he knew all too well, one contorted with hatred. In the instant it took for the concrete to crash into his skull, I wonder if everything made sense - this pointless journey to an isolated piece of waste ground. By then it was too late. Cartland dropped to the floor, his remarkable life at an end.

Investigators never wavered in their belief that Jeremy had committed the deed. If that was the case, the teacher-poet would have needed to cover his tracks. 'I would dearly love to know,' wrote Jeremy,[3] 'how the French investigators ... would have explained how, had I committed the deed as they chose to think, I could have done it without being covered in my father's blood.'[4]

To be fair, it wouldn't have been *that* difficult. I imagine a young man carefully removing his pyjamas and socks as he stands in the thicket, shivering in the bright moonlight, before he returns to the Sprite, barefoot and half-naked, to clean himself up. Having done this, I suppose next he would have changed into a pair of clean pyjamas and blue corded trousers before slipping into his desert boots. Then he would have been faced with a very urgent problem: how to dispose of these incriminating items, blood-stained pyjamas and possibly a pair of socks also soaked in blood.

Fire ...

Is that what happened? It seems plausible. I'd go further: it's a course of action that seems *logical*.

Had the deed been committed by assassins or prowlers, likely there would have been no need to torch the caravan. There would, however, have been plenty of other considerations: clothes and a getaway vehicle saturated in the victim's blood for starters. Further, these two (or more) perpetrators would have been absent from home at work around midnight – surely somebody must have seen or known something? Added to which, the case was about to explode across France. The ensuing publicity was massive. Virtually the whole of the country would have known who was doing what as the clocks struck midnight on Sunday, 18th March. So, just how did the perpetrators manage to avoid rousing suspicion? Police never received a single tip-off or information that could have led to the perpetrator(s). The guilty party melted into the moonlight, literally.

No doubt this is why police focused their attentions on Jeremy; it was much easier than explaining the movements of what appeared to be phantoms who, after killing Cartland, set the caravan alight before vanishing into thin air leaving not a single clue in their wake.

Dramatic and somehow unnecessary, the fire immediately alerted detectives that all was not how it might have appeared. It seemed a bizarre if not illogical way for nocturnal visitors to act, not least because a midnight inferno such as this would immediately draw attention to the crime scene. The conclusion seemed clear: it must have been set to conceal evidence.

Assuming that whoever had committed the murder had also set the fire, discovering how the blaze had started could only progress the murder enquiry. The most obvious assumption involved the jerrycan. Presumably, the prowlers had stumbled upon the container during the course of the night. Left carelessly outside the caravan, it had been an open invitation to create mischief, an *Alice in Wonderland* moment almost: *Drink Me*.

'Look, my dear fellow.' I can almost hear Paul Lombard's suave intonations in conference with his Viking client. 'What about if your father – in his haste to come to your rescue – what if he knocked over the paraffin heater? Could a fire have started that way?' The jerrycan made him uneasy. The hotshot lawyer knew from experience when and if something sounded implausible.

But my imagination is running away with itself! However it occurred, the fire did indeed destroy most if not all of the evidence. Almost all. How did blood – Jeremy's own blood - end up inside the teacher's desert boot? Now that *was* odd.

Recall what the teacher told police upon being woken that night: that he had put on shoes *without socks*. On a night of chaos and blurred memory, it does seem a rather irrelevant detail to remember. Was it somehow important? And if so, why? Although the implication draws me uncomfortably close to resolution, the probable reason cannot be ducked: in all the excitement, the killer, *wearing socks but no sboes,* had failed to notice he had nicked the sole of his foot on some object or other strewn across the rocky terrain. Back in the caravan, he exchanged old for new pyjamas. However, as he put on his desert boot, a few spots of blood transferred from the sole of his foot into the shoe.

Of course, all this is mere speculation, just one of several possible scenarios as is the last scene.

Stabbing oneself goes against every human instinct yet it is the only explanation police had for what occurred next. Only the insane could even contemplate such an act according to one commentator. Is this then the point at which the police hypothesis crumbles? Then it must also be the point where my imaginings ought also come to an end.

Before closing there are, however, a few final observations I would ask the reader to reflect upon, which may or may not help toward clarification or even closure.

In an affair with so many unanswered questions, arguably the most perplexing is the issue of why Jeremy never stood trial in France. Just as inexplicable – perhaps more so - and much to the disbelief of the French media, just a matter of days after the murder the police's 'witness no. 1' and against whom they held strong presumptions of guilt, flew back to the UK for rest and recuperation! If nothing else police would have appreciated the murder before them was no ordinary case, the young British teacher no ordinary suspect. From Benham and Edmonds through Lombard and Chiappe, team Cartland was a formidable prospect. As impressive as his list of supporters was, did the cool, phlegmatic Viking have someone else on his side with even greater influence than Vice Consuls as well as some of the finest legal minds available, an ally unseen?

Disappointingly, John Cartland is not mentioned in any of the many biographies of former British Prime Minister, Edward Heath. Were the two men friends then as rumours suggested? Or was this another red herring in a tale where fact and fiction interchange so often to render dizziness? Absent from the biographies, a single fleeting reference to Cartland is found in the politician's own 1998 biography: 'Meanwhile, I had to find another job,' writes Heath reflecting on his precarious situation prior to entering politics full-time just after the war. 'I sought, once again, the aid of John Cartland, head of the Oxford University Appointments Board, later tragically murdered in the south of France, to find me something which could be combined with politics.'[5]

Political pressure never was far away from the case. The Drummond affair resurrected at every possible juncture by a relentless media machine, the jitters of those higher up the judicial and political hierarchy soon cascaded down to those on the ground. Nor was this the only shadow looming over the authorities. In April 1972, a 15-year-old girl had been strangled to death in the town of Bruay-en-Artois. Based on the intimate conviction of the presiding judge, a local dignitary had been arrested and held in prison for several months before being released due to lack of evidence. The Bruay affair had caused a scandal. The entire French judicial system had been under intense scrutiny ever since. 'Handling of Murder Case Arouses Storm in France,' reported the *New York Times.'* Gonzalves, Krikorian and Delmas had in fact been walking on egg shells throughout the entire investigation.

That just leaves a few more unresolved issues, ends that will invariably remain loose and which I suppose provide a suitably enigmatic coda to this endeavour.

The first point concerns Mme Chauvet the pump attendant whose contribution did so much to unsettle Jeremy. He never could quite recall the location of that final petrol stop. In *The Cartland File* it is located 'somewhere near Salon.' In police statements the location is described variously as being 'a little after Salon' and 'a little before we arrived in Pélissanne.' I am left wondering why French police did not simply take their 'witness no. 1' to the place itself for verification purposes – perhaps they did.

But it's something else that sticks in my mind about this lady's observations, an apparent triviality. In her statement, Mme Chauvet mentions how it was the driver of the English vehicle who produced the money to pay for the petrol, passing it through the vehicle's window to his older companion who stood on the blustery forecourt. Something about that inconsequential observation rings true. But what? Eventually, I find it: in *The Cartland File* (p. 8) Jeremy makes the following observation upon checking out of the hotel in Toulouse on March 14th: 'I paid the bill (I kept all the money, traveller's cheques etc.)' Nikko Lyon confirmed that the younger Cartland did indeed hold the purse strings. Is it enough to place the Cartlands on the forecourt of the Total garage that afternoon?

Possibly. One thing though must be borne in mind and it is this: even if the caravan's curtains were yellow as appears to have been the case and as indicated by Mme Chauvet, Sprite Musketeer caravans of the era were invariably liveried in pale green, just as Jeremy said. The years having gone by, it is impossible to assess the reliability of this lady and that of her testimony. Green or pink, somehow that key fact regarding colour never did get established. Loose ends indeed.

Another outstanding issue concerns Professor Cameron's alleged remarks. Did he make those comments about his patient's character or not? When Jeremy consulted him, the doctor suspected the wounds presented to him may well have been self-inflicted. If that was so, the rest of his story was clearly a pack of lies. According to one source, Cameron *did make* those comments.[6] Made 'off the record' thereafter they somehow found their way to Interpol. Whichever way events occurred, it must have come as an awful shock for the professor to receive an urgent phone call from France asking him to effectively withdraw the comments, that Jeremy's freedom depended upon him doing so. Whatever the professor's private thoughts, the young teacher was his patient. If he had made the comments, I believe Cameron had no choice but to retract them such was the pressure he had been placed under.

Next, it's a comment from Paul Lombard that teases. Many decades after the extraordinary events in spring and summer of 1973 and with my work nearing completion, I am reading one of the Marseille master's many books chronicling his fascinating career. Within these pages I come across the following startling comment: 'I have been a professional liar since November 1952,' writes Lombard looking back on his long and illustrious career . . . How else can this statement be read if not as emanating from a man troubled by his conscience, an admission that he had knowingly colluded with those seeking to thwart truth and justice? He goes on: 'I hate lying, but like everyone else, I practice it. I like the truth, but it scares me.'[7] These revelations transport me back to his master stroke, that ingenious *partie civile* which so audaciously snatched his British client from out of police jaws.

Around the same time another mini revelation comes my way. Will they never stop occurring? Watching television one afternoon, a black and white programme airs entitled 'The Blazing Caravan.' It tells a story of a murder for financial gain. Having committed the deed and in order to conceal his crime, the perpetrator sets the victim's caravan on fire. Thereafter, he heads off to spend his ill-gotten gains in Brighton. Broadcast in 1954, it's part of a series called 'Scotland Yard.' If the young Jeremy had watched that programme along with millions of other British school children, the author of this book might not have been the only ten-year-old whose dreams were haunted by images of burning caravans.

It doesn't end there. Just as I am wrapping up, relieved to have reached the end of a long and arduous journey, I receive an e-mail with the subject line '*L'Affaire Cartland*.' I can hardly believe my eyes. It's from an individual who has contact with a third party who claims to have 'information about that night.' Attached is a scan of a letter in neat, quite legible hand-written French. The writer remembers driving past the crime scene on the night of the murder. This I did not expect! It continues:

> I saw a man walking fast on the side of the road, looking strange. He was wearing a white shirt, open, dark trousers,

> he was going towards Pélissanne, I was driving towards Saint Cannat. At the time I didn't tell anyone, because normally I should have been at work (I worked from 9pm to 5am). I have always felt remorse for not having testified, you are giving me the opportunity to make amends.

It was around midnight that he saw this individual, continues the writer, adding that he 'looked worried.' Judging the veracity of this account is nigh on impossible: what happened to the second attacker? Why, having just committed murder, would the perpetrator walk along a main highway? As ever with this case, the anomalies keep on coming and the enigma, well, it just keeps on growing.

All of which leaves the question of who committed the murder tantalisingly out of reach. Ultimately, the identity of John Basil Cartland's killer shall never be known. With the passing of time the case has faded away. There it now rests on a shelf, gathering dust, neither a cold case ripe for re-investigation nor one which resulted in a conviction. What else is there to say?

It is Jeremy Cartland himself who, in that tale of his entitled *The Cartland File*, sums up better than anyone the sense of emptiness which surely follows from such blatant injustice. 'What is left?' rhetorically asks a dispirited author at the end of his tract: 'The unalterable facts are that my father is dead, and that whoever did it is free.'

Bibliography

Bianchini, R.L. (2005) 13 Mystères de la Côte: Fayard.

Buckmaster, M. (2014) They Fought alone: The True Story of SOE's Agents in Wartime France: The Story of British Agents in France: Biteback.

Canning, J. (2003) Unnatural Death and Unsolved Murders and Mysteries: Time Warner.

Cartland, J. (1978) The Cartland File: Linkline.

Deacon, R. (1980) Escape! BBC.

Ferguson, J. (2008) The Vitamin Murders: Who Killed Healthy Eating in Britain? Granta Books.

Heath, E. (1998) The Course of My Life: Hodder & Stoughton.

Hutchinson, G. (1970) Edward Heath: A Personal and Political Biography: Prentice Hall Press.

Innocenzi, P-C (1973) L'Énigme de Pélissanne: J'ai Lu.

Kirby, D. (2020) Scotland Yard's Murder Squad: Pen and Sword True Crime.

Laborde, J. (1974) The Dominic Affair: Collins (trans Waldman, M)

Lombard, P. (1977) Mon Intime Conviction: Robert Laffont.

Lombard, P. (1997) Ma Vérité sur le Mensonge: Plon.

Wilson, D. (2020) Signs of Murder: A small town in Scotland, a miscarriage of justice and the search for the truth: Sphere.

Notes

1: In the forest of the night

[1] The distance from the farm to the concrete pylon near to which the Cartlands had camped being approximately 440 metres, the farmer's judgement was sound.

[2] Police and media reports usually refer to 'Jas de Dames' and other variations. However, according to contemporary ordnance survey maps the area is indeed called *Jas de Dane*. In Provencal dialect this approximates to 'sheepfold of Monsieur Dane.'

2: Daybreak

[1] Jeremy would later dispute that he had given Brighton as his birthplace citing the fact that he, like his father, had been actually born in London.

3: Jeremy's tale

[1] Equivalent to just over £3,000 in 2021.

[2] The following events are based on Jeremy's various police statements as well as *The Cartland File* - his 1978 account of the affair.

[3] Now the site of El Farallo restaurant, Carrer Fenix.

4: Manic Monday

[1] In *The Cartland File* Jeremy devotes a whole chapter to a critique of the report. What, if any value investigators would later attach to this report by local police is not known.

[2] Madame Chauvet's official statement would be taken the following day.

[3] Given his receding hairline Jeremy would later call into question this recollection of 'long hair.' However, as contemporary images reveal, forehead apart, his hair was in fact quite voluminous at the side and back of the head.

[4] Of course, what exactly Mr Cartland meant by 'far' is not known.

[5] This detail does not appear in any of Jeremy's police statements, but does appear in *The Cartland File*.

[6] In his police statement of 28th March Jeremy states that the Cartlands 'arrived in Pélissanne.' However, it appears that when he says 'Pélissanne' he means in fact La Barben the actual location of *Jas de Dane.* This small commune lies a mile or so east of its larger neighbour. Indeed, Jeremy does not mention La Barben by name in any statement, but refers instead to Pélissanne e.g.

To be precise it was not I who was tired but my father, that is what made me decide to stop at Pélissanne rather than Jouques.

Although it might seem that Jeremy is acknowledging he and his father did indeed drive through Pélissanne and by implication did refuel at the Total garage, this is not necessarily the case.

[7] With a population of about 100,000 at the time, driving through the city on a Sunday afternoon would surely not have presented too many problems even for a touring caravan.

[8] In order to avoid Aix, the most obvious place would have been junctions located around the town of Célony, all of which would have led to the N 296 and on to Jouques.

5: 'With savage fury'

[1] The Habitat Co-operative had been founded in 1965 by a certain Jacques Nahmans with just 700 francs capital. The company constructed properties on behalf of small investors. Six years later, after defrauding these same investors on a massive scale, Nahmans was living the life of a multi-millionaire. He was jailed in 1972. The

investigation by Krikorian's team also exposed corruption on a massive scale involving senior police and political figures.

[2] *Signs of Murder*, p. 264.

[3] *The Cartland File*, p. 26.

7: Worshipper of the Provence sun

[1] Not quite everybody. The Swiss-Italian artist and writer Franco Beltrametti, later married to Cartland's former stepdaughter Judith and through whose prism his view was presumably coloured, refers to him somewhat dismissively as, 'that uptight Englishman killed in his trailer in southern France.'

[2] A certain J B F Cartland of the Worcestershire Regiment served as both Captain and Major in the 1914-18 war.

[3] Born Leila Nash in 1916, John Cartland became Ms Hirschfield's third of four husbands. Upon their marriage he became step-father to his wife's two daughters, Judith (b. 1942) and Elizabeth (b. 1947) from her first marriage to a Jacob Danciger.

[4] Cartland was not an actual professor of course. The title stuck no doubt because of mistranslation i.e. the French media referred to him as a 'professeur' – a much more generalised word for 'teacher' than its English counterpart.

[5] Equivalent to about £4,400 in 2020.

[6] Cartland sold his share to the school's then headmaster, a Mr Alexander, whose son who would go on to marry Cartland's first wife Joan.

8: The gangbuster

[1] The young British couple had been hitch-hiking back from a holiday on the Costa Brava when they were picked up by two gypsies just outside Toulouse at around midnight on the evening of 29 August 1972. The gypsies had been

waiting at the road with the intention of kidnapping unwary hitch-hikers.

[2] The dirt track has since disappeared – one of many topographical changed to have occurred in the area in the succeeding decades.

[3] It was only after having performed the manoeuvre that Mr Cartland was allegedly told by strangers that he was on the wrong road. Had the Cartlands turned around after this meeting, rather than immediately upon their arrival at *Jas de Dane*, the manoeuvre would have made more sense.

9: Under pressure

[1] Such is Olivia's devotion to her brother in *Twelfth Night*, the lovesick Duke Orsino is moved to observe: 'She that hath a heart of that fine frame/To pay this debt of love but to a brother.' Orsino is amazed that a sister could be so attached to a mere brother that she has vowed to spend the rest of her life mourning his loss.

[2] 'At no time did he tell me had received a blow on the left side of the jaw,' so testified Dr Louvard who examined Jeremy at Salon hospital. 'And in particular he did not complain of pain in the lower left jaw.' (Official report of interview with Jean Louvard, 20th April 1973.)

10: Rendezvous a Marseille

[1] The equivalent of approximately £16,000 in 2020. The average UK house price in 1973 was £9,942.

[2] *Mon Intime Conviction*, p. 176.

[3] The French state carrying out the execution of a British subject would have been of course unimaginable. Nonetheless, the death penalty was a theoretical possibility.

11: When the inspectors called

[1] *The Cartland File*, p. 79.

[2] Negotiations might also have involved Paris and even London.

12: Attack, the best form of defence

[1] Commenting on Heath's complete lack of journalistic skills or qualifications prior to landing the job at *Church Times* i.e. his unsuitability for the role - in his book, *Edward Heath: A Personal and Political Biography*, Hutchinson calls the future Prime Minister's engagement as the paper's editor a 'bizarre appointment,' pp. 59-60.

[2] *The Cartland File,* p. 90.

[3] The reason why the report did not surface is almost certainly due to Cameron's conclusions not helping, but quite possibly implicating the same client who had commissioned him in the first place. In *Scotland Yard's Murder Squad* Dick Kirby confirms as much. Having assessed Jeremy's wounds (i.e. those requiring suture) the pathologist came to the conclusion the wounds could indeed have been self-inflicted. However, due to the rules governing doctor-patient confidentiality he only disclosed this information once the case had been dismissed.

[4] And yet the police arrived at the scene at 1.30 am, finished searching at 5am, posted guards throughout the night and resumed the search of the murder location at 9am. It is not exactly clear then what, if any opportunity, the public had to contaminate the site.

[5] In Innocenzi's book *L'Énigme de Pélissanne,* the author relates how, upon hearing this news, a colleague immediately claimed to know the identity of the murderer: a chimpanzee from the nearby La Barben zoo!

13: Intimate convictions

[1] Statement by Arlette Blasco, 23 March 1973.

[2] *The Cartland File*, p. 94.

[3] Statement by Jeremy Cartland at Palais de Justice, Aix-en-Provence, 28 March 1973.

[4] *The Cartland File*, p. 106.

[5] The following witness testimonies demonstrate the difficulty placing the original position of car and caravan:

> *There was an English car near the caravan, about two metres away. It was unhitched, the front pointing towards the road.* (Chambonnet)
>
> *An English car was 2 or 3 metres from the caravan, pointing towards the road.* (Lorenzo)
>
> *The tow bar was pointing towards the way into the patch of waste ground, that is to say towards the road in the direction of Pélissanne.* (Delaude)

In Jeremy's sketch car and caravan are lined up behind one another parallel with, rather than pointing towards the road. Meanwhile, in the police sketch the Hillman is also parallel with the road while the caravan lies behind, almost perpendicular to it. Of the two sketches, Jeremy's appears closest to the truth though neither one is 100% accurate.

[6] *The Cartland File*, p. 20.

[7] Ibid. p. 108.

[8] In 1988 Relton would be sentenced to 12 years imprisonment for his involvement with the Brinks-MAT robbery of 1983 in which £26 million was stolen from a facility close to Heathrow airport.

14: A dish best served exceedingly cold?

[1] In what is the definitive book on the case, *L'Affaire Dominici* (1972) Jean Laborde presents a cast iron case

that the right man was indeed convicted of the murders i.e. Gaston Dominici.

[2] 'Cartland killing said to be linked to Resistance,' The *Guardian*, 29 March 1973.

[3] Ms. Marshall is still invariably referred to as 'Jane' and occasionally 'June' and erroneously linked to Drummond by various writers and journalists.

[4] *The Cartland File*, p. 123.

15: She said, he said

[1] Madame and Jeanine Sobansky.

[2] There was another explanation: perhaps the Blascos had not arrived until after Delaude's departure to Salon hospital in which case a red car could have parked up in the meantime. However, the Blascos testified to watching two men attempting to push the Hillman forwards. Delaude did not escort Jeremy to Salon hospital until after this event i.e. after the Beaucaire youths had obtained the Hillman's keys from Jeremy having not succeeded in moving the vehicle manually. Therefore, Delaude's grey 2CV must have been parked next to the white 4L while the Blascos were observing events.

[3] With the odds stacked against him, it seems odd that Jeremy would continue to insist the left front door had been unlocked. Presumably this is because he had already committed himself to the story as early as (or earlier than) the time of his first statement given at Salon hospital. Was Jeremy's version therefore correct? In order to corroborate his prowler story, he would most certainly have ensured the left front door was unlocked before flagging down the witnesses. Perhaps then one of the witnesses had, as the defence would suggest, inadvertently locked the door during the ensuing drama.

[4] Thus, it appears that the Blascos arrived at the precise moment Delaude and Weltman had gone to retrieve the

keys from Jeremy. Although M. Blasco thought he had been at the scene for 5-7 minutes, given that Delaude and Weltman returned immediately with those keys, he had likely been present for a shorter time than he estimated.

[5] If it was Jeremy who retrieved the jerrycan it must have been pure opportunism. His window of opportunity had, after all, been very small – in the moments before the Beaucaire youths succeeded in moving the Hillman. This means that upon their arrival, Jeremy must have followed the youths at a safe distance over to the caravan. Presumably he'd been curious to see what would unfold – whether they would succeed in taming the fire. He must have seized his chance the moment Delaude discarded the container. If Jeremy had been responsible for retrieving the container, as well as lucky (no witness recalled seeing him near the car) he must have indeed been very quick. No doubt with this proviso in mind, Dick Kirby thinks a police officer had placed the container in the Hillman and then forgotten doing so. A plausible scenario but with one problem: the jerrycan was already in the car when the youths succeeded in moving the vehicle – a manoeuvre they executed well before the arrival of police. Of course, there could have been a much simpler explanation: there had been two – maybe more – jerrycans all along.

16: Munitions de Delmas

[1] Statement by Joan Elizabeth Cartland, Court of Appeal at Aix-en-Provence, 4th April 1973.

[2] *The Cartland File*, p. 132.

17: Showdown

[1] Brighton solicitor Frederick Scales testified that he – not the dead man's next of kin - had officially identified Mr Cartland's remains at the London Hospital on April *16th* in the presence of Professor Cameron and Det. Chief Super-

intendent Page. The error remained both uncorrected and unexplained.

[2] 'English Autopsy on the Body of Mr John Cartland by Professor Cameron,' Mortuary of the Institute of Pathology, The London Hospital, 24 April 1973.

[3] In his interview with Krikorian on Tuesday 20th March, Jeremy claimed he was asked if he had had a discussion with his father on the night of the murder, to which he had answered in the affirmative. He then claimed the translator told him the meaning of 'discussion' in French was closer to the English sense of 'argument.'

[4] Delaude claimed the next car to stop – that of the Sobansky's – was an 'undeniably red,' Renault 4L. Curiously, in his interview of 4 April, Jeremy would also state that the colour of the Sobansky car was red. The Sobansky car was in fact pale blue.

[5] *Mon Intime Conviction*, p. 205.

[6] *The Cartland File*, p.143.

18: The colour pink

[1] 'Trial by Terror,' The *Daily Express*, 27th April 1973.

[2] 'The Enigmatic Jeremy Cartland,' *Paris Match*, 21st April 1973.

[3] Interview with Renee Ripert, 2nd May 1973.

[4] *The Cartland File,* p. 36.

[5] If Gonzalves did establish the caravan's colour, the information will no doubt be contained in the case notes located at the National Archive in Kew. Still, it seems odd that this crucial information never found its way into the media. Stranger still, in his statement provided in *The Cartland File,* Lyon makes no mention of the caravan's colour; however, as with several witness statement included in the book it is not entirely clear whether his statement had been in some way edited or truncated prior to their inclusion.

19: John n' Jerry: 'diabolical fermentations?'

[1] For a more extensive list of Jeremy's criticisms of the article see *The Cartland File*, p.186. Oddly, having pointed out that the article is 'riddled with errors and mis-statement of facts' he does not correct the record. With regards to the interview itself, according to Jeremy the *Paris Match* journalists had to be 'thrown out' of the hotel while conducting it.

[2] 'The private world of Janet and John,' The *Daily Express*, 8th June 1973.

[3] Apocryphal? If *Paris Match* had plucked this story out of thin air, then one can only admire the imaginative powers of its journalists. And yet stories of Jerry driving a Roller around Brighton's streets are invariably in extremely short supply.

[4] 'The private world of Janet and John,' The *Daily Express*, 8th June 1973.

20: Flirting with Madame Guillotine

[1] *Mon Intime Conviction*, p. 211.

[2] 'A free day for the man on Europe's wanted list,' The *Daily Express*, 21st May 1973.

21: Entente uncordial

[1] Interestingly, when asked by the paper to describe the position of the car and caravan when he came upon them, M. Blasco replied that the Hillman had been 'square' to the caravan, 'forming with it almost a right angle.' If so, then it is an observation that would tend to support the police sketch of the murder scene.

[2] A native of Beaucaire.

[3] 'Cartland case demand for witnesses to be reheard,' The *Times*, 21st May 1973.

[4] Hansard, Volume 857: debated on Tuesday, 22 May 1973, Q 10, col 56.

[5] *The Cartland File*, p. 156.

[6] That the Cartland children had not been informed of their father's funeral and cremation is dealt with in a single paragraph in *The Cartland File* peculiarly bereft of criticism or outrage.

22: End of the beginning

[1] According to this testimony at least one aspect of the case would have thus been confirmed: the Cartlands *had driven* through Pélissanne that afternoon.

[2] More witnesses would emerge even later. Dick Kirby relates how a couple from the nearby village of St Cannat, passing *Jas de Dane* on the night of the murder at around 11pm, reported seeing a light on in the caravan parked there – presumably that of the Cartland's. If so, then the Cartlands had clearly not been asleep as per Jeremy's testimony.

[3] Slang in French for police, similar to 'cops.'

[4] The stain had been discovered by world-renowned forensic scientist Margaret Pereira of The Metropolitan Police Forensic Science Laboratory. Early in her career she had developed the N & P (Nicholls and Pereira) method of detecting minute bloodstains which had gone on to be adopted worldwide. Thus, the dossier had been expanded by the inclusion of a testimony from a truly expert witness making the DPP's 'insufficient evidence' judgement all the more baffling.

[5] *The Cartland File*, p. 166.

[6] The transcript of the interview taken by Troon, and agreed with Jeremy while 'resisting the urge to correct the spelling mistakes,' will no doubt shed light on the importance attached to these notes.

[7] The remark related to Delmas who, much to Jeremy's disdain, had not been familiar with UK quarantine laws as pertaining to canines. The judge had apparently wanted to

know whey Jeremy had not taken his pet dog Lara with him on the camping trip.

[8] Chronicled in Dick Kirby's *Scotland Yard's Murder Squad* pp. 171-73.

[9] *Mon Intime Conviction*, p. 212.

[10] 9 Highcroft Villas – Jeremy's address at this time - was in fact a large semi-detached, not terraced property.

[11] 'Whodunnit?' The *Observer*, 29 Dec 1974, p. 24.

23: The Cartland File

[1] On page 181 of *The Cartland File* Jeremy alludes to this interview dismissing it as 'full of unpleasant innuendos.'

[2] 'I don't mind if the world thinks I killed my father,' The *Daily Express*, 26 June 1976.

[3] *Contemporary Review* 1979, vol 234/1357, pp. 109-110.

[4] Lombard is quite explicit on this point: Delmas was convinced of guilt whereas he, Lombard, thought Jeremy was innocent. When he took out the *partie civile* suite, Lombard reported that Delmas twice referred to Jeremy as 'the guilty party.' See *The Cartland File*, p. 79.

[5] *Mon Intime Conviction*, p. 191.

[6] *The Cartland File,* p. 108.

[7] Ibid. p. 190.

[8] Statement by Jeremy Cartland, Court of Appeal at Aix-en-Provence, 28th March 1973.

[9] *The Cartland File*, p. 7.

[10] Meanwhile the statement Jeremy made on Wednesday, 21st March contains elements of both versions: 'I noticed as we were loading the car that my father had put a big axe in the boot of the vehicle. I asked him what it was for and he said for our protection. I said 'Why the axe?' and took it out of the boot . . . The big axe was left in the house.'

[11] French police methods of the time surface in popular culture in which they are if not celebrated then at the very

least tolerated, the means to an end. For example, the 1975 film *Adieu Poulet* tells the story of a couple of Rennes police officers who think nothing of using intimidation and low-level violence to close a case.

[12] *The Cartland File*, p. 146.

[13] If so, the Cartlands could not have intended taking the alternative route to Jouques via the D15 which is nowhere near Aix and would therefore not have involved by-passing the town, further evidence that their decision to take the RN 572 had almost certainly been deliberate.

[14] *The Cartland File*, p. 12.

[15] A minor road, the D17 also runs from Pélissanne south-easterly, but goes directly through and beyond Aix. Furthermore, as a minor road it would hardly have been suitable for a touring caravan.

[16] Which makes perfect sense given that Mr Cartland was under the impression he was now en route to Jouques. The older man knew perfectly well how to get from Salon to the village – via the RN 572.

[17] *The Cartland File*, p. 98.

[18] For example, consider the issue of toileting. Police strongly suspected John Cartland had been murdered while in the process of *faire ses boissons*. On March 21st Jeremy stated that, 'The caravan had no toilet and so *we* (my italics) went outside into the countryside when we stopped.' No mention of chamber pots or tin cans at this point . . . this element would emerge later, after police had expounded the *faire ses boissons* theory. So too would the tin can.

[19] *The Cartland File*, p. 111.

[20] For Jeremy's actual words see p. 136 endnote no. 3.

[21] *The Cartland File*, p. 13.

24: Murder triangles

[1] 'Why John Cartland feared for his life,' The *Daily Express*, 4 Oct 1973.

[2] If the claim that Mr Cartland took his personal papers to a dinner party where he allowed a complete stranger to read them seems a trifle far-fetched, then what to think of the rendition of Mr Cartland's actions when leaving the party? Checking for supposed assassins in the manner described by Mr Sparrow seems comical, absurd even - straight from the script of an Austin Powers' film.

[3] 'Marseille's Corsicans Make Informing a Fatal Business,' *Asbury Park Evening Press*, 21 Feb 1973.

25: Mythologies

[1] *Escape*, p. 153.

[2] Liz Cartland was a lawyer (teacher), the Cartlands had picked up their caravan from Benidorm (Denia) – are amongst several other factual errors in this account.

[3] Examples are quoted from *Unnatural Death and Unsolved Murders and Mysteries*, pp. 76-84.

[4] 'Jeremy Cartland - Lives in brief,' The *Times*, 29 Aug 2014.

Postscript: Imagining a murder

[1] *The Cartland File*, p. 5.

[2] In his statement of 6th June 1973, Nicholas Lyon mentions 'the Cartlands' had told him they intended moving the caravan to 'their land in France.' This could only mean Jouques. From the way it is told several interpretations are possible. Does 'the Cartlands' literally mean father and son had both spoken of Jouques together and/or separately? Or perhaps when he says 'the Cartlands' Lyon simply means Jeremy, who was after all co-ordinating all aspects of the journey – logistical and financial.

Some clarity is found in Lyon's next sentence in which he states that, 'I recall Jeremy Cartland told me that he was anxious to take the caravan to their land in France.' Quite possibly, Jeremy imparted this information to Lyon out of Mr Cartland's earshot, casually - part of an alibi that might just come in useful at a later date: *We'd always planned to stop at Jouques – ask Mr Lyon*. The distinction between 'the Cartlands' speaking for themselves separately and Jeremy speaking on behalf of himself and his father collectively might not have struck Lyon as worthy of clarification.

One day later John Cartland sent a postcard home. It made no mention of Jouques. Similarly, in Marseille Mont-Reynaud expected his friend's imminent arrival some time on Sunday 18th or Monday 19th. If Jouques had indeed been discussed as a possible location in front of Lyon by either one or both of the Cartlands, come Saturday 17th March, the day he wrote the postcard to Janet Gibson, Cartland senior must have dropped the idea.

For the record, the Nikko Lyon statement presented in the appendices of *The Cartland File* and cited here is not the official police statement, but rather one obtained by Jeremy's lawyer, Michael Relton. Mr Lyon's official police statement would no doubt make interesting reading if only to compare with this version.

[3] *The Cartland File*, p, 33.

[4] Whoever committed the murder, the fact remained that no bloodied footprints were discovered anywhere at the scene of crime. Not only had the killer likely worn socks which had then been burnt in the fire, but as observed in the autopsy report, the majority of blood from Mr Cartland's carotid injury seeped directly into the earth where it formed a large pool of blood by the victim's head.

However, if Jeremy's assertion is true that the killer(s) should have left bloodied footprints all over the site, ironically, it's a contention that hardly helps his cause: how then did the prowlers manage to avoid doing so? The only explanation would appear to be that Mr Cartland was not murdered by prowlers but by someone who *did manage* to avoid leaving footprints i.e. an individual(s) who had prepared for such an eventuality and also had sufficient time to ensure this objective was achieved.

[5] *The Course of My Life* p. 121. Interesting to note the phrase 'once again' with its implication that Cartland had assisted the ambitious young politician on more than one occasion. Unfortunately, Heath does not provide any detail of how Cartland had previously assisted his career.

[6] In *Scotland Yard's Murder Squad*, Dick Kirby reveals the identity of the possible intermediary.

[7] *Ma Vérité sur le Mensonge*, p.11.

Printed in Great Britain
by Amazon